A DOG LOVER'S GUIDE TO HIKING

Wisconsin's State Parks

A DOG LOVER'S GUIDE TO HIKING
Wisconsin's State Parks

Danielle St. Louis

THE UNIVERSITY OF WISCONSIN PRESS

The University of Wisconsin Press
728 State Street, Suite 443
Madison, Wisconsin 53706
uwpress.wisc.edu

Gray's Inn House, 127 Clerkenwell Road
London EC1R 5DB, United Kingdom
eurospanbookstore.com

Printed in the United States of America
This book may be available in a digital edition.

Library of Congress Cataloging-in-Publication Data
Names: St. Louis, Danielle, author.
Title: A dog lover's guide to hiking Wisconsin's state parks / Danielle St. Louis.
Description: Madison, Wisconsin : The University of Wisconsin Press, [2022] |
Identifiers: LCCN 2021038678 | ISBN 9780299336646 (paperback)
Subjects: LCSH: Hiking with dogs—Wisconsin. |
Parks—Wisconsin—Guidebooks.
Classification: LCC SF427.455 .S7 2022 | DDC 796.5109775—dc23
LC record available at https://lccn.loc.gov/2021038678

To all people who just want to do right by their dog.
And to our dogs for making us better people.
Specifically, to my dogs, Lucky and Little Man.

In every walk with nature,
one receives far more than he seeks.

—JOHN MUIR

Contents

THE WEST-CENTRAL REGION

Preface

Before adopting a dog, I thought I'd be that person who took my dog everywhere with me. We'd be inseparable—best friends. But then I adopted Lucky, and I soon discovered I couldn't take him anywhere. A border collie/Labrador retriever mix, he is as high-energy as they come, so exercise is a must—but even walks around our neighborhood were stressful. I'd have to take specific routes to avoid the house with the chain-link fence patrolled by another reactive border collie. And then I'd take the long way around to avoid the other house with the six-foot privacy fence that barely contained the massive Great Dane behind it. Those were the knowns. Stray dogs, feral cats, kids on skateboards, squirrels—I never knew what we'd run into and how Lucky would react. Having a reactive dog made me feel isolated. I wanted to meet my neighbors when we were out for walks, but they couldn't get close to me without Lucky barking and lunging. I wanted to take Lucky out to parks and dog-friendly patios, but I didn't know if I'd be able to control him. Even though he clearly had issues, I was wrong to think he wasn't the kind of dog I could take everywhere. He just wasn't ready. And neither was I.

When I first adopted Lucky, we did a basic obedience course, but I knew Lucky and I both needed something else if we were going to make significant improvements. I investigated some local dog training companies and found a series of force-free courses that train owners to modify behaviors such as reactivity and develop dogs' trust in their owner. The training we did through the courses helped me keep Lucky focused and gave me the confidence I needed to take Lucky into unknown environments.

No longer an adolescent dog, Lucky still requires a lot of exercise, and after moving back to Wisconsin after twelve years away, I wanted to get to know my home state better. I figured the best way to get Lucky exercise and explore my home state would be to hike its state parks. Despite feeling more confident in our abilities to navigate the unknown, I still like to have information about what I'm getting us into. After a couple of unsuccessful attempts to find specific information about some of the parks I wanted to visit with Lucky, I realized the resource I wanted didn't exist. And so here we are! I think dog people, whether your dog is reactive or not, can benefit from dog-centric resources. I hope that you and your four-legged fluffer feel empowered to adventure in Wisconsin's state parks because of this guide.

This book is not associated with the Wisconsin Department of Natural Resources (DNR). The views expressed here are mine and do not represent the views of the Wisconsin DNR.

Thanks go to everyone who kept Lucky and me company on these state park adventures, including my parents, Richard and Kathy; my sisters and their families, Natalie, Sean, Ahsoka, Zoolander, Klaus, and Tedd; Marisa, Nate, Fletcher, and Baxter; Nicole, Clint, and Colton; and my friends Jamie, Raven, Jane, J, Alex, Alison, Jess, Thea, Ellen, Bailey, Ceeanna, Justin, Liesl, Luna, Susan, and René. I owe an extra special thank-you to my friend Angela McNutt, who endured countless hours in the car with Lucky, spent an entire summer being our personal navigator on both roads and trails, and camped with us weekend after weekend. Additional thanks to my family and friends for their support and understanding throughout the process of researching and writing this guidebook.

Thank you to the Board of Regents of the University of Wisconsin System and the University of Wisconsin Press for seeing the value in this niche guidebook and agreeing to publish it. Thanks to Dennis Lloyd, for his encouragement and faith in this project, and to Nathan MacBrien, for his guidance as an editor and dog lover. Thank you to the extremely talented Patrick Smyczek for contributing the quirky illustrations and to my brilliant artist sister Marisa St. Louis for expanding her repertoire to include cartography. Thanks to Jess and Local Dog Training and Adventure for teaching us how to be successful as a team out exploring the world. Thanks to our "group therapy" friends, human and canine, for your friendship and support. Thanks to Odyssey Vet for helping keep Lucky in tip-top hiking shape. Thanks to the former HIVE Social Club for surrounding me with people who were pursuing their dreams. And thanks to Lucky for teaching me about myself, making me a stronger person, and bringing this project into existence, all just by being himself.

Wisconsin's state parks occupy the ancestral homelands of the Ho-Chunk (Winnebago) and Menominee nations and were home to the Dakota, Fox, Kickapoo, Mascouten, Mesquakie, Ojibwe, Ottawa, Potawatomi, and Sauk refugee nations. European settlers and the US government exploited and forcefully removed these people to acquire the land that we now recreate on. I acknowledge the land is sacred to its original inhabitants and implore all park visitors to respect it as such and to learn more about the history and culture of its indigeneous people.

A DOG LOVER'S GUIDE TO HIKING
Wisconsin's State Parks

Introduction

The Wisconsin Department of Natural Resources (DNR) offers this blanket statement concerning dogs in state parks: "Pet owners are not allowed to let their pets interfere in any manner with other people's enjoyment of the park. Pet owners who fail to properly control a pet or whose pet creates a public nuisance or other disturbance may be asked to leave the park or may be issued citations."

This policy feels a bit discriminatory, considering the plethora of ways one's enjoyment of the parks could be disturbed. For some, it could be children tearing through the campgrounds at dawn on their bikes like banshees out of hell. But the policy stands, and if we want our dogs to continue to be welcome in Wisconsin's state parks, it's important to be shining examples of well-behaved, rule-abiding patrons and canine companions.

Other state park rules to know:

- "Pets must be on a leash no longer than 8 feet at all times."
- "Loose pets may be seized and are subject to local laws pertaining to stray animals. Owners of loose pets may be ticketed."
- "Pet owners are responsible for proper removal and disposal of their pets' waste products. Waste should be disposed of in dumpsters or trash receptacles."

In summary, whenever you're visiting a Wisconsin state park, leave your flexi leashes at home, always keep your dog on a leash, bring poop bags and use them. And in most cases, take your poop-filled bags with you when you go, since trash receptacles are uncommon in state park day use areas. Some state parks have additional rules regarding dogs, so make sure to check in at the office when you arrive to find out about any park-specific rules and to determine if designations have changed since this guide went to press.

This book is not meant to be a standalone navigation guide. Rather, it should be used to supplement the information provided at each park. Additionally, I've specifically focused on parks that are state parks in name and have not included state recreation areas, though I am aware these are also technically state parks. Finally, dogs are not allowed anywhere in Copper Culture State Park or Heritage Hill State Park, so clearly these parks are dead to us and will not be mentioned again in this book.

A GUIDE TO THIS GUIDE

The parks are organized alphabetically by region. Regions include northern, northeast, southeast, south-central, and west-central.

The #wistateparkdogs project was born out of necessity and desire: the necessity of getting Lucky exercise and the desire to learn more about my home state. I've enjoyed learning about each park's history, so I've included some highlights at the beginning of each park's entry. The information in this section may not enhance your dog's experience of the park, but I hope it enhances your experience. I've tried to mention what I found most interesting or compelling about each park, which was a struggle of another kind. I am aware there are many stories, people, and perspectives I am leaving out of each park's entry. I hope the choices I've made provide value, and if you're interested, you'll seek out more comprehensive histories.

WATER AVAILABILITY: It's always best to drink water from reliable sources, so I've indicated where water can be found in each park. Water can typically be found in campgrounds, but I specifically focus on water that can be accessed in day use areas. Water spigots may be turned off during the winter, in which case your best bet is bringing water from home. Natural/untreated water sources such as streams and ponds can contain leptospirosis, giardia, and cryptosporidia, so avoid letting your dog drink from these sources whenever possible.

BATHROOM AVAILABILITY: Because humans can't just pee on a tree stump along the trail (or at least they shouldn't), I've indicated where flush and vault toilets are in each park. Toilets can typically be found in campgrounds, but I specifically focus on those that can be accessed in day use areas. Some bathrooms may be closed during the winter, though most vault toilets are open year-round.

TRASHCAN AVAILABILITY: Day use areas in Wisconsin's state parks are typically carry-in/carry-out. Some parks will provide plastic trash bags at picnic areas but don't usually provide cans for those bags once you've filled them up. The exception is for campers, who typically have access to garbage and recycling dumpsters in the campgrounds. Some parks are becoming more dog friendly by providing dog waste bags and trash bins. I'll make a note in this portion of the entry if that's the case.

DESIGNATED DOG SWIMMING AREA: Lucky loves to wade in water. Calling it swimming would be generous—it's more like walking around submerged chest deep and gulping huge mouthfuls of water—but he loves it. So, Lucky and I are particularly interested in the pet swimming areas. These areas are often described as beaches, but we've discovered this term is used very loosely. I've tried to include more accurate descriptions, so you have a better idea of what to expect. If a park doesn't have a designated dog swim area, I also inquired about unofficial areas and rules. Some parks are more lenient than others. When applicable, I've included information about unofficial swimming spots. When you visit, check with park staff in case designations have changed. General rules for pet swim areas instruct that your dog can be off leash while in the water but should be on leash whenever they're not actively swimming. This is always a bummer for Lucky, who enjoys running and chasing between dips in the water. Before letting your dog swim in and lap up any lake water, make sure to check water quality reports. Some parks have signs at the beach indicating water quality or may include water quality information on their website.

DESIGNATED DOG PICNIC AREAS: General Wisconsin state park pet rules prohibit dogs from being in picnic areas. Some parks have designated a picnic area—typically one of the least desirable or least scenic—as a "pet picnic area." This is the spot where dog owners are free to picnic with their leashed pets. In cases where there is no designated pet picnic area, dog owners' options can be limited. In these cases, we've opted to picnic along the trail or at our car. When applicable, I've included suggestions for picnic spots along the trail.

Some parks are more lenient than others and don't mind dogs in regular picnic areas. For example, when I asked about specific pet picnic areas at Rib Mountain State Park, the park attendant looked confused. He assured me leashed pets could go anywhere in the park. Apparently, dog segregation hasn't yet reached the Wausau area, but when you visit, check with park staff in case designations have changed.

RECOMMENDED HIKE: The recommended hike is often our favorite hike of those available to patrons with dogs during the summer. We are suckers for loops and try to create them whenever possible. Sometimes it's hard to pick a favorite, especially if there is a nice recreational rambler trail and a great avid adventurer trail, so I try to mention these other trails in the Worth a Mention section. I also mention ways to shorten/extend a hike in the Experience section in case you're looking for a shorter or longer hike. Ultimately, we want more Wisconsinites and Wiscodogs of all fitness levels to get out and enjoy the state parks, so while we forced ourselves to pick a hike to recommend, we want to offer options so you can hit the trails, no matter your and your dog's fitness levels.

Generally, dogs are not allowed on nature trails in Wisconsin state parks, but there are a few exceptions. If you're interested in hiking a nature trail with your dog but it's unclear whether the trail allows dogs, check with park staff.

HEADS-UP: This is usually where I mention trails I wouldn't recommend, provide disclaimers, or offer rationale for my recommended hike. Something I've learned over the course of visiting so many state parks: trails that double as cross-country ski trails in the winter are typically not my favorite. The characteristics that make these trails great for skiing in the winter make them relatively boring, buggy, and downright bummers in the summer. I may mention these trails in the Heads-Up section as trails I don't recommend. But that's just my opinion, and if you're into those types of trails, more power (and certainly more hiking options) to you. Because they tend to be very wide, these types of trails are especially well suited to reactive dogs who need a lot of space for passing other hikers and dogs.

DISTANCE AND ELEVATION GAIN: This is roughly the distance you'll go if you stick to the recommended hike and roughly how much climbing you'll do if you stick to the recommended hike. The distance is based on what my GPS measured when we hiked the trail. Your experience may be plus or minus some distance depending on how much meandering you do. We typically do a lot of meandering, exploring little offshoots and photo opportunities.

The elevation gain is based on what my GPS measured when we hiked the trail. Your experience may be plus or minus some elevation gain depending on how much meandering you do. This information is most useful in determining, generally, how strenuous the hike is.

I considered including how long it took us to do these hikes, but our "time on trail" is all over the place. Some trails we stopped to take photos every three steps. On other less interesting trails, we set the cruise control and just went on our way. Rather than provide you with a time that may or may not be anywhere close to how long it would take you to do these hikes with your dog, I've decided to let you estimate for yourself, based on the trail length and elevation gain. Time some walks around your neighborhood to determine how fast

you and your dog walk. If there's more elevation gain, guess that
you'll be moving slower than normal.

DOG AND HUMAN FITNESS LEVEL: I developed three categories for
classifying hikes based on difficulty: recreational rambler, weekend
warrior, and avid adventurer.

A "recreational rambler trail" is typically two miles or less and flat.
There may be slight undulations along the trail but no significant
elevation gain. This is the kind of trail I hike with my parents who are
in their late sixties and don't exercise regularly.

A "weekend warrior trail" is typically a distance between two and
four miles and/or may have moderate elevation gain. I consider Lucky
and myself weekend warriors. We walk a couple of miles a day
regularly during the week and hike on the weekends but don't do a lot
of strenuous exercise.

An "avid adventurer trail" is typically a distance that's more than
four miles and/or may have significant elevation gain. In my opinion,
there aren't many avid adventurer trails in Wisconsin.

Some trails don't fall squarely into one of these categories, and
obviously difficulty levels are subjective. These designations are
meant to provide you with a general frame of reference and are
relative to hiking in Wisconsin. It's true that the most challenging hike
in Wisconsin would likely be a recreational rambler trail in the High
Sierra, for example. Additionally, most hikes in Wisconsin are
appropriate for dogs of all sizes. You might have a small dog that is
super athletic or a large dog that is arthritic or out of shape, so I
encourage you to make decisions based on your dog's abilities as well
as your own.

TRAIL CONDITIONS/MATERIALS: In one of Lucky's "learning how to be
calm in public" classes, the instructor had us walk our dogs through
a sand volleyball court and across other types of materials. Thankfully,
Lucky's neuroses don't include an aversion to walking on
unconventional materials, but other dogs have issues with sand,
rocks, wooden bridges, grates, and so on. I've included information

about what kinds of materials you'll find along the recommended hike, so you can prepare for or avoid them, depending on your dog's comfort level. This information may also come in handy when selecting your own footwear for the hike.

I also include information about the width of trails. As the owner of a reactive dog, I like to know what my options are if there is another dog approaching us head-on. There have been many times when we haven't encountered a single person, much less another person-dog duo, on the trail. But on other outings we've had to navigate numerous groups with and without dogs. When we do have to pass others, I try to stay on designated trails and stairways to prevent erosion. But if I have to step off the trail, I will. And hopefully it won't mean tumbling down the side of a cliff. While I recommend staying on designated trails, I also recommend being smart and doing what's safest and best for the other hikers and for you and your dog. Finally, trail conditions will vary based on weather.

TRAIL MARKINGS/EASE OF NAVIGATING: During one visit to Rib Mountain State Park with my sister Natalie, we were ten minutes into our hike when she started laughing out of nowhere. Curious, I asked what was up, and she explained, "I always hear about these people who go out for a hike and get lost in the woods, and I always wondered how that's possible. How hard can it be to follow a trail? But I keep looking up and wondering, 'Is this the trail or is that the trail?' and now I understand how people get lost!"

The Wisconsin Department of Natural Resources hasn't standardized state park trail markings or maps, so each park takes its own approach—some of which are more intuitive than others. While I think I have a decent sense of direction, there have been times during hikes that I've looked at a park map and been utterly confused. I've tried to indicate when trails have a more foolproof marking system and when trails are less obviously marked. That being said, this book is not meant to be a standalone navigation guide to the trails of each park. Rather, it should be used to supplement the map provided at each park.

Example of user-friendly trail marking system from Whitefish Dunes State Park
(Danielle St. Louis)

THE EXPERIENCE: If you decide to do the recommended hike, the Experience section provides chronological details about the route. I often provide tips on where to park, whether to do a loop clockwise or counterclockwise, options for shortening or lengthening the hike, and other observations about the trail. I'll mention turns we missed, sections of the hike we liked or disliked, and everything in between (literally, everything). Depending on the trail, this section might be super short or rather long but, I hope, always helpful.

WHILE YOU'RE IN THE AREA: Sometimes we recommend other state parks that are nearby. Occasionally we recommend other nearby dog-friendly places we've stumbled upon during our adventures.

WORTH A MENTION: This is where I share other relevant or interesting information that may not fall into any of the other categories because, sometimes, I just had more to say.

TRAIL ETIQUETTE

If we want our dogs to continue to be welcome in Wisconsin's state parks, it's important to be shining examples of well-behaved, rule-abiding patrons and canine companions. We don't have to be perfect (even with all of the training we've done, Lucky is still a work in progress), but we do need to be especially considerate of other park users—even if other park users aren't being particularly considerate of us. Here are some trail etiquette basics to follow while out adventuring.

Keeping Your Dog on Leash

State parks are not dog parks, and they have many legitimate reasons for requiring dogs to be on leash. I can vouch for these reasons. During a visit to Kohler-Andrae State Park, just as Lucky and I came out of the woods and back into the prairie, we both spotted four white-tail deer further down the trail. The deer spotted us as well and took off, quickly bounding back into the thick understory. I was thinking "How cool! I wish I had been able to get a photo!" Lucky was thinking "MUST CHASE!!"

If he hadn't been on leash, he would have, because frankly his impulse control sucks. Me telling him to stay would not have kept him from his pursuit. He was so riled up we had to take a timeout and do some focus exercises before continuing. And even then, I could tell he was keeping an alert eye out for the big brown bouncy things. Being a good steward of our environment and an ambassador for dogs in state parks means keeping our dogs from chasing after and disturbing the local fauna. And for most dogs, a leash is the best way to keep them from chasing and disturbing.

On another hike, Lucky met an off-leash Japanese Chin. The Chin's owner informed me he was happy with the dogs' positive interaction, since the Chin had previously been attacked by a big dog and still has some residual fear of larger mutts. I was completely baffled as to why this owner would let his off-leash dog approach my on-leash dog (or any dog/leash combo), given this previous experience. I also couldn't help but wonder if that previous experience had been the unfortunate consequence of an off-leash interaction. Your dog may be friendly, but strangers' dogs might not be. Don't risk it. Keep your dog on leash.

Here's yet another reason to keep your dog on leash in state parks: Your dog might be friendly and love saying "Hi" to other humans, but not all humans love dogs. We can't know other visitors' experiences with and feelings toward dogs, so we shouldn't assume they are comfortable being approached by our dogs, even when our dogs are on leash. Respecting other visitors' personal space is always incredibly important and another good reason for requiring dogs to be leashed while in state parks.

And then there's the matter of respecting the flora. Lucky is pretty good at identifying and sticking to the trail, but he's sometimes tempted by smells to depart from the trail. Departures from the trail can be harmful to plant life and cause erosion, which are things we want to avoid as much as possible. Keeping your dog on leash helps keep them on designated trails. So, for these reasons and the fact that it's a rule, Lucky and I always encourage #wistateparkdogs to be on leash. This applies to winter hikes as well. Just because there may be fewer people out in the parks doesn't mean leashes are optional.

Passing on the Trail

Passing on the trail can be challenging. While I recommend staying on designated trails, I also recommend being smart and doing what's safest and best for the other hikers and for you and your dog. If that means stepping off the trail to let others pass, do so as safely and respectfully as possible.

Many state park trails are multiuse, so it's good to know the hierarchy of trail users and these general rules for passing:

- Faster users yield to slower users, which means bikers should yield to hikers.
- Downhill traffic yields to uphill traffic. This is important to keep in mind for steep climbs on narrow trails at many of the state parks.
- All users yield to horseback riders. Riders should advise hikers of the horse's temperament and other information to assist in passing. If a horse has a red ribbon in its tail, that means it tends to kick.
- Listen for other trail users. Wearing headphones or anything that impairs your hearing could be hazardous.
- When in doubt, yield to others.

Generally, we suggest groups with dogs always yield to groups without dogs. Not everyone is a dog lover and other visitors may even be fearful of dogs. By yielding to oncoming hikers, you'll stay on everyone's good side, and I bet they'll comment on what a good boy/girl your dog is! When two groups with dogs are passing, we've found a little communication goes a long way. Just like horseback riders, dog owners can advise others of their dog's temperament and request others take certain actions/precautions when passing.

Picking Up Poop

If you're venturing out into nature, it's important to be familiar with the principle of Leave No Trace. This principle is the basis for most park's carry-in/carry-out trash policies, and the principle applies to our dogs too. Dog poop is the one of the most visible, stinky, dirty, and convincing points in the argument for banning dogs from public spaces. So, protect our natural spaces and make sure dogs continue to be welcome in them by picking up after your dog. This applies to winter hikes as well. Just because that poop fell into some snow and isn't as visible, doesn't mean it's okay to leave it for the spring thaw.

Here's a helpful tip: rather than transporting smelly bags full of poop in the cabin of the car, I place them between the hood of the car and the windshield, securing the bag with the windshield wiper blade. This way, my car doesn't end up smelling like poop, and I remember to throw the bag out when we get someplace with a trashcan because it's there, right in front of me. This method obviously does not work in the rain or any other circumstance in which you'd need to engage your windshield wipers.

ESSENTIAL SKILLS

There was a time when I would never have attempted to take Lucky hiking—or to any public place for that matter. Lucky is reactive, which means he overreacts to certain situations. His reactivity used to be triggered by people walking by us on the sidewalk, dogs, skateboards, bicycles, squirrels, children, and really anything that moved. His overreactions included barking, lunging, pulling on the leash, charging (if off leash), and just general hysteria. Reactivity is not the same as aggression, and with the right training and attention reactivity can be addressed and managed. Lucky is much less reactive now because we've learned how to manage his reactivity. So I asked my friend and dog trainer extraordinaire Jessica Cady-Bartholomew, KPA CTP, CPDT-KA to go over a few skills for you that we learned during our classes with Local Dog Training and Adventure. These skills empowered us to get out of the house and onto the trail, and while not required, I hope they will empower you and set you and your dog up for success in Wisconsin state parks too.

It's important to train behaviors before you go out on a hike. Work on developing the fundamental understanding of the skills in a comfortable and stimulus-free environment (like your house) before you go to a more challenging environment like the trail. As your dog picks up the behaviors, gradually move to more exciting environments like your backyard or out on a walk. Also, when you're training behaviors, you need to have a marker to let your dog know they are doing the behavior you want. This marker can be a dog training clicker or a marker word. I use the marker word "yes" to let Lucky know he's doing what I want him to do. Use whatever marker is most comfortable for you. And while you can work on these behaviors by yourself, I highly encourage you to take your dog to classes. It's always a good idea to work with a professional trainer, plus your dog will benefit from learning and practicing with other dogs around and you'll benefit from meeting other dedicated dog people who might turn into hiking companions.

Look

This skill is great for refocusing your dog's attention on you. I use this a lot when we pause to let other hikers and dogs pass us on the trail. Lucky doesn't even notice people and pups walking by when he's staring deeply into my eyes and drooling because he knows a treat is sure to follow. To train "look," toss a piece of food on the floor to distract your dog. Let your dog eat the food, and then as soon as they look back in your direction, click or mark and then give them a piece of food. Repeat and continue until they nibble the floor food and look back superfast (in a second or less). Once they are looking back super fast consistently, you can add the verbal cue. So now, you toss the food to the floor, let your dog eat the food, and then say "look" as soon as your pup is about to look back at you. Then, reward with food. Continue repetitions with the verbal cue and then start working into real life situations. Again, start to practice the behavior in less exciting environments before moving to exciting environments. For example, when your dog is casually looking out the window, ask for "look," mark, and then treat.

Leave It

When you happen upon gross things along the trail, this is a great way to keep your dog from eating them—and we've come across plenty of gross things. It might be goose poop landmines at Lakeshore State Park or someone's discarded catch of the day at Big Foot Beach State Park. To

Danielle pulled off to side of trail with Lucky using "look" to keep his attention as other people and dogs pass (Angela McNutt)

train "leave it," start with some food in your closed hand. Keep your hand still while you let your dog sniff. The very second your dog leaves your treat-filled hand alone, mark the action with a clicker or verbal marker and offer a food reward. Continue with a closed-hand sniff for multiple repetitions and then move to an open handful of food. When your dog pulls away, mark the behavior and offer a food reward. Add the cue "leave it!" and continue practicing until you can drop treats on the ground and your dog won't dart after them.

To take this behavior to the next level, plant smelly distractions along your walk, so you know where the distractions are. Keep your eyes peeled for your dog's body language that they've smelled something attractive and use your verbal cue "leave it." When your dog abandons the pursuit of the smelly distraction, reward with a treat. If it's a highly tempting smell/object, you can use your "leave it" command and then encourage your pup to continue walking by luring with the food reward. When "leave it" fails, you need "drop it!"

Drop It

When "leave it" isn't 100 percent effective, this is the next best thing. Sure, that owl pellet might be in Lucky's mouth, but at least it's not going to end up in his stomach. When you're working on developing this behavior (and when you're out there using it IRL), it's important to have some high value treats on hand. Jess, dog trainer extraordinaire, has offered this friendly advice, "If it's an owl pellet, Danielle, a dry biscuit isn't going to cut it." And she's right. The best way to train "drop it" is to offer your dog a swap of a toy or snack of equal or greater value. When your dog has an object in its mouth, offer a big handful of food/treats as the swap. If you have a toy-motivated dog, you could use a tug toy in lieu of food if your dog finds a lot of value in it. This should feel like a win-win: your dog drops the gross thing (win for you) and gets a super yummy thing (win for dog). Aggressively grabbing at items or forcing your dog's mouth open (unless it's life threatening) may encourage your dog to swallow or guard the item.

After plenty of repetitions, start introducing the verbal cue before you present the food to exchange. I use the cue "drop it" because that's what I learned in Lucky's basic obedience class, but Jess recommends using the cue "thank you" because you can't say it like a jerk. No matter what cue you decide to use, use the cue and then give your dog a big handful of high value treats in exchange.

Leash Walking and On-Leash Recall

These are important behaviors to master because dogs are always required to be on leash in Wisconsin state parks. You and your dog will enjoy your hiking experiences so much more if you've mastered leash walking and on-leash recall. Walking on leash with your pup should be enjoyable for you both. Most dogs find walking at a human pace boring, so increase fun levels and enrich the on-leash walking experience with opportunities to sniff and explore. Don't just stop to smell the roses—stop and smell all the things. Also, most humans don't like their shoulder getting pulled out of its socket by their dog. If you have a strong puller, a front clip harness is a great piece of equipment. While it won't eliminate pulling completely, it will spare your shoulder and increase comfort for your dog by taking pressure off their neck.

Making walking on leash fun by letting your dog sniff and explore is important, but getting their attention again is also important. To train on-leash recall, work on calling your dog to your side while on-leash in a less exciting environment. When you call your dog, use a super excited voice and a fun noise, sound, or word that catches your dog's attention. This could be a bird noise or a whistle and then your dog's name and verbal cue like "come," "here," or "this way." Encourage your dog to run all the way over to you and always reward them for coming when called. Then start practicing their on-leash recall in slightly more distracting environments. The important thing here is for your dog to come back to you, and then you can add a "look" or ask for a sit and then reward while the distraction passes. Developing solid on-leash walking and recall skills will set you and your pup up for success hiking and yielding to other hikers.

HEALTH AND SAFETY

Before you head out into the Wisconsin wilderness with your dog, it's not a bad idea to familiarize yourself with some basic health and safety information. The information I provide here should serve as the starting point for a more in-depth conversation with your veterinarian. But here are some basics from Lucky's veterinarian, Kaitlin Young, DVM.

Fitness

Dr. Young says that dog fitness is much like human fitness; what is an appropriate length or difficulty of a hike depends on the dog's condition, which varies from dog to dog. "If your dog is overweight, they will need more conditioning to safely lose the weight before extensive hiking to prevent joint injuries, but even a thin dog might not be well conditioned if she or he is a couch potato. On the other hand, a dog that regularly walks multiple miles a day is going to be in better condition to get out and hike." It's also important to not rush young puppers into strenuous exercise. "Dogs should reach full skeletal maturity (usually around one year) before doing extensive hiking of more than 2–3 miles," explains Dr. Young. Your dog's age can be a helpful metric for determining general fitness. Dr. Young suggests thinking about your dog as a person when it comes to their age. "If your dog is young, would you ask your child to do the hike? If your dog is older, would your grandparents be able to do the hike?" If you're not sure where your dog falls in the fitness spectrum, work with your veterinarian to determine what distances and difficulties are appropriate.

It's always a good idea to gradually build up to longer and more strenuous hikes and different environments. Your own neighborhood is a great place to start. You can begin with shorter walks and introduce any new gear you'll be using for hiking. Let your dog get comfortable wearing a backpack, first empty and then carrying lighter items. Use your training walks to practice walking on leash, determine potential triggers, and practice modifying/managing behaviors before you get out on the trail.

It's also important to be able to recognize signs of overexertion in dogs; even the fittest dog can reach its limit. Dogs overheat much faster than people do because of their heavy coats and lack of sweating, and Wisconsin's hot and humid summers can be particularly taxing on dogs. Dr. Young offers this rule of thumb: "If you're feeling hot and exhausted, assume your dog is probably feeling worse." Signs of overexertion include lagging behind, trying to lie down flat on a cool surface, and being unable to stop panting once given water and shade.

Hydration

Staying hydrated is just as important for your dog as it is for you. Dr. Young offers these guidelines, "Most dogs drink around 60ml/kg per day, so if needing to pack water, take 100ml/kg to be on the safe side." To make your calculations easier, I'll put these guidelines into more familiar units of measure. One kg is about two pounds, and sixty ml is about two ounces. Lucky is about 64 pounds (29 kg), so he'd normally drink about 1740ml (58 ounces) a day. To be safe, I'd want to bring about 2900ml (97 ounces) along for a day of hiking. While each state park entry includes information about water availability at the park, I suggest always bringing some water from home just to be on the safe side. This water can come in handy on the drive to and from the park and will be a lifesaver if, for whatever reason, water is not available at the park. Water from home is also going be safer for your dog than water from streams and ponds. A good rule of thumb is if you wouldn't drink the water, your dog shouldn't either. They can get the same diseases people can get—icky stuff like leptospirosis, giardia, and cryptosporidia—when drinking from natural/untreated bodies of water. Giardia and cryptosporidia cause nasty diarrhea and can lead to dehydration, which can be serious. Leptospirosis causes kidney and liver disease, so don't skip that Leptospirosis vaccine just in case your pup does end up drinking from natural/untreated bodies of water. Another concern is blue-green algae blooms, which can be toxic to dogs if they drink contaminated water.

Once you're out on the trail, Dr. Young recommends offering water breaks at least every hour, but more frequently depending on the weather and difficulty of hike. It's always better to offer water too often than not often enough, so let's talk human and dog water logistics. I love hiking with my Camelback because I don't have to stop hiking to take a sip. But I find that when I use my Camelback and don't have to stop to drink, I tend to stop less often for water breaks for Lucky. I'm aware of this tendency and do my best to be super attentive to his water needs. When he's wearing his backpack, he carries a water bottle on each side, and I alternate bottles at each stop to try to keep his load as evenly distributed as possible. But if it's too hot for him to wear his backpack, I will carry his bottles in my backpack or use my own Camelback as a spigot into his doggie bowl. That's my favorite option if I have plenty of water in my Camelback. I just squeeze the mouthpiece and bend over his bowl and voilà!

Some signs of dehydration to watch out for include dry gums, reduced energy, sunken eyes, and when dehydration is severe, skin that becomes less elastic. Signs of heat exhaustion can include collapse, seizures, and vomiting. Dr. Young notes a normal dog rectal temp is 101.5 and says, "I'd be concerned and getting my dog rest, shade, and cooling with temps over 102.5." Let's be real—it's unlikely you're going to go hiking with a doggie rectal thermometer, so just make sure you are carrying plenty of water and offering frequent breaks. Given Dr. Young's previous point— "If you're feeling hot and exhausted, assume your dog is probably feeling worse"—it would follow that if you're feeling thirsty, your dog probably is too. Finally, be okay ending your hike early if you dog seems tired or hot.

Ticks and Other Insects

After an Easter Sunday visit to Richard Bong State Recreation Area, I spent an hour picking ticks off Lucky. As he lay in the bathtub wondering why he was getting such a thorough massage, I seriously questioned whether I had the stomach to continue with this project. Then there was the traumatic trip to Governor Thompson State Park. After that Tick-Palooza, it took mustering every bit of courage and applying three different kinds of tick repellent to get me back out into nature the very next weekend. (I went with a combination of Coleman spray to pre-treat our clothing, some Deep Woods OFF! and essential oil drops, plus essential oil sprays for the dogs. We were probably radioactive when it was all said and done.)

The unfortunate reality is that the tick situation in Wisconsin is only getting worse. Over the past ten years, the number of cases of Lyme disease in Wisconsin has more than doubled. In 2018, Wisconsin ranked fifth in the nation for confirmed cases. Lyme disease in Wisconsin has gotten to the point of being a legislative issue. Two bills were approved by Governor Tony Evers in January of 2020 to increase awareness of ticks and Lyme disease. As a result, you should start seeing educational signs and brochures about ticks and preventing tick bites at state parks, and state parks should now be selling bug spray with DEET. Even if you take precautions, it's likely you'll encounter a tick or two (or more) while you're in Wisconsin's state parks. If you don't have the stomach for these pesky buggers, hiking might not be the right activity for you and your dog.

While we mostly hear about Lyme disease, ticks can spread other bacterial infections: anaplasma, Rocky Mountain spotted fever, ehrlichia, and more. The best first line of defense against ticks is preventative tick treatments. It's important to consistently use a tick preventative, especially during the spring, summer, and fall months. In recent years, ticks have been found on dogs in Wisconsin in every month of the year, so if you get out into the woods in the winter, you may want to continue the tick treatments. A good second line of defense against Lyme disease is the Lyme vaccine for your dog, which Dr. Young says is quite effective.

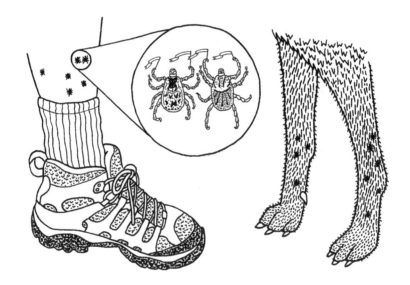

The first series for the Lyme vaccine is a two-dose regimen, followed by an annual revaccination booster.

Even if your dog is on a tick preventative and has gotten the Lyme vaccine, you should still always check for ticks on both you and your dog after every hike, so a tick doesn't end up hitching a ride home and into your house, or even worse, your bed. I've refined my tick removing technique over the years and found this to be the most effective method when dealing with a significant number of ticks while still at the park: fill a bowl/Tupperware with water, use tick removing tool to remove tick, shake tick off of tool in water, repeat until all the ticks have been removed, dispose of tick water in woods or fire depending on what's available and how much you value these arachnids' lives. At home, I'll put Lucky in the empty bathtub, pull the ticks off of him, and dispose of them in the toilet.

In the event your dog is not on a preventative and hasn't gotten the Lyme vaccine, here are signs of Lyme disease to watch out for: fever, lameness, and generally just not being quite right. Lyme can also present as acute renal (kidney) failure, which is a very severe situation. Most dogs, however, will show no symptoms. For this reason, I recommend using a preventative and getting your dog vaccinated.

Other nuisance insects include mosquitos, gnats, fleas, spiders, and horseflies. I've spent many a mile feeling incredibly sorry for Lucky as he's been swarmed by these pesky buggers. Swatting the bugs away while we hike is not very effective, so I've tried using essential oil sprays like Vet's Best Flea and Tick Home & Go Spray and Pyranha's Zero-Bite Natural Insect Spray, which make Lucky smell super pungent and seem to deter some insects, though not all. While most of these nuisance insects aren't hazardous to our dogs' health, mosquitoes can spread heartworm disease, which is becoming increasingly common in Wisconsin. So in addition to a tick preventative, it's a good idea to have your dog on a year-round heartworm preventative.

Plants

At some state parks, an interpretive sign on a post will warn about poison ivy, quoting the mnemonic device, "Leaves of three, let it be." Then as an additional identification aid, the sign will say "Poison ivy surrounds this sign." I look at the variety of plants around these signs and am still utterly confounded by which plant is the poison ivy. Did you know there are at least *seven* different mnemonic devices to help identify poison ivy? The fact that there are so many mnemonic devices makes me feel better about my inability to ID the darn thing. I find it so difficult to spot that I even had some poison ivy included in one of my tattoos, so I could use my arm as a field guide while we're out on the trail. I'm not joking.

While dogs are less susceptible to poison ivy and poison oak, it's possible for a dog to get a rash in areas with less hair. If your dog gets a rash that won't go away, contact your vet for further treatment. The biggest concern related to your dog being exposed to poison ivy or poison oak is the potential for the plants' oils to spread from your dog's fur to you. If you know your dog has been rolling around in these plants, it's a good idea to wash them with soap to remove the oils from their fur. If you don't know what your dog has been rolling around in, it's probably not a good idea to jump straight into a sleeping bag with them after hiking.

Another plant-related piece of advice is to avoid letting your dog ingest plants while hiking; it's what's best for the environment and for your dog's health. Dr. Young's advice relating to plants echoes her advice about drinking from natural water sources: "If you wouldn't eat it, don't let your dog eat it!" But dogs will be dogs, which means they might eat something they shouldn't. According to Dr. Young, a small amount of most plants probably won't hurt your dog; the main side effects will likely be vomiting or diarrhea. In the event your dog does eat something and is acting sick, take pictures of the plant, including its flowers, stems, leaves, and any identifying marks to help with identification, and seek veterinary care. If you have a smart phone, you might also download a plant identification app, of which there are many. Do not remove plants from state parks.

One specific plant Dr. Young warns about is the black walnut tree. Black walnuts and the wood and shells of black walnut trees can be poisonous to dogs, so she advises being especially watchful around these trees. Black walnut is mostly found in the southwest and southeast regions of Wisconsin, but since the species is growing twice as fast as other species in the state, it's likely you'll come across a black walnut tree at some point in your adventures.

Animals

You and your dog may encounter animals while out hiking in Wisconsin's state parks—both living and dead. During one visit at Merrick State Park we encountered a turtle, a snake, and a deer all in one hike. We've been harassed by blue jays and squirrels and stalked by baby racoons. Thankfully, we have yet to encounter a bear. During a visit to Rib Mountain State Park, Lucky managed to sniff out a deer leg along the side of the trail. That's right, just a leg—bone, skin, flesh and a hoof. And then there are the dead fish washed up on dog beaches and occasionally along the trails at Big Foot Beach State Park.

If your dog gets sprayed by a skunk, gently rinse out their eyes with saline or water and bathe when possible using a skunk remover product, such as Nature's Miracle Skunk Odor Remover. If your dog has a run-in with a porcupine, try to keep them as still as possible. If there are just one to two spines, you can attempt to remove them on your own if your dog will let you. If there are multiple spines, your dog will probably need to be sedated to remove the spines safely, so get to the nearest emergency vet as quickly as possible. Thankfully, there are only two species of venomous snake in Wisconsin, and both are very reclusive, so the chance of running into one is unlikely. However, if your dog is bitten by a snake, or any wild animal, flush out the wound with clean water or saline and seek veterinary care to have their wound assessed. In general, if either you or your pup is injured in an encounter with an animal, call the park emergency number, 911, and/or the nearest vet (contact information is included at the end of the book).

More likely than encounters with animals are encounters with the byproducts of animals. Lucky is particularly fond of scat in general and goose poop in particular. He's also foraged out a few owl pellet trail snacks in his day. All of these animal byproducts can cause GI upset in dogs and can pass along parasites and other infections. If your dog is like Lucky, it's a good idea to use a regular heartworm preventative, get regular fecal exams (at least annually, more frequently for highly exposed dogs), and do routine deworming through your vet.

Whether you encounter live animals or animal byproducts while out on the trail, the "leave it!" command really comes in handy—see the Trail Etiquette section for more on "leave it!"

IN CASE OF EMERGENCY

I often felt guilty leaving my chihuahua, Little Man, at home while Lucky and I were out adventuring. So one weekend I decided to bring him along on a visit to Governor Thompson State Park. The trip started out normally. We spent the afternoon hiking, Lucky on his leash and Little Man in my backpack, and then we went back to our campsite to get a fire going and to cook our dinner. This is when our weekend took a detour. We were just finishing the final rotation of the pizza over the fire when Little Man had a seizure. Little Man was epileptic, so I was prepared. At the time, I had diazepam to administer to Little Man in the event of a seizure. I gave him a dose of diazepam. His seizure stopped. I continued to monitor him, and five minutes later, he had another seizure. I administered the second dose of diazepam, and his seizure stopped. But now, I was out of diazepam. I had never had to use both doses in one day before. At this point, if Little Man were to have another seizure, I'd have had no way of stopping it.

I started to mildly panic. In the middle-of-nowhere Wisconsin, my phone was virtually useless. I couldn't Google anything, and I barely had enough service to get through to my parents. I walked around our campsite trying to find the strongest and most reliable signal while my dad looked for emergency vets on his stable internet connection at his home in civilization. He provided me with a couple of phone numbers and addresses, and, staying as still as possible so as to not lose my one bar of cell service, I called the first number. By now, all the local veterinarians were closed. I made it through to the emergency veterinarian in Green Bay. My call intermittently broke up as I spoke with the receptionist. We went over the options: stay at the park and hope Little Man doesn't have another seizure or drive to Green Bay, have the vet assess him, and then possibly give me more diazepam. I made the decision to pack up both dogs and people and drive the hour and twenty minutes into Green Bay to go to the emergency vet. We arrived at the vet at 11 pm and were informed they had several critical patients, so we waited. Just as we were next up to see the doc, Little Man had another seizure. The technician took him to the back to hook him up to an IV and administer medicine to stop the seizure. The doctor came and talked to me, and we decided to have Little Man stay for what was left of the night for observation and to make sure he didn't have any more seizures. We ended up spending the night in a hotel in Green Bay rather than in our tents at Governor Thompson.

While Little Man's medical emergency was related to a preexisting condition and required specific intervention, it's smart to bring a first aid kit for both people and pets along on a hike. You can purchase pet-specific first aid kits, or just make sure your kit includes these pet-specific items: bandage material (gauze pads, telfa, cling gauze, vetwrap/coban, and bandaging tape), a syringe and sterile saline (to use for eyewash and for flushing wounds), nail trimmers and styptic powder, tick removing tool, and a towel or sling that can be used around a dog's middle to help support their weight if they are having trouble walking. If camping overnight, you could also bring along some prescription GI food from your vet to have on hand in case your dog has an acute attack of diarrhea. In addition to having the right supplies, you'll want to become familiar with basic dog first aid skills so you can administer care when needed: bandaging, nail trimming in the event of a broken nail, and how to remove a tick. Ask your vet for a tutorial or find a reliable YouTube video.

If a first aid kit isn't going to cut it and your dog needs medical attention, I've included the closest local veterinarian and 24-hour emergency veterinarian offices (based on travel time from the park) at the end of this guide. Since we do most of our hiking on weekends, local veterinarian offices typically aren't open. I hope you don't ever need to use this information, but it's here for you in case of an emergency. If there's a human emergency, call the park emergency number or 911.

WHAT TO PACK

I always thought I was that person who overpacked. Then I found out one of my coworkers always brings a water filtration system and three weeks' worth of dehydrated food with him whenever he hikes. I often take for granted the "safety" of going out for a day hike in one of Wisconsin's state parks—it's probably not a bad idea to bring a water filtration system and three weeks' worth of food. But typically, here's what I would consider essential items:

- Dog's collar with tags
- Dog's leash (max 8 feet long; no flexi leashes)
- Poop bags
- More poop bags—they come in handy for a lot of other things too
- Water (enough for human and dog)
- Collapsible water dish
- Training treats/positive reinforcement
- Training pouch for treats
- Towel in case of muddy/wet conditions
- Tick removing tool
- Dog and person first aid kits. Dog first aid items include:
  - bandage material (gauze pads, telfa, cling gauze, vetwrap/coban, and bandaging tape)
  - a syringe and sterile saline for flushing wounds
  - nail trimmers and styptic powder
  - a towel or sling that can be used around a dog's middle to help support their weight if they are having trouble walking
- Compass
- Knife
- Trail maps
- Snacks for humans
- Bug spray
- Sunscreen

Here's other items I've found useful in our hiking experiences:

- Dog backpack for carrying water and full poop bags
- Hands-free leash
- Dog booties (Lucky only uses these occasionally in the winter)
- Extra battery pack for my phone (though service is often unreliable anyway)
- GPS

Have I gone out for hikes without most of these items? Yes. One time I even left the house without Lucky's collar and had to stop at a hardware store along the road to pick one up. You can make do without, but I typically like to be a little more prepared and well-equipped.

And now, without further ado, let's get on to adventuring in Wisconsin's state parks!

	Designated Pet Picnic Area	Designated Pet Swimming Area	Dog Waste Bags and Trash Bins	Recommended Trail Difficulty
Amnicon Falls State Park				RR
Aztalan State Park	X			RR
Belmont Mound State Park				RR
Big Bay State Park	X		X	RR/WW
Big Foot Beach State Park	X			RR/WW
Blue Mound State Park				RR
Brunet Island State Park	X	X		RR
Buckhorn State Park	X	X		RR
Copper Falls State Park	X			RR
Council Grounds State Park			X	RR
Cross Plains State Park				RR/WW
Devil's Lake State Park	X	X		WW/AA
Governor Dodge State Park	X	X		WW
Governor Nelson State Park	X	X	X	RR
Governor Thompson State Park			X	RR
Harrington Beach State Park	X	X		RR
Hartman Creek State Park	X			RR
High Cliff State Park	X	X		WW/AA
Interstate State Park	X			RR/WW
Kinnickinnic State Park	X	X		RR
Kohler-Andrae State Park	X	X	X	RR
Lake Kegonsa State Park	X	X	X	RR
Lakeshore State Park				RR
Lake Wissota State Park	X	X	bags only	WW/AA

	Designated Pet Picnic Area	Designated Pet Swimming Area	Dog Waste Bags and Trash Bins	Recommended Trail Difficulty
Lost Dauphin State Park				RR
Merrick State Park	X			RR
Mill Bluff State Park				RR/WW
Mirror Lake State Park	X			WW
Natural Bridge State Park				RR
Nelson Dewey State Park				RR
New Glarus Woods State Park				WW
Newport State Park		X		RR
Pattison State Park	X			RR/WW
Peninsula State Park	X		X	AA
Perrot State Park				AA
Potawatomi State Park				WW
Rib Mountain State Park				WW
Roche-A-Cri State Park				RR/WW
Rock Island State Park			X	WW/AA
Rocky Arbor State Park				RR
Straight Lake State Park				RR/WW
Tower Hill State Park				RR/WW
Whitefish Dunes State Park	X	X	X	RR/WW
Wildcat Mountain State Park				WW/AA
Willow River State Park	X			RR
Wyalusing State Park				WW
Yellowstone Lake State Park	X	X		RR

DOG LOVER'S STATE PARK QUICK REFERENCE GUIDE

THE NORTHERN REGION

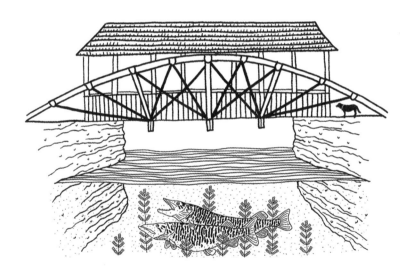

Amnicon Falls State Park

Maybe the quaintest of Wisconsin's state parks, Amnicon Falls doesn't rely on any one feature to leave a dramatic impression. Instead, the sum of Amnicon's parts creates a charming world befitting a fairytale and deserving of a stop on a family vacation. The histories of Amnicon's parts are also mildly fascinating, depending on how interested you are in geology and civil engineering.

The falls themselves are a byproduct of a cluster of geological activity over the course of a billion years. Volcanoes erupted, oceans advanced and receded, sand compressed into sandstone, earthquakes forced rock masses up, and glaciers steamrolled through the area. Evidence of these ancient processes are present throughout the park, including a portion of the Douglas Fault, the line along which great earthquakes used to rumble, which extends from Ashland, Wisconsin, to the Twin Cities. You might even be able to see the Douglas Fault, if you know what you're looking for.

The covered bridge is the legacy of Charles M. Horton, whose patented bridge design is characterized by arched beams, hooks, and clips. The Horton design didn't achieve widespread application. The bridge was built probably sometime in the early 1900s and is one of only six known Hortons. The cover isn't part of Horton's original "bow-string" design; it was added later, and wisely so, as it contributes to the idyllic atmosphere of the park. The only thing about this park that isn't very romantic is the meaning of its name. *Amnicon* is derived from the Ojibway words for "where fish spawn." This area is home to an uncommon freshwater fish, the muskellunge. But since the muskellunge dating pool is limited to the Amnicon watershed and four of its lakes, maybe the name of this park is romantic after all.

WATER AVAILABILITY: Water is available at the main parking lot that provides access to the covered bridge, at the reservable picnic shelter, and at two spots along the walking trail.

BATHROOM AVAILABILITY: Vault toilets are available at the main entrance to the park, at the parking lot that provides access to the covered bridge, and at the reservable picnic shelter.

TRASHCAN AVAILABILITY: There are dumpsters and recycling in the parking lot on the west side of the river, between the reservable shelter and the campground. This parking lot and its dumpsters are also accessible from the walking trail.

DESIGNATED DOG SWIMMING AREA: At the time of our last visit, there was no designated dog swimming area. There is no specified human swimming area either, but swimming in the river is allowed. I let Lucky wade into the lower falls on leash only if there were no people trying to swim in the area at the same time. Check with park staff when you visit in case designations have changed.

DESIGNATED DOG PICNIC AREA: At the time of our last visit, there was no designated pet picnic area. Check with park staff when you visit in case designations have changed.

RECOMMENDED HIKE: Walking Trail

DISTANCE AND ELEVATION GAIN: 1 mile, 76 feet

DOG AND HUMAN FITNESS LEVEL: recreational rambler

TRAIL CONDITIONS/MATERIALS: The walking trail is mostly dirt, pine needles, and spotty grass in some areas. There are stone stairs on either side of the bridge that takes you over to the island and stone stairs down from the walking trail to the edge of the river downstream from the upper falls. Stone stairs also take you down to the base of the Upper Falls. There are some wooden riser stairs along the walking trail. The trail is flat and is wide enough to accommodate you and your dog walking side by side. There are many areas for stepping aside to let others pass.

TRAIL MARKINGS/EASE OF NAVIGATING: The walking trail on the east and west sides of the river is well established and easy to follow. Once you are on the island, the trail seems to dissolve into a network of paths, each leading to a view of the river or of the falls and each only a short walk to another. Infrequent hiker icons are attached to trees to suggest the park's preferred route for visitors.

HEADS-UP: Water levels at Amnicon vary depending on the time of year, which explains how Now and Then Falls got its name. Exercise caution around the falls, which can turn treacherous when water levels are high.

THE EXPERIENCE: Park at the north lot near the covered bridge. Because it will take you two minutes, go down the very short paved trail at the southeast side of the parking lot to view Now and Then Falls. As the name suggests, Now and Then Falls are dependent on the river's water level and are most impressive during times of high water. Walking this short segment of trail will also acclimate you to the scale of the map. Distances between objects are shorter than they appear. Then, go back through the parking lot and descend another short trail and stone stairway to a platform adjacent to the base of the Upper Falls. Retrace your steps up the trail and head over to the covered bridge. Crossing the covered bridge takes you over to the island, and here you can try to follow the walking trail along the perimeter of the island or you can meander through the pine stands on the various social trails. These unofficial trails function much like the indirect routes of theme parks designed to keep visitors ambling through the attractions and extending their stay. Here the attractions are three sets of falls—the Upper, Lower, and Snake Pit falls and different views of and points of access to the river.

Cross over the second, smaller bridge to the west side of the river and continue on the walking trail, which is more defined here than on the island and runs parallel to the edge of the river. When the trail splits at the water fountain, stay to the left and continue following the edge of the river until you emerge from the woods into the picnic area and playground. You can either backtrack on this segment of trail or cross the picnic area and take a short segment of trail back to the water fountain to complete the loop. From the water fountain, backtrack to the bridge, back across the island and the covered bridge, and then take a left. Follow the trail northwest past the picnic area to explore the top of the sandstone cliff and view the falls and covered bridge from another vantage point before returning to the parking lot to complete your hike.

WHILE YOU'RE IN THE AREA: You should also visit Pattison State Park and Wisconsin Point.

Big Bay State Park

When I was traveling in Brazil, a fellow lodger at a hostel in Rio described Iguazu Falls as a "magical place full of butterflies and rainbows." I wrote off his ethereal description as a byproduct of his marijuana-induced high, until I saw Iguazu Falls. It was literally full of butterflies and rainbows, which made it feel downright magical. I mention this because I don't want you to dismiss this description. Believe me when I say Big Bay State Park is a magical place—the views, the vegetation, and the emerald green water have a combined effect that can very accurately be described as a natural high, no smoking required.

There's inherent charm in a place that can only be reached by ferry. Big Bay State Park is on the eastern side of Madeline Island, the largest of the Apostle Islands and the only island open to commercial development and private ownership. Probably for this reason, Madeline Island isn't included as part of the Apostle Islands National Lakeshore, but that doesn't mean Big Bay State Park isn't worthy of national recognition. When I first laid eyes on the lake through the trees at Big Bay, I knew it was love at first sight. I've seen plenty of lakes before—big lakes, small lakes, other Great Lakes. I've even visited the shores of Lake Superior before. But this was different. It didn't feel like Wisconsin. It didn't feel midwestern. It felt like paradise.

The tourists can have the Apostle Islands National Lakeshore, and us Wisconsin natives can keep Big Bay our very own secret. Something else I'm keeping secret? The location of our favorite spot along Bayview Trail. This little nook is perfect for lazy afternoons, alternatively wading in the cool waters and basking in the summer sun on surrounding rocks. A tip

I'm happy to share? After long relaxing days at Big Bay, you must go to Tom's Burned Down Café, which is everything the Yelp reviews say about it and more. With an art car parked out front, this spot is a cross between Margaritaville and Burning Man. The vibe is chill, and the place is super dog friendly.

WATER AVAILABILITY: Water is available at the park office, the day use picnic area, and the pet picnic area.

BATHROOM AVAILABILITY: Flush toilets are available at the park office and day use picnic area. Vault toilets are available at the pet picnic area.

TRASHCAN AVAILABILITY: Garbage, recycling, and a pet poop bag dispenser are available at the day use picnic area and the pet picnic area.

DESIGNATED DOG SWIMMING AREA: At the time of our last visit, there was no designated dog swimming area. Along Bayview Trail there are several social trails down to the water. Use discretion when letting your dog go for a paddle. And check with park staff when you visit in case designations have changed.

DESIGNATED DOG PICNIC AREA: The Point Picnic Area is the pet picnic area. There are picnic tables, vault toilets, a water pump, trash and recycling receptacles, and even a poop bag dispenser available in the picnic area—everything you could possibly need. To get there, drive into the park and take a right at the first intersection. Then continue straight on the park road until it dead ends at the parking lots for the Point Picnic Area.

But why eat next to a parking lot when you can picnic in paradise? Lucky and I recommend finding a spot along the trail to enjoy lunch with a view.

RECOMMENDED HIKE: Point Trail + Woods Trail + Bayview Trail

DISTANCE AND ELEVATION GAIN: 4.1 miles (includes going out to Outlook Picnic Area), 122 feet

DOG AND HUMAN FITNESS LEVEL: recreational rambler/weekend warrior

TRAIL CONDITIONS/MATERIALS: Point and Bayview trails are mostly dirt and forest floor. Woods Trail is a combination of dirt, moss, and grass. There are several wooden footbridges along Bayview Trail. Point Trail is wide enough to accommodate you and your dog walking side by side. Woods and Bayview trails have shorter sections that are wide enough to accommodate you and your dog walking side by side, but longer sections of these trails are narrow and walking single file will be more comfortable. Even along the narrower stretches of trail, there is room to step off the trail to let others pass if needed.

TRAIL MARKINGS/EASE OF NAVIGATING: The trails are well established and easy to follow, though Woods Trail may be a bit overgrown in places. The trails are marked with brown wooden signs that designate the trail name. Many of the signs also include a trail map and icons indicating what activities are allowed on the trail.

THE EXPERIENCE: Park by the Point Picnic Area, which also happens to be the pet picnic area. Don't take the most direct path to the lake from the parking lot. Instead, for a more dramatic reveal, began on Point Loop Trail at the south end of the parking lot. The trailhead is marked with a wooden "Point Trail Loop" sign, a trail map, and an assortment of activity markers. Point Trail Loop starts out routinely enough: trees, ferns, you know, the usual. At the first T-intersection, take a left onto Cut-Across Trail and get ready. As you get closer, you might notice a bright twinkle visible in the distance, just beyond the trees. Go toward the light. And then, with a chorus of angels, you'll arrive at Lake Superior.

Take a right to continue south along Point Trail, but we recommend proceeding at a leisurely pace so you can become more acquainted with the shoreline and ponder the deep emerald greens of Lake Superior against the warm browns of the ancient sandstone cliffs that date back 500 million years or more. The first intersection on Point Trail is a Y-intersection, stay to the left to continue along the shoreline. The next intersection is with Woods Trail. Here, you can either continue straight on Point Trail to check out the Overlook Picnic Area before doubling back to Woods Trail or take the right onto

Woods Trail immediately and skip the Overlook Area. There are many amazing views along the trails that offer stiff competition to the view from this overlook. But it's only about another 0.2 miles to the overlook, so we recommend you go check it out so you can form your own opinion.

Back at the intersection with Woods Trail, take a left. Now, you may feel a twinge of sadness as you turn inland away from the water. But appreciate Woods Trail for what it has to offer. Ferns and moss abound (and maybe bugs too). The trail crosses the park road and then it's just a bit further to the short connecting trail for the Day Use Picnic Area. Take the left and head for the picnic area if you want to use a flush toilet or get some water. Otherwise continue straight on Woods Trail, which is especially narrow and overgrown in this section. Woods Trail comes to an end just a short distance later, and a wooden footbridge leads to a clearing at the northern end of the Day Use Picnic Area. In this clearing there's a nice spot to sit with your dog if someone from your group wants to take the stairs down to take a peek at the barrier beach.

From this clearing, head right (east) toward Bayview Trail, which is marked with a wooden Bayview Trail sign and a trail map. It will only take a moment for the giddiness to return now that the trail has you back along the water. Along this stretch of Bayview there are plenty of vistas worth stopping at to appreciate, and even some historical wind damage to examine. A helpful wooden sign explains how this area of the island was badly beaten up by a storm in 1991. Giant trees uprooted by 100 mph winds lay vulnerable, their entire undersides exposed—now walls of earth and root and reminders that sometimes there's trouble in paradise.

The next section of Bayview Trail includes a series of wooden footbridges. Near these bridges you may notice social trails leading down to the water. One of these paths takes you down to a small inlet frequented by hikers and kayakers, as evidenced by the colony of cairns.

Next, Bayview Trail intersects with the short path to the parking lot, but I recommend skipping this direct route and instead continuing on Point Trail back to Cut-Over Trail so you don't miss a single inch of shoreline. When you reach the intersection with Cut-Over Trail, take a right to backtrack to Point Loop Trail, and then take a right again at the intersection with Point Loop Trail to backtrack to the parking lot, finishing this recommended hike.

WHILE YOU'RE IN THE AREA: You should also visit Copper Falls State Park, Town Park, and Tom's Burned Down Café.

Copper Falls State Park

Like many of Wisconsin's state parks, the story behind Copper Falls goes back millions of years and involves the usual players: transient mountains, ancient seas, Canadian glaciers, and oozing lava. The telltale signs of this historical drama are the black and red lava, granite boulders, shale, and sandstone that can be seen throughout the park. And, of course, the waterfalls! While we have nature to thank for the waterfalls, we owe a debt of gratitude to World War I veterans for developing the park for public enjoyment. In the 1920s, thousands of war veterans, or doughboys, were employed on conservation projects and park development, including developing Copper Falls State Park. In the 1930s, the Civilian Conservation Corps (CCC) completed much of the infrastructure and many of the park's structures that remain today. In homage to these laborers, the trail through the park's main attractions—Copper Falls, Brownstone Falls, Devil's Gate, and the cascades—is named the Doughboys' Trail.

Unfortunately, the Doughboys' Trail is off limits to dogs. There is a giant pet picnic area nearby, but if you don't have friends or family to trade off dog-sitting with you, here's what you're missing: The Doughboys' Trail is one of the most manicured and well-maintained trails I've seen in a Wisconsin state park. Between the smooth and uniform log railings, the even path that skirts the edge of the bluff overlooking the falls, and the groups of people lining the railings to take photos, it feels a bit like waiting in line for the flume ride at Disney World. Despite the somewhat commercial feel of the trail, it's surrounded by a forest, navigating along the edge of a cliff, overlooking a river and occasionally providing glimpses of waterfalls, making this trail a solid runner up for the most magical place on Earth. On the other hand, the views from the top of the Observation Tower are not as advertised. Any views of Lake Superior, the Apostle Islands and the surrounding Penokee Range have long been obscured by the tops of the surrounding trees.

WATER AVAILABILITY: Water is available at the park office, at the concessions stand, and in the pet picnic area.

BATHROOM AVAILABILITY: Flush toilets are available in the park office, at the beach, and by the main parking lot/concession stand. Vault toilets are available at the end of the park road near the Brownstone Falls and in the North Camp Area.

TRASHCAN AVAILABILITY: No trashcans on site; plan on carry-in/carry-out, but there is a trash bag dispenser on a post at the Loon Lake Picnic Area.

DESIGNATED DOG SWIMMING AREA: At the time of our last visit, there was no designated dog swimming area. Dogs are not allowed anywhere past the bathrooms on the paved path to Loon Lake. Unofficially, there's a tiny riverside beach partially hidden from view just beyond the pet picnic area. From this hidden beach there is a clumsy and rocky access point to the river, but the current is stiff. Lucky hasn't been interested in swimming at this spot, but I've seen other owners cast their dogs out into the river on flexi leashes and then reel them back in when they begin to flounder. This itty-bitty beach is a better picnic spot than swimming hole. Check with park staff when you visit in case designations have changed.

DESIGNATED DOG PICNIC AREA: The pet picnic area is the large field just south of the main parking lot near the concessions stand. The area comes equipped with picnic tables, a park-style charcoal grill or two, and a water fountain. I'd recommend bringing all the necessities: camp chairs, cooler, food, and activities to entertain you and your dog while members of your hiking party check out the Doughboys' Trail. And, of course, bring treats and water for your dog too. Skip the hammock though; unfortunately, none of the trees in the pet picnic area are appropriately spaced to set up a hammock.

To get to the pet picnic area, take the park road past the south and north campgrounds and then to the left, to the main parking lot for the concessions stand. Since there isn't a separate parking lot for the pet picnic area, pick a spot as close to the southwest corner of the main parking lot as possible. Then walk down the path and stone stairs to the pet picnic area. If you don't want to schlep all your belongings down the path and stairs, there is an access road that runs adjacent to the pet picnic area. Use discretion when driving on the access road, and of course, move your car back to the lot once you're done unloading.

RECOMMENDED HIKE: Red Granite Falls Trail

HEADS-UP: While you have the option of hiking the Takesson and Vahtera trails, these trails are primarily intended for cross-country skiing, which means that in the summer, the grass is long. Where there's long grass there are more bugs, and where there's no grass, there's dirt which turns into mud in wet conditions. We didn't particularly enjoy these trails for these reasons. Also, Takesson and Vahtera are multiuse trails, so you may encounter bicyclists.

DISTANCE AND ELEVATION GAIN: 2.5 miles, 239 feet

DOG AND HUMAN FITNESS LEVEL: recreational rambler

TRAIL CONDITIONS/MATERIALS: The trail is mostly dirt and rocks—the ratio of dirt to rock fluctuates, with some sections being mostly dirt and other sections being mostly rocks. There are occasional wooden poles embedded at an angle across the trail in these rocky sections, which I assume are to prevent erosion. Additionally, there are some sections where grass encroaches on the trail to varying degrees. The grass completely consumes the trail in a few sections, save parallel dirt ruts from vehicle wear. The trail is wide enough to accommodate you and your dog walking side by side, and there is enough room to step off the trail to let other groups pass.

TRAIL MARKINGS/EASE OF NAVIGATING: The trail is well established and easy to follow. There are brown wooden signs marking the trailhead and at various points along the trail. Some indicate mileage to destinations along the trail. There's a post with a trail map along the way, as well as posts indicating what activities are permitted along the trail.

THE EXPERIENCE: Park in the lot used to access the beach at Loon Lake. The sign for the Red Granite Falls trailhead is near the bathrooms, so this is a convenient opportunity to use a flush toilet before you head out on the trail. To get to the trail proper, walk west across the picnic area and the road. On the other side of the road, the trail is marked with another brown sign. Follow the wide and mildly undulating trail through the forest.

The trail arrives at a Y-intersection; take the right branch to keep heading in the direction of the falls. Then, when the trail splits again, beginning the loop portion of Red Granite Falls Trail, stay to the right to complete the loop counterclockwise. You'll get to the falls faster this way. A bit further down the trail, the trail passes under a high-voltage powerline corridor. A gaping bald swath of land goes on as far as the eye can see to accommodate the powerlines. Despite the obvious intrusion, the forest has begun to reclaim its territory. Prairie grasses, ferns, and even some conifer saplings are opportunistically moving into the void.

After crossing under the powerlines, the trail goes back into the forest and about a mile into the hike, it reaches the area of the falls. A blue arrow on a wooden post points to the left, indicating the trail. But to the right, a short scramble takes you down to the edge of the Bad River and to views of the rapids. This is a scenic place to stop for water and a snack. Calm waters puddle in rocky basins along the edge of the riverbank, while only a few feet away excited water tumbles swiftly north on its way to Copper Falls. After taking in Red Granite Falls and some exploring, head back to the official trail, which continues south parallel to the river but not close enough to offer additional views. Eventually the trail turns east and crosses the high-voltage powerline corridor again. Pass under the powerlines again and continue through the woods.

Once back at the intersection where the Red Granite Falls loop began, stay to the right to backtrack on a familiar segment of trail. At the next intersection, stay to the right to complete the second half of this other smaller loop. And then stay to the right to retrace your steps from the very first intersection back to the parking lot. For a longer hike, double back for a second visit to the falls.

WHILE YOU'RE IN THE AREA: You should also visit Big Bay State Park.

Council Grounds State Park

There's some lore behind the name of Council Grounds State Park, and even though the lore hasn't been substantiated, I think it must be true. As the stories go, Native Americans would canoe down the Wisconsin River to the site that is now Council Grounds to gather for their annual festivals. After visiting this park, it's hard to deny the sacred feeling that permeates the forest and spills out onto the water of the Wisconsin River and into Lake Alexander. If I were to select an epigraph for this park, it would be this line from Edgar Allan Poe's "The Fall of the House of Usher": "There are combinations of very simple natural objects which have the power of thus affecting us, still the analysis of this power lies among considerations beyond our depth."

Walking through a dense forest of mixed hardwood and hemlock— trees that are in some cases as large as two feet in diameter and that shelter many a treasure at their feet, including wild blackberries and day-glow orange fungus—it's easy to understand why Native Americans would have chosen this location for their meetings. Council Grounds possesses a light that the dreariest of days couldn't snuff. Even the occasional dead hemlock tree looming stoic between towering red and white pines has a strangely positive effect. Council Grounds is a modest park, but that modesty is endearing. If I lived in the area, I would visit regularly to read on a bench, to run on the park road, to stand in contemplation on the pier, or to find my muse among giant pines.

WATER AVAILABILITY: Water is available by the beach shelter and the shelter-house picnic area.

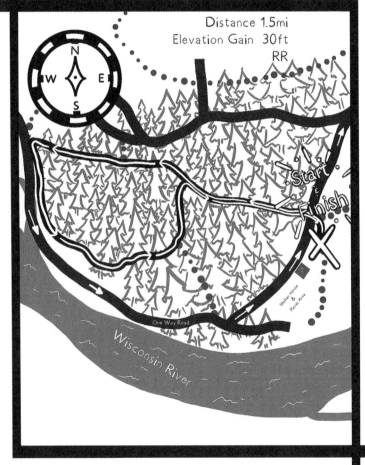

Council Grounds State Park

Distance 1.5mi
Elevation Gain 30ft
RR

N
W E
S

Start
Finish
X

Shelter House
&
Picnic Area

One Way Road

Wisconsin River

BATHROOM AVAILABILITY: Vault toilets are available by the boat landing/fishing pier, the beach, and the shelter-house picnic area.

TRASHCAN AVAILABILITY: There's a pet waste station, with poop bags and a trashcan, just past the entrance station in a small clearing by the information kiosk. For all other trash, plan on carry-in/carry-out.

DESIGNATED DOG SWIMMING AREA: At the time of our last visit, there was no designated pet swim area. Check with park staff when you visit in case designations have changed.

DESIGNATED DOG PICNIC AREA: At the time of our last visit, there was no designated pet picnic area. Check with park staff when you visit in case designations have changed.

RECOMMENDED HIKE: Blue Trail + Green Trail

DISTANCE AND ELEVATION GAIN: 1.5 miles, 30 feet

DOG AND HUMAN FITNESS LEVEL: recreational rambler

TRAIL CONDITIONS/MATERIALS: The trails are mostly dirt and forest floor. Some sections of trail are grass and weeds. A portion of this hike is on paved road. The trails are predominantly flat and are wide enough to accommodate you and your dog walking side by side. There is enough room to step off the trail to let other groups pass.

TRAIL MARKINGS/EASE OF NAVIGATING: The trails are well established and easy to follow. There are brown posts along the trail marked with colored arrows indicating which trail you are on as well as icons indicating what activities are permitted on the trail.

THE EXPERIENCE: There are infinite ways one could navigate the various spokes of these trails, but I'm a sucker for hiking a loop. To get to the start of this Blue/Green loop, drive almost all the way around the park to the very last pull-off along the side of the road. It is just after the drive to the shelter-house picnic area. After parking at the pull-off, walk north/northeast on the road (going with traffic), until you reach the first access point for the Blue Trail. From the road, take a left onto the Blue Trail and follow it into the Krueger Pines Scientific Area. Along this section of trail, you'll be dwarfed by pines on all sides. If your neck starts to kink from looking up, the understory through this section is also impressive. At the three-way intersection, stay to the right to take the Green Trail. A little bit further there is another three-way intersection with a short connector trail. Stay to the left to continue west on the Green Trail until it intersects with the park road near the river. Reaching the road is the midpoint of this hike, so turning left onto the road begins the return trip. Watch for passing cars as you walk along the road, but also check out some amazing views of the Wisconsin River.

Head back into the forest by taking a left at the next access point to the Green Trail. Then, at the next trail intersection, stay to the left to follow the trail back to the first three-way intersection, which should look familiar. Finally, take a right onto the Blue Trail to backtrack through the Krueger Pines Scientific Area. When you reach the road, take a right and head back to your vehicle at the pull-off, completing this recommended hike.

Interstate State Park

This piece of trivia might be useful someday: Interstate is Wisconsin's oldest state park. It's technically not Wisconsin's first; that title goes to the short-lived State Park, which was in north-central Wisconsin and fell swiftly to the axes of lumber companies in 1897. Thankfully, the same fate did not befall Interstate, which was granted state park status in 1900. It's not surprising that Interstate was the second pick for a state park. The St. Croix River and Dalles of the St. Croix gorge are impressive by any standards and are jewels of natural Wisconsin. Speaking of jewels, you may notice some very hefty, round, polished rocks in front of the Ice Age Center and Gift Shop. These are grinders, or small boulders that were caught in whirlpools of melted glacial water as it rushed through the valley. Stuck in the swirling waters, the grinders bored into the bedrock and created massive potholes, which you can view on the aptly named Pothole Trail.

Lucky and I recommend taking plenty of time to explore Interstate State Park and the surrounding area. Despite the noise from US Highway 8, this park offers a welcome respite from the daily grind. Amble up to the overlooks for sweeping views of the Dalles of the St. Croix or launch a kayak or canoe for a more intimate encounter with the Old Man of the Dalles. Put aside any rivalry and visit Minnesota's Interstate Park and Taylors Falls. Take your dog along on a riverboat tour. Head into St. Croix Falls for some ice cream or venture further along the St. Croix Scenic Byway to Stillwater, Minnesota, for some sightseeing. You won't be disappointed; Lucky guarantees it.

Interstate State Park

Dalles of St. Croix

Short Cut

Bonus Route!!!

Lake O' the Dalles

Park Rd

Start & Finish

Distance 1.3 mi
Elevation Gain 431 ft
RR/WW

WORTH A MENTION: Just because we didn't pick Pothole Trail as the recommended trail doesn't mean we don't love it. But it's at most a half-mile long, so we wanted to recommend a hike that covered more ground. You should hike Pothole Trail while you're visiting Interstate State Park. Not only can you stand at the western terminus of the Ice Age Trail but also you and your pup can sit in a giant pothole!

WATER AVAILABILITY: Water is available at the park office and by most of the picnic areas.

BATHROOM AVAILABILITY: Flush toilets are available at the park office and near the amphitheater. Vault toilets are available at the picnic areas by the boat launch, near the trailhead for Pothole Trail, and by the Camp Interstate picnic shelter.

TRASHCAN AVAILABILITY: There are no trashcans on site; plan on carry-in/carry-out. There are trash bag dispensers at some of the picnic areas by the boat launch.

DESIGNATED DOG SWIMMING AREA: At the time of our last visit, there was no designated pet swim area. The boat launch is an unofficial option, but it can get crowded as outfitters launch their kayak and canoe rentals from this location. However, when no one is using the boat launch, I've let Lucky wade around in the calm waters of the St. Croix. There is a short length of shoreline south of the boat launch that is accessible from the boat launch or from a couple of the picnic areas above. However, dogs are not allowed in those picnic areas, so if you're going to access the water and shoreline, I recommend doing so via the boat launch. The shoreline is not accessible from the pet picnic area, and the section of shoreline below the pet picnic area is not very inviting. When you visit, check with park staff in case designations have changed.

DESIGNATED DOG PICNIC AREA: The pet picnic area is the southernmost picnic area in the group by the boat launch and the River Picnic Shelter. Take the road through the park toward the boat launch. You'll end up on a one-way loop that goes past the boat launch and several picnic areas along the river. Take this loop past the second picnic shelter. The pet picnic area is to the right of the final parking lot, before the one-way road loops back out to the main road.

The pet picnic area is equipped with picnic tables, a charcoal park grill, and a few benches that overlook the river. Across from the pet picnic area are vault toilets and a trash-bag dispenser. There is no water in the pet picnic area, but you can get water at one of the other picnic areas nearby. There is no access to the shoreline from the pet picnic area, but the views of the river are nice. As far as pet picnic areas go, this is one of the more scenic ones we've experienced.

RECOMMENDED HIKE: Summit Rock Trail + Echo Canyon Trail + River Bluff Trail

DISTANCE AND ELEVATION GAIN: 1.3 miles, 431 feet

DOG AND HUMAN FITNESS LEVEL: recreational rambler/weekend warrior

TRAIL CONDITIONS/MATERIALS: These three trails are mostly dirt with sections of stone, crude asphalt, and some gravel. There are stone stairs throughout all three, and Summit Rock Trail includes a few flights of wooden stairs. Many of the stone stairs are uneven and at odd intervals and heights. The wooden stairs along Summit Rock Trail include handrails. In sections of Echo Canyon Trail, crude asphalt has been put down. There is some fine gravel along the ridge of River Bluff Trail. These trails are moderately steep in places and are narrow as they climb to the top of the bluffs, making hiking single file most appropriate. It may be challenging to find somewhere to pull off to the side to let others pass in the lower sections of the trails where they are narrower. However, once the trails get toward the top of the bluffs and near the observation points, they become wider and there is more room for passing, pulling aside, and picking a spot to rest and enjoy the view.

TRAIL MARKINGS/EASE OF NAVIGATING: The trails are well established and easy to follow as you ascend the bluffs. It can be more challenging to find and follow the official trail once you are on top of the bluffs. The trails are marked by a combination of signs. Wooden signs with trail maps can be found at the trailheads. Along the way, metal signs are either nailed to posts or directly to trees; when on a post, the sign is often accompanied by a trail map in a tarnished fiberglass casing. Along the tops of the bluffs, where the trails are less obvious, small hiker icons are tacked to trees to suggest the correct path.

HEADS-UP: What we loved about these trails is that they are all short loops, so you can do one, two, or three depending on how far you'd like to hike. Each trail offers enjoyable hiking that isn't too strenuous, plus spectacular views of the St. Croix River gorge.

THE EXPERIENCE: After entering the park, follow the park road around to the first small pull-off parking lot on the right, which is located just below the trailhead for Summit Rock Trail. The trailhead is marked with a wooden "Summit Rock Trail" sign and other signs providing information about the Dalles of the St. Croix River State Natural Area.

The trail starts out with a modest flight of stone stairs that takes you up to the first Y-intersection with Echo Canyon Trail. Stay to the right to continue hiking on Summit Rock Trail, which goes through Canyon Valley. It's not immediately obvious, but you'll know you're in the valley when you pass along a stone wall to your left and the temperature drops a few degrees. Just as soon as you arrive in the valley, you'll climb out of it on a crude and narrow flight of stone stairs. The trail returns to a thin dirt track with occasional stone steps as you get closer to the top of the bluff. The first observation point is marked by wooden rails and offers views of the Dalles of the St. Croix. You can see the overpass of Highway 8 in the distance, and you may see the tour boats making their way along the river to and from the boat launch. From this overlook, go up the multiple flights of wooden stairs to another observation point that offers similar views from a higher vantage point. From here, follow the trail as it turns back, away from the ridge, and descends to the second intersection with Echo Canyon Trail.

At this intersection Summit Rock Trail ends, and Echo Rock Trail goes in either direction. Take the right onto Echo Canyon Trail. Echo Canyon Trail is a gravel and dirt trail that gradually descends into an extinct riverbed. Once level with the river, the trail offers opportunities to get right along the edge of the St. Croix. You can watch as the tour boats, kayakers, and canoeists glide by before going back into the extinct riverbed, which is flanked by canyon walls and punctuated with pine stands. The stone and shade make this area cool, in terms of both temperature and ambiance. You may spot a rocky talus that looks remarkably like the Old Man of the Dalles, though this is not *the* Old Man of the Dalles. As you exit Echo Canyon, the trail transitions to a combination of crude asphalt and pine needles before it finally dead-ends at The Lake O' the Dalles. From here, you can shorten your hike by taking a left and going back to the parking lot along the Lake O' the Dalles Trail. Otherwise, take a right at this intersection to pick up the Lake O' the Dalles Trail momentarily.

Walk along the edge of the lake a short way until you reach the trailhead for River Bluff Trail. Take a right onto River Bluff Trail to head back into the forest and back up the bluff. The trail is an especially narrow dirt track as it sets out through the forest. It widens a little when it begins its ascent up to the top of the bluff on a combination of manmade and natural stone steps dispersed along the dirt and gravel trail. Once up the bluff, the trail becomes less apparent as it parallels the ridge. Small hiker icons are nailed to trees to help you find your way, but you may miss them if you're distracted by the views of the lower gorge. Along the edge of the ridge are several exceptional places to stop for a bit and enjoy the view. You might even be able to see rock climbers on the bluffs across the river in Minnesota. From here, follow the little hiker icons to the official trail and back down to the bottom of the bluff.

When you get back to the bottom of the bluff and River Bluff Trail dead-ends at Lake O' the Dalles Trail, you have a couple of options. To complete the recommended hike, take a left onto Lake O' the Dalles Trail, heading around the north side of the lake to get back to the parking lot. If you'd like to extend the recommended hike, you can take a right onto Lake O' the Dalles Trail, heading counterclockwise around the south side of the lake. Going around the southern side of the lake adds an additional 0.8 miles to the recommended hike. Whether you go north or south around the lake, once you reach the clearing with the picnic area and beach house, take the path east toward the park road, and then take either the path or the park road north back to the parking lot to complete the hike.

HEADS-UP: At the time of our last visit, the trail maps inconsistently marked the lengths of some of the trails. The map we were using indicated the Eagle Peak Trail was 0.8 miles linear, so we anticipated a 1.6 mile hike roundtrip. However, GPS indicated that the hike was more like 0.8 miles roundtrip rather than 0.8 miles linear. Next, we decided to hike Silverbrook Trail. The map said 1.2 linear, so we anticipated 1.2 roundtrip. One mile into the hike and not yet to the midpoint of this out-and-back route, we were starting to think this time it actually was 1.2 miles linear.

Silverbrook Trail is not as exciting as advertised. It is described as a wildlife viewing trail that passes by an abandoned copper mine and the grounds of Silverbrook Mansion, and it supposedly offers a view of the 18-foot Silverbrook Falls. The description of this trail totally oversells it. The sights are really some fenced-off holes in the ground and stone walls that could have been the remains of a copper mine, two stone pillars that possibly marked the drive to the mansion back in the day, and a modest waterfall in the distance obscured by forest. It's fine for an out-and-back if you're just looking to do some walking. But if you're looking for scenery, stick to the trails on the bluffs.

WHILE YOU'RE IN THE AREA: You should also visit Willow River State Park and take a dog-friendly Taylors Falls Scenic Boat Tour. And if you have a lot of time to explore, you might make the trek to Straight Lake State Park as well.

Pattison State Park

Big Manitou Falls, the main attraction at Pattison State Park, is a thing of beauty, but it may take some getting used to. The water that plummets down 165 feet from the Black River is brown. Root-beer brown. And where it crashes against rocks, it froths and foams, resembling a root-beer float. When I first saw Big Manitou Falls, I had to recalibrate my eye to appreciate this giant cataract's majestic beauty—root-beer brown beauty.

The water is tinted brown because of tannins—yes, the same tannins being discussed during wine tastings. Tannins are organic substances found in some tree bark, plant tissues, leaves, seeds, and fruit skins. Tannins constrict the mucus membranes of the mouth, causing dry mouth. This same organic substance that makes wine taste dry makes the waters of the Black River brown. Tannins from decaying leaves and roots along the river seep into the water as it flows from its source in Minnesota to Lake Superior. I imagine this is why Lucky didn't care much for Black River water. He's more a pinot noir kind of guy.

Big Manitou Falls is the highest waterfall in Wisconsin, so it may be surprising that the park isn't called Manitou Falls State Park. But the park might not exist if it hadn't been for the park's eponym, Martin Pattison. Pattison was a successful lumberman and miner back in the late 1800s and early 1900s, and he spent a lot of time around the falls. When he learned of a plan to build a hydroelectric dam on the Black River, he secretly purchased 660 acres of land to save the waterfall. He donated the land to the state, and so Pattison State Park became Wisconsin's sixth state park in 1920.

Pattison State Park

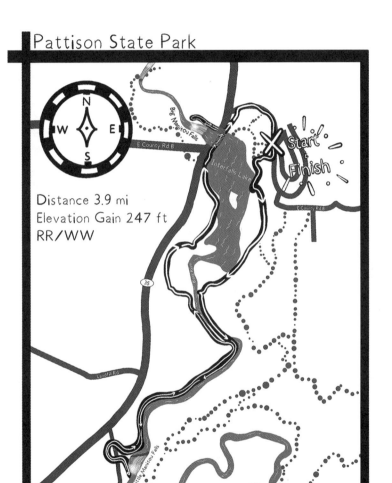

Distance 3.9 mi
Elevation Gain 247 ft
RR/WW

Big Manitou Falls

E County Rd B

Interfalls Lake

Start & Finish

E County Rd B

35

Landfill Rd

Little Manitou Falls

While Big Manitou Falls may be the main attraction at Pattison, Lucky and I much preferred Little Manitou Falls. Despite being the smaller of the two Manitous, the vantage points for viewing Little Manitou Falls are much closer than those for viewing Big Manitou, and there's just something to be said for feeling the mist of a waterfall on your face. The temperature and dew point around Little Manitou can also be a welcome relief from the heat and humidity of a Wisconsin summer day.

HEADS-UP: On nice summer days, the observation platforms overlooking Big Manitou Falls can get Disney World–level crowded with park visitors. If crowds aren't your or your dog's thing, consider visiting during a shoulder season or during off-peak hours.

WATER AVAILABILITY: Water is available at the park office and main picnic area, at the pet picnic area, and near the parking lot for Little Manitou Falls.

BATHROOM AVAILABILITY: Flush toilets are available in the park office. Vault toilets are available at Big Manitou Falls picnic area, the Little Manitou Falls picnic area, near the parking lot for the beach/main picnic area, and at the bath house.

TRASHCAN AVAILABILITY: No trashcans on site; plan on carry-in/carry-out.

DESIGNATED DOG SWIMMING AREA: At the time of our last visit, there was no designated pet swim area. If you take Big Manitou Falls Trail down to the Black River, you eventually descend a flight of wooden stairs that deposits you along the edge of the Black River. Water levels and conditions vary depending on the time of year, but I've let Lucky wade in along the edge of the river here. Apparently, you can also view the Douglas Fault from this location, though I am not exactly sure what to look for. I guess just the cliff in front of you? As always, check with park staff when you visit in case designations have changed.

DESIGNATED DOG PICNIC AREA: The pet picnic area is across from campsite number 1. Park in the southwest corner of the main parking lot and walk south, following the wooden split-rail fence past the horseshoe pits that are between the parking lot and the road into the campground. The pet picnic area is on your right. There is a brown metal sign near the entrance to the picnic area indicating which trails are accessible from this spot, and a paved trail leads into and through the pet picnic area and connects to the Beaver Trail. The pet picnic area comes equipped with picnic tables, a charcoal park grill and a water fountain.

WORTH A MENTION: Pattison State Park has added white paw prints to the paved path to guide visitors with dogs from the pet picnic area around the main picnic and beach area, around the shelter, and then to the tunnel to go under the road to Big Manitou Falls. That's how seriously they take keeping dogs out of the picnic area and away from the beach. So, follow the paws and be shining examples of rule abiding #wisconsinstateparkdogs.

RECOMMENDED HIKE: Beaver Trail + Little Manitou Falls Trail + Checking Out Big Manitou Falls

HEADS-UP: Overlook and Oak Ridge trails are less overlook and ridge and more tall grass and dirt. If it's rained recently, you may encounter a particularly challenging stretch of trail: parallel tracks of quicksand-esque mud with unreliable tufts of grass sporadically serving as a median. The only way through it is to channel your inner Indiana Jones and attempt to calculate each precarious step through this booby-trapped quagmire.

DISTANCE AND ELEVATION GAIN: 3.9 miles, 247 feet

DOG AND HUMAN FITNESS LEVEL: recreational rambler/weekend warrior

TRAIL CONDITIONS/MATERIALS: This route contains stretches of gravel, dirt, pavement, wooden boardwalks, and stone stairs. It also goes through a tunnel. These trails are mostly flat and most comfortably hiked single file. Throughout most of the hike it's possible to find somewhere to pull off to the side to let others pass. There is a catwalk of metal grating to get from one side to the other of Interfalls Lake Dam. If you or your dog are not comfortable walking on the metal grates, your other option is to walk up to Highway 35 and walk along the highway to the other side of the dam.

TRAIL MARKINGS/EASE OF NAVIGATING: The trails are well established and easy to follow. Along the trails there are large brown wooden signs that indicate trails and distances to destinations. However, at the time of our last visit, some of trail names on the signs didn't match the trail names on the park map. For example, some signs refer to the Beaver Slide Trail and the Logging Camp Trail, while park maps refer to Beaver Trail and there is no mention of Logging Camp Trail. Based on the distance, I'm assuming Logging Camp Trail is the combination of Overlook, Oak Ridge, and River View trails. Brown posts with North Country National Scenic Trail markers indicate where the scenic trail overlaps with Beaver and Little Manitou trails. Other posts host icons to indicate activities that are or are not permitted on the trails. Trail intersections are well marked with signs and/or trail maps.

THE EXPERIENCE: Park in the southwest corner of the main parking lot and walk south, following the wooden split-rail fence past the horseshoe pits that are between the parking lot and the road that leads into the campground. Take a right into the pet picnic area and follow the paved trail that goes through the pet picnic area toward Interfalls Lake. Where the paved trail connects with Beaver Trail and transitions to gravel, take a left to head south on Beaver Trail, with Interfalls Lake to your right. There are a couple of opportunities to take in views of the lake along this stretch of the trail, including an earthen dock defined by tread edging of wooden planks and posts. This plot of dirt is not conducive to entering the lake as it is mostly surrounded by shoreline plants, but it's a nice place to stop for photos. In the lake, the brown water looks more like Willy Wonka's Chocolate River than root beer, but flowing along the Black River, it thins out into frothing root beer once again.

Continuing south on Beaver Trail, you'll cross two wooden footbridges before arriving at a three-way intersection with the connector trail that leads from Beaver Trail to Overlook Trail. Stay straight/to the right to continue on Beaver Trail (or Beaver Slide Trail) toward Little Manitou Falls. You'll go over another wooden footbridge and then down a small hill with wooden stairs and two wooden boardwalks. This section of trail skirts the marshy area along the Black River and can get muddy after wet weather, which explains the boardwalks. Beaver Trail then continues west/southwest rather than following the river and returns to a predominantly gravel trail. The trail also narrows through this section and has occasional wooden water bars that have been embedded in the trail at an angle to divert surface water and prevent erosion. Careful stepping on the water bars; they can be slippery when wet.

Next, the trail resumes following the river's edge, and there's a social trail that allows for river access. The water along the riverbank is calm due to the barrier created by a handful of boulders, but just past the boulders, the current can be swift. Back on the trail, at just under a mile into this hike, you'll reach the CCC Bridge. The bridge consists of stone stairs leading up to a wood planked bridge with wooden split railings. After crossing the bridge, you can shorten the recommended hike by taking a right to complete the second half of Beaver Trail now, or you can continue on the recommended hike by taking a left onto Little Manitou Falls Trail. We recommend taking the left onto Little Manitou Falls Trail. It makes for a longer hike, but the spectacular scenery is totally worth it.

You are rewarded very soon after taking the left with a pleasant and scenic trail that runs along the west bank of the Black River. Little Manitou Falls Trail is narrow and mostly dirt and gravel. In places where the river water churns more aggressively over the rapids, clumps of foam catch along the riverbank. Eventually, the trail departs the shoreline and goes up the riverbank. It passes by a bench that offers a partially obstructed view of the river. Past the bench is a clearing in the trees and a large boulder, which offers a much better view. After passing over another wooden footbridge, the trail is back alongside the river near a segment of stronger rapids. From here, the gravel trail transitions to a narrow strip of blacktop that takes you to a clearing and a great view of Little Manitou Falls.

From this vantage point, go straight to see the falls from every possible angle. The next photo opportunity includes a remarkable view of the falls framed by the forest and the official Little Manitou Falls sign. Stone stairs take you down closer to the falls, and a steep rocky social trail on the left takes you all the way down to the base of

Little Manitou Falls. There is no sign suggesting that accessing the falls via this trail is prohibited, but there is a sign along the descent that lets the most adventurous of visitors know that diving into the water is not allowed. This social trail is crude and clunky and should be traveled with caution. But if you can make it down to the base of the falls, you'll be rewarded with amazing views, a cooling mist, and a lot of root beer river foam.

Take caution getting back up the steep rocky trail and then go the rest of the way on the stone trail up to the crest of the falls. Explore the network of short social trails at the top of the falls but be careful if you walk out around the crest. After getting your fill of Little Manitou Falls, head back along the stone trail and either immediately start retracing your way north on Little Manitou Falls Trail or, if you'd like to refill water or use the vault toilets, take the stone stairway on the left up to the parking lot. From the parking lot, you can follow the handicap accessible trail back to the first vantage point of the falls and start retracing your way north on Little Manitou Falls trail from here.

Back at the CCC Bridge, stay to the left to complete the rest of the Beaver Trail loop. This half of Beaver Trail includes sections of stone stairs that take you up and down the undulating terrain. Most of the trail goes through the woods rather than hugging the bank of the river, providing mostly obstructed views of the water off in the distance. The trail returns to the water's edge at the southwestern corner of Interfalls Lake, where the narrow gravel path follows the lake around until it reaches the intersection of Highway 35 and County Road B.

Following the trail will take you across the metal grating over Interfalls Lake Dam. If you or your dog are not comfortable walking on the metal grates, your other option is to cross Highway 35 and walk the short distance along County Road B to the Big Manitou Falls trailhead. If your dog is large enough, the metal grate shouldn't be a challenge, but smaller dogs may need to be carried over the grates lest their wee paws fall through the holes. On the other side of the dam, the trail is paved and leads to a tunnel on your left. The tunnel takes you under Highway 35 and, once on the other side, take a right to get to two different platforms overlooking Big Manitou Falls.

The views of the falls and of the surrounding area are remarkable. A paved trail and some wooden stairs lead to a clearing with commemorative plaques and park signs explaining the geology of the falls. A wide concrete and wooden stairway on the left leads to the first observation platform for Big Manitou Falls. It's difficult to see the actual crest of Big Manitou from this concrete platform because of the surrounding trees and the platform's proximity to the falls, but the views of the gorge and the upper half of the falls are impressive. Taking the paved trail further leads to the second observation platform, which is at the bottom of a short flight of concrete stairs. This wooden observation platform has been built out further into the gorge, making it feel like you're suspended over the river as it tumbles down the rapids. You can see how the water splits into different chutes as it descends the 165 feet and marvel at the trees growing out of the rock face of the gorge. The view downriver from this vantage point is spectacular. This observation platform is our favorite, but on a nice summer day the platform can get crowded with park visitors.

To finish the recommended hike, go back through the tunnel and then take a left. Follow the white paw prints up the concrete stairs and then around the shelter and back to the parking lot, completing this recommended hike.

WORTH A MENTION: If you decide to log more miles by going to the other side of the gorge to hike Big Manitou Falls Trail, you'll see additional views of the falls from a greater distance. Big Manitou Falls Trail is a combination of pavement, dirt, and gravel, with occasional water bars, wooden footbridges/boardwalks, and some steep wooden stairs. The trail is narrow through some sections, making passing other groups more difficult. Going all the way to the end of Big Manitou Falls Trail adds a little over a mile of moderately challenging hiking to your trip, but it is well worth it to see if you can spot the Douglas Fault and to relax for a moment next to the calmer waters downstream from the falls.

WHILE YOU'RE IN THE AREA: You should also visit Amnicon Falls State Park and Wisconsin Point.

Straight Lake State Park

From Madison, Straight Lake State Park is a trek. I'm not going to lie; it took a lot to get me up there. We had plans to visit Straight Lake one long weekend but got sidetracked with a second day at Willow River State Park. And then every time I was planning weekend adventures, it just seemed so far to go for an out-and-back on the Ice Age Trail. But after another 2.7 miles of trails were added to the park, we finally made the trek.

Before it was a state park, the land was owned by the founder of Reader's Digest magazine. Before that it was owned by the Boy Scouts of America, and before that it was almost developed as a golf-equestrian community. And before that it was a popular plot of land with logging companies. And before *all* of that it was along an Ojibwe route to visit Lake Superior tribes. Since the park's founding in 2005, basic improvements have been made—including vault toilets, the trails, picnic areas, and campsites. But much like Newport State Park, the plan is to keep things rustic. There's not going to be electricity hook-ups at campsites, showers and flush toilets, or even a park office. There might be wells in the future for water, but for now you have to BYO. Visitors need to use a self-registration station for day passes, though campsites can be reserved online.

Given the park's relative newness, location, and rustic conditions, it's no surprise that it's a pretty quiet spot. At present, there are a mere 100-plus #straightlakestatepark posts on Instagram. And a check of the DNR's records of state park attendance data from 2005 on shows nothing for Straight Lake State Park. So, if you want a quiet spot in the woods à la Walden Pond, Straight Lake is your best bet of all of Wisconsin's state parks.

Straight Lake State Park

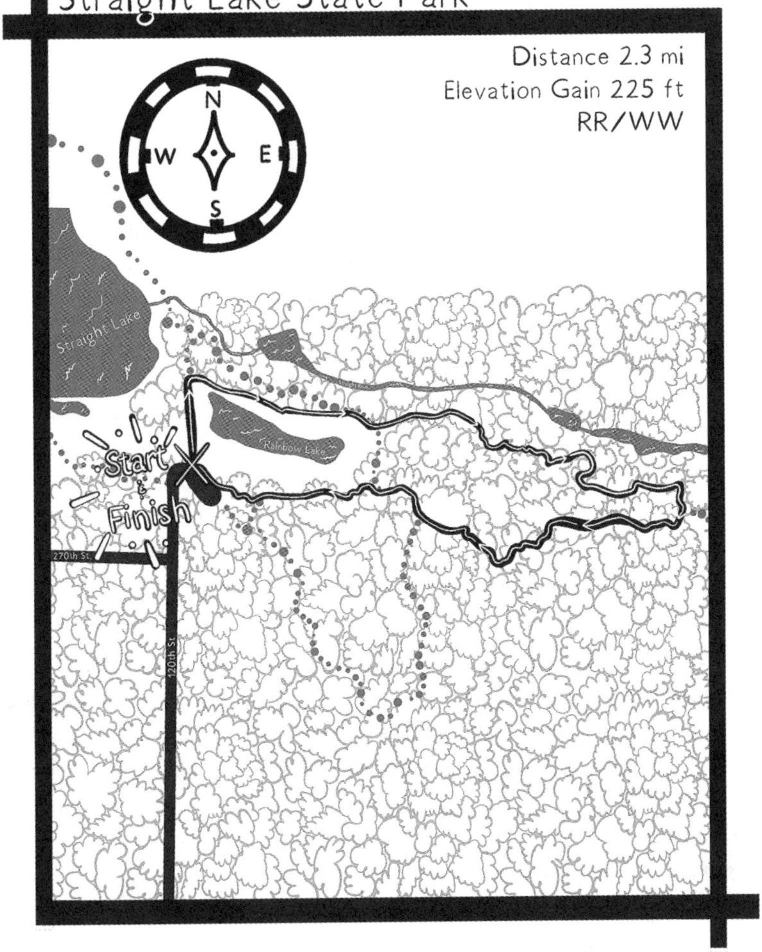

Distance 2.3 mi
Elevation Gain 225 ft
RR/WW

N
W E
S

Straight Lake

Rainbow Lake

Start & Finish

270th St

120th St

WORTH A MENTION: It's only 20 miles on the Ice Age Trail from Straight Lake State Park to the western terminus of the Ice Age Trail at Interstate State Park. Anyone interested? Straight Lake is remote, but there was at least a Kwik Trip about 20 miles from the park. I thought I'd mention it in case you forget something or get sick on the way to the park and desperately need a box of tissues and some cold medicine like I did. #lifesaver

WATER AVAILABILITY: None. BYOW.

BATHROOM AVAILABILITY: Vault toilets are available at the picnic area parking lot, at the campground parking lot, and along Straight Lake Trail near campsite number 8.

TRASHCAN AVAILABILITY: No trashcans on site; plan on carry-in/carry-out.

DESIGNATED DOG SWIMMING AREA: At the time of our last visit, there was no designated pet swimming area, but the carry-in boat launches at both Rainbow Lake and Straight Lake are small sandy entry points into the water that work just as well for a dog as a canoe or kayak. And as there were no park staff around for us to ask, we assume it's permissible to let your pup in the water. As always, be respectful of other park visitors, and if you do see a park employee, be polite and ask so my assumptions don't make an ass out of you, me, and your pooch.

Of these unofficial dog swimming area options, our favorite is the western carry-in boat launch on Straight Lake. It's very secluded, especially scenic, and the water is crystal clear. However, I once found a leech on my foot after wading in the water, so be on the lookout if you take a dip. Park in the campground parking lot and take Straight Lake Trail west, past hike in campsites 4–8. After passing campsite 8, take the trail to the right and down to the water.

DESIGNATED DOG PICNIC AREA: At the time of our last visit, there was no designated pet picnic area. But there are two picnic tables and a park grill at the western carry-in boat launch on Straight Lake, which makes this our favorite unofficial dog swimming area as well as our favorite unofficial dog picnic area. Plus, this is the best picnic area option for enjoying Straight Lake, the park's eponym. Park in the campground parking lot and take Straight Lake Trail west, past hike in campsites 4–8. After passing campsite 8, take the trail to the right and down to the water. As always, check with park staff when you visit in case designations have changed.

RECOMMENDED HIKE: Rainbow + Ice Age + Glacial + Rainbow Loop

DISTANCE AND ELEVATION GAIN: 2.3 miles, 225 feet

DOG AND HUMAN FITNESS LEVEL: recreational rambler/weekend warrior

TRAIL CONDITIONS/MATERIALS: These trails are a combination of dirt, grass, leaf litter, and pine needles—but mostly dirt. There are some rolling undulations along this route but no major elevation gain, despite what the DNR website might say about "steep terrain." There are several bridges along the Ice Age segment, including a bog bridge (a log that's been sliced lengthwise and the two halves are laid side by side, flat sides up), a curving length of boardwalk reminiscent of an old wooden rollercoaster, and a couple other shorter and less exciting wooden footbridges.

The segment of Rainbow Lake Trail on the northern side of Rainbow Lake is the widest of the trails along this route, so you and your dog could walk side by side along this segment. However, the trails on the southern side of Rainbow Lake are all narrow and best navigated single file. Despite the narrow trails, there are plenty of places to step aside if you need to so others can pass, but it's unlikely that you will need to because this is one of Wisconsin's quietest state parks.

TRAIL MARKINGS/EASE OF NAVIGATING: The trails are well established, frequently marked, and easy to follow. There is a wooden sign at the trailhead for Rainbow/Ice Age trails pointing in the direction for each option. Brown hiker icons are tacked frequently to trees on Rainbow and Glacier trails. Ice Age is well marked, as usual, with yellow blazes. There are signs and trail maps at most intersections, except where Ice Age Trail meets up with Glacial Trail. At this intersection there are brown posts with yellow blazes, Ice Age emblems, and arrows pointing in the directions of Ice Age. The path not marked is Glacial Trail, but once you head in that direction, you'll soon start seeing the brown hiker icons again.

HEADS-UP: At the time of our last visit, the DNR map included a "High Point Trail." We hiked what the map indicated was High Point Trail but didn't see a single sign calling it High Point Trail. Even the sign at the trailhead in the upper parking lot called it Rainbow Lake Trail.

THE EXPERIENCE: Park in the main lot (lower lot) and head toward the information kiosk and then north on the road/trail to the right of the information kiosk. Stay on this wide road until you reach the three-way intersection marked with a wooden sign. If you continue straight ahead, you'll get to the Ice Age Trail. If you take a right, you'll be on Rainbow Lake Trail. Rainbow Lake Trail essentially runs parallel to the Ice Age Trail here, along the northern side of Rainbow Lake, so we recommend taking Rainbow Lake Trail to start your hike with as many glimpses of the water as possible. But don't worry, you'll get on Ice Age eventually.

Rainbow Lake Trail follows around the edge of the lake, but you're not on the shoreline. It's a bit above the water, but it's a decent vantage point of the lake. The trail gradually moves a little further inland from the lake, and the view is mostly obstructed by trees, but you can still see occasional glimpses of the water. There are some rolling undulations as the trail makes its way through the woods. Then Rainbow Lake Trail meets up with the Ice Age Trail. Take a left to follow the yellow blazes and log a segment of the Ice Age Trail.

I'm always excited when we get to jump on a segment of the Ice Age Trail while on a state park adventure, and this opportunity is no exception. In my opinion, this portion of the hike is the most interesting and entertaining. The trail is narrower now, but it continues to meander through the woods with a few easy rolling hills. The first bridge you'll come to is the bog bridge. With its moss edging and the surrounding ambiance, I could imagine seven dwarfs going off to work across this bridge. Then the trail goes back to curving through the forest for a while before reaching the second and possibly my favorite Wisconsin state park bridge of all time. This boardwalk-style bridge reminds me of an old wooden roller-coaster track curving through the woods. It doesn't seem necessary—a straighter bridge could get hikers from point A to point B much more directly—but a more direct route would be much less entertaining.

A little bit further down the trail, you'll reach another segment of boardwalk, but it is much shorter and not nearly as reminiscent of a roller coaster. And then even further down the trail, there's an even more basic wooden bridge. After crossing this basic bridge, the narrow trail begins a gradual ascent.

The next intersection is where the Ice Age Trail meets up with Glacial Trail. Off to the left through the trees, you can see some of the ponds of Straight River. There are several Ice Age posts with arrows indicating that trail's course, and then there is a trail that goes to the right. This is Glacial Trail. Take the right, departing from the Ice Age trail, and soon you'll begin to see the brown hiker icons on the trees again. The next intersection is where Glacial Trail meets High Point Trail. If you want to add a little more mileage, you can take the left at this intersection and finish your hike on High Point Trail, which would make your total distance about a half-mile longer than the recommended hike.

Otherwise, stay to the right to keep going on Glacial Trail until the next intersection where Glacial meets up with Rainbow Lake Trail Loop. Take a left to continue on Rainbow Lake Trail. At this point in the hike, things may start to feel a bit monotonous: a narrow trail meandering through the woods. At times like this, I try to look for funky mushrooms or forest critters. Rainbow Lake Trail delivered on both for me—I hope you see some shrooms and critters too. Continue following the brown hiker icons, and when you reach the intersection marked with a post indicating "upper lot" and "lower lot," stay to the right, following the sign for the lower lot. Then just a bit further down the trail there is a final sign for "Rainbow Lake Trail" and "Shelter." Keep to the left, and you'll end up back in the parking lot where this hike started.

WHILE YOU'RE IN THE AREA: You could also head over to Interstate State Park or even Willow River State Park. We initially planned on doing all three parks in one long weekend, but it ended up being a lot to cram into four days. If you have more time to explore and don't get out to this part of the state very often, I recommend trying to explore all three parks because, as I've learned, it can be hard to get out to this neck of Wisconsin woods again.

THE NORTHEASTERN REGION

Governor Thompson State Park

One of my favorite things about exploring Wisconsin's state parks is learning about my home state along the way. In the case of Governor Thompson State Park, I even learned a little about my ancestry. Attempting to keep up with my adventures, my dad asked, "Where are you off to this weekend?" I said "Governor Thompson State Park. It's by Crivitz?" I had never heard of Crivitz, Wisconsin, and was sure my dad had never heard of it either. To my surprise, my dad said, "Oh, Crivitz!" and then told me his parents were both from that area. When times got tough, their families sold off their farms and moved to Milwaukee in search of work. My dad recounted many of his memories of the area, while I mentally recorded this newly discovered tidbit of family history.

Personal ancestry aside, Governor Thompson State Park speaks to Wisconsin's history, as the park bears the name of the state's forty-second governor, Tommy Thompson. Governor Thompson is the longest-serving governor in the state's history; he was in office from 1987 to 2001. The park was established in 2000, making it one of Wisconsin's newest state parks, and while it boasts 16 miles of hiking trails, the water seems to be where most of the action is—if your dog is into it, canoe, kayak, and stand-up paddleboard rentals are available at the park and are reasonably priced.

HEADS-UP: While ticks have been found year-round in Wisconsin, if you hike at Governor Thompson State Park in the spring, be prepared to do multiple tick checks of both you and your dog. During a visit to Governor Thompson on a Memorial Day weekend, we noticed the prolific tick population right away. They started crawling up the outer walls of our tent only moments after having staked it down. Despite the heat that weekend, I wore long spandex pants tucked into my crew socks. There was practically a tick on every blade of long grass that blanketed the trails. I'd watch as the ticks climbed up my hiking boots and then my crew socks, and when they reached the top of my sock, I'd stop to flick them off. Then, I'd repeat this exercise of watching, waiting, and flicking.

After each hike, I'd spend up to an hour picking ticks off Lucky. After one of our hikes, the backs of his legs looked like they had scales. I filled a bowl of water with all the ticks I could find on Lucky, and then I stripped down to my underwear and changed my clothes along the side of the road. Despite these measures, days later I continued to find ticks crawling on the ceiling in my car and across the floor in my kitchen.

WATER AVAILABILITY: Water is available at the park office and at the Woods Lake Picnic Area.

BATHROOM AVAILABILITY: Flush toilets are available at the park office. Vault toilets are available near Woods Lake Picnic Area and at Boat Landing 13.

TRASHCAN AVAILABILITY: There are poop bags and a specific dog waste trashcan available at the Woods Lake Picnic Area.

DESIGNATED DOG SWIMMING AREA: At the time of our last visit, park staff informed us that dogs could go anywhere in the park if they were on leash and under the owner's control. They even said dogs could swim at the beach at Woods Lake. Apparently pet segregation hasn't yet come to Governor Thompson State Park. But rather than disturb anyone swimming, we recommend doggy paddling at the canoe/kayak launch just north of the beach. When you visit, check with park staff in case designations have changed.

DESIGNATED DOG PICNIC AREA: At the time of our last visit, there was no designated pet picnic area, but the poop bags and trashcans at the Woods Lake Picnic Area make it pet friendly. And with only one other picnic shelter in the park (also by Woods Lake), this is your best

Governor Thompson State Park

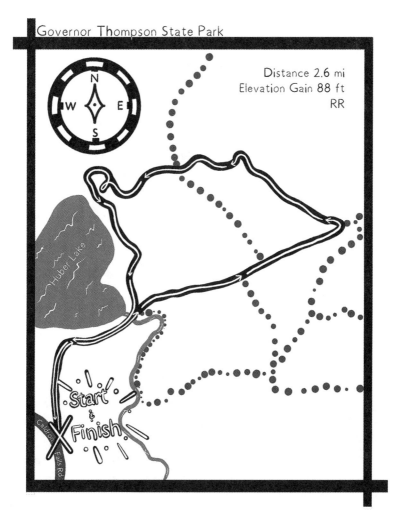

Distance 2.6 mi
Elevation Gain 88 ft
RR

Huber Lake

Start & Finish

Caldron Falls Rd

option. When you visit, check with park staff in case designations have changed.

RECOMMENDED HIKE: Part of Flowage Trail + Sunset Trail

DISTANCE AND ELEVATION GAIN: 2.6 miles, 88 feet

DOG AND HUMAN FITNESS LEVEL: recreational rambler

TRAIL CONDITIONS/MATERIALS: The trail is mostly grass with some sections of sand. This route is predominantly flat, but the recommended section of Flowage Trail includes a couple of small hills. The trails are wide enough to accommodate you and your dog walking side by side, and there is enough room for passing other hikers and dogs.

TRAIL MARKINGS/EASE OF NAVIGATING: The trails are well established and easy to follow. The trail intersections are marked with wooden posts with trail names atop them. The posts also have icons indicating activities that are permitted on the trails.

THE EXPERIENCE: You don't have to go into the park to get to the Flowage Trailhead on Caldron Falls Road. Park on the side of Caldron Falls Road by the gate and signs that mark the trailhead. The trail is wide and grassy as it heads north to Huber Lake. There are few undulations of the trail in this section, and the grass is replaced with sand in some spots. The trail then turns east when it hits the lake, and though it doesn't stick closely to the edge of the lake, it offers some partially obstructed views of the water. Cross a short gravel bridge, and then continue straight. The trail here is wide enough for a vehicle, and it's apparent that vehicles frequent this trail as it's mostly grass except for parallel tire tracks of sand. A bit further, the trail returns to consistent grass but remains wide enough for walking side by side with easy passing.

You have many opportunities to extend this hike and explore trails that split off from Flowage Trail, but to follow the recommended hike, go straight at the first four-way intersection as well as at the next two three-way intersections. The first intersection is with Sunset and Thunder Mountain trails, the second is with Hills Trail on the right and the third is with North Trail on the left. At the next intersection, Flowage Trail meets up with Sunset Trail for a second time. At this intersection, take a left to begin a counterclockwise hike of Sunset Trail. Follow the wide grass trail through the woods to Sara's Rock. Most of Sara's Rock is obscured by overgrowth, but just past Sara's Rock the trail takes you over some exposed rock that looks like bald spots swelling from beneath the grass. These bald spots dappled with moss and grass are an interesting feature along an otherwise ordinary trail. At the next intersection where North Trail crosses Sunset, continue straight.

Further along Sunset, you'll reach a short offshoot that takes you to a bench and a vista of Thunder Mountain, which is best seen off in the distance by standing on the bench. Sunset Trail finally brings you back along Huber Lake, and once again you'll be able to take in some semi-obstructed views of the water on your way back to Flowage Trail. When you reach the intersection with Flowage Trail and Thunder Mountain Trail, take a right onto Flowage and begin backtracking toward the road. Cross back over the gravel bridge and backtrack to the trailhead to complete this hike. And once you're back to the road, make sure to do a thorough tick check before getting in your vehicle.

Hartman Creek State Park

Hartman Creek State Park has classic Wisconsin roots: beer and cheese. The land that is now Hartman Creek State Park was once owned and farmed by the Allen family, and their primary crop was hops. In the late 1800s hops production on the east coast was going gangbusters, until drought and aphids decimated the eastern hop yards, creating an opportunity for farmers in Wisconsin. George Allen (the OG) got in on the action in the 1870s and ended up having the largest hop house in Waupaca County. When the farm changed hands from George to his son Merrick, it also transitioned to dairy farming, and the hop house was replaced with a creamery. John J. Windfeldt, an award-winning cheese and butter maker, was brought in to run the creamery until the next generation's George Allen took over and turned the creamery into a fish hatchery. The land was eventually purchased by the Wisconsin Conservation Department in 1939 and then turned over to the State Parks and Recreation Division in 1960. The state park officially opened in 1966.

The park is located near the Chain o' Lakes, a series of lakes formed when chunks of ice melted in the valleys carved out by the Cary Glacier 12,500 years ago. The glacier also tapped natural springs as it scraped across the earth's crust, and now those springs supply the lakes with super pure water. The water is incredibly clear, and the park ranger told us that on a sunny day, you can look down on Allen Lake from the trail above and see fish swimming around. We haven't been able to make out any fish on our visits, but when you're standing on the fishing pier, you can unmistakably see the underwater lake weeds that surround it.

WATER AVAILABILITY: Water is available at the park office and at picnic areas, including the pet picnic area by Allen Lake.

BATHROOM AVAILABILITY: Flush toilets are available in the office and at the Whispering Pines picnic area. Vault toilets are available at the picnic areas and shelters, including the pet picnic area.

TRASHCAN AVAILABILITY: Always plan on carry-in/carry-out, but the trash/recycling station is outside of the family campground, right along the south side of W. Windfeldt Lane. Technically, dumpsters at state park campsites are for registered campers only, but they're right on your way out if you park at the Campground Overflow Parking/Playfield lot to do a hike. I think if you're dumping one bag of poop, you're ok. Just don't bring all your trash from home to their dumpster.

DESIGNATED DOG SWIMMING AREA: At the time of our last visit, there was no designated pet swimming area, but there's a canoe/kayak launch on Allen Lake that, when not being used by anyone else, could be a spot for your dog to take a quick dip. The pet picnic area is nearby on a smaller, unnamed pond, which I imagine could make an improvised dog swimming area for undiscriminating dogs. There's no official entry point or beach, but when it comes to dogs and getting into water, where there's a will, there's a way. As always, check with park staff when you visit in case designations have changed.

DESIGNATED DOG PICNIC AREA: The pet picnic area is on the north side of the parking lot for Allen Lake. It's a pretty decent spot for a pet picnic area. There's a water spigot close by, vault toilets a short walk away, and a handful of picnic tables shaded by some giant pines. Between the pond and Allen Lake, no matter where you sit, you have a water view.

RECOMMENDED HIKE: Deer Path Trail

HEADS-UP: When it comes to restaurant menus, I hate having too many options, but when it comes to trails, I'm over the moon to have lots of options—and the trail system at Hartman Creek reads like a choose-your-own-adventure book. So, while I'm recommending Deer Path Trail as an easy and scenic loop, Lucky and I like to add on to Deer Path to get in a little more mileage. If you're looking for a longer hike, we'd suggest adding on some combination of the Oak Ridge

Trail System and the Ice Age Trail. Between the two, we prefer spending more time on Ice Age Trail because it's more technical and interesting. The Oak Ridge system is groomed for skiing in the winter, which means it has classic cross-country ski trail characteristics— it's wide, grassy, and predominantly flat. If you get out into the Oak Ridge Trail system, there are maps and letter markers at all major intersections. The short extension from Deer Path up the red trail to Oak Ridge (near letter N) is not marked on Deer Path. The Ice Age trail is well marked, with yellow blazes painted on trees at regular intervals along the route.

DISTANCE AND ELEVATION GAIN: 1 mile, 45 feet

DOG AND HUMAN FITNESS LEVEL: recreational rambler

TRAIL CONDITIONS/MATERIALS: Deer Path Trail is mostly a dirt trail, with some pine needle–laden segments, some sandy segments, and some weedy grass segments closer to the lake's edge. The trail can get muddy, especially closer to the lake's edge. The trail is predominantly flat, but there's a moderate grade as you get around to the western side of the lake. There are also some wooden stairs on the southern section of Deer Path Trail that are eroding and not very uniform in height and spacing.

As the name suggests, the trail looks a lot like the path deer might carve out as they navigate the terrain single file, so the trail is narrow. It is not wide enough to accommodate you and your dog walking side by side, but there is usually someplace for you and your dog to step off the side of the trail to let others pass.

TRAIL MARKINGS/EASE OF NAVIGATING: The trail is well established and easy to follow, especially because it follows the edge of the lake. Along Deer Path there are infrequent posts with arrows and hiker icons.

THE EXPERIENCE: Park in the lot at Allen Lake, by the pet picnic area. We recommend going counterclockwise on Deer Path, so take the paved walkway toward the lake and then take a right at the water fountain. Allen Lake, the canoe/kayak launch, and Travel Wisconsin's selfie station are to the left, and the pet picnic area and unnamed pond are to the right. Straight ahead is a wide dirt path that cuts between these two bodies of water and is bordered on either side by a single row of tall pines. This is a pretty cool start to the hike because it feels like you're being ushered into the grand hall of some outdoor palace. Once you reach the other side of the grand hall, take a left onto the narrow dirt trail. You're now on Deer Path Trail.

The trail is very narrow through this initial section and stays close to the water's edge. Soon enough, it puts more distance between you and the water and passes through the edge of a pine stand. The trail is a little wider here and covered in pine needles. This cycle repeats a few times—the trail narrows and gets closer to the water's edge, going through understory, before turning more inland and back into and along the pine stands. Eventually, as you reach the northwestern side of the lake, the trail begins a subtle ascent. You'll know you've reached the top of the climb when you see the descent ahead of you. It's short but also sort of steep. Also, at the top of the hill and to the right is the short trail extension that connects Deer Path Trail to the Oak Ridge Trail System. If you're going to extend your hike, now is a great time to part ways with Deer Path. There are a lot of options that can keep you busy for a bit and then bring you back to this same spot to finish this hike, if that's what you want to do.

To complete the recommended hike as-is, go down the hill in front of you. While most of Deer Path is one narrow path, erosion by water and foot traffic has created a couple of different flows down the hill. At the bottom, the various flows merge back together, and the trail continues through the understory. The trail is still very narrow and is a bit further from the water on this side of the lake. Also, the pine stands are replaced with mixed hardwood saplings and lots and lots of ferns (we love ferns). You'll pass a bench with a vista of the lake, and the trail will take a right and go up another low-grade hill with exposed roots that serve as natural stairs. Then the trail turns back toward the lake, where it continues along a ridge above the lake.

Next, you'll arrive at a three-way intersection. Stay left, and head down the gradual descent that includes some wooden stairs that are eroding and not very uniform in height or spacing. The trail gets closer to the water once again and eventually passes by another small canoe/kayak launch point. The dirt trail reaches and runs alongside a wooden fence, which ushers you past the official Deer Path Hiking Trail sign and to a short connecting trail. Stay to the left on the trail and pick up the paved walkway that cuts through the picnic area and past the vault toilets to get you back to the parking lot at Allen Lake, completing the loop.

WORTH A MENTION: The park has about 12 miles of single-track mountain bike trails. These trails are open to hiking but are very popular with bikers. We recommend only hiking on the mountain bike trails at nonpeak times, like weekdays in early spring and fall.

High Cliff State Park

Peninsula State Park has claimed the moniker "Wisconsin's most complete park," but High Cliff could easily compete for the title. In fact, the parks have a lot in common. Both are located on a body of water. Peninsula State Park is on the eastern side of Green Bay, and High Cliff is on the northeastern side of Lake Winnebago, Wisconsin's largest lake. Both parks host a portion of the Niagara Escarpment, the long cliff that stretches all the way to New York (and yes, the very same cliff that Niagara Falls cascades over). Both parks offer visitors a variety of recreational opportunities. But where High Cliff has the advantage, in my opinion, is in its dog-friendly features. High Cliff is one of the most pet-friendly parks in Wisconsin, with three separate pet picnic areas and a legitimate dedicated pet swim area. Plus, dogs are allowed on all trails. Because it is so dog friendly, you can usually expect to run into some other #wistateparkdogs during your visit.

The park also has two distinctive levels—lake level and escarpment level—and each level tells a story of the park's history. The lake level bears the remains of a once-booming mining town. The limestone mine operated for about one hundred years, and at its peak, the town had a tavern, dance hall, and even an amusement park. The only structure that remains intact is the general store, which has been restored and now serves as a museum. The last load of lime went into the kilns in 1956, and since then, the kilns have been left to deteriorate. Now, hawks perch on the ruins looking for their next meal.

The escarpment level bears the remains of an even older civilization— but in this case, not the actual human remains. Nine effigy mounds have been preserved along Indian Mound Trail, but they contain no human remains or artifacts. At one time there were thirty mounds in this area, but early developers of the land didn't have the same deference for these sacred structures. The escarpment level also features an unrelated and more contemporary structure honoring a Native American. The statue of Chief Red Bird that stands at the top of the escarpment was dedicated in 1961. Red Bird was Chief of the Ho-Chunk in the 1820s, but he and his people actually lived on the western side of Wisconsin in Prairie du Chien. As the story goes, Red Bird was caught up in a misguided revenge killing, so he surrendered himself to prevent a war between the Ho-Chunk and the white men. He ended up dying in prison in 1827. Then the George Banta Foundation commissioned the Red Bird statue in 1953. George Banta was a Kentuckian who moved to Menasha in 1885, opened a printing company, and helped create the Phi Delta Theta fraternity and Delta Gamma sorority. The connection between Red Bird and Banta remains a mystery, but the statue helps elucidate the story of Chief Red Bird and the history of the Ho-Chunk people in Wisconsin.

WORTH A MENTION: You'll probably spend most of your time on one of the park's two levels, but did you ever consider what happens between these levels? During one of our visits, we noticed a picnic table that had been thrown over the edge of the escarpment precariously perched halfway down the cliff. But that's not the strangest thing that's ever been tossed over the side of the escarpment. Apparently in the 1920s people drove cars over the edge for fun on the Fourth of July. Throughout history, where there's a cliff, there will be people doing stupid things over the edge of it.

WATER AVAILABILITY: Water is available at the park office, near the lower shelter, and near the Red Bird statue on top of the escarpment.

BATHROOM AVAILABILITY: Flush toilets are available at the park office, by the pet picnic area at the marina, and at the picnic area near the Red Bird statue on top of the escarpment. Vault toilets are available at the pet picnic area on top of the escarpment.

TRASHCAN AVAILABILITY: Most picnic areas are carry-in/carry-out, but there is a dumpster at the marina parking lot.

High Cliff State Park

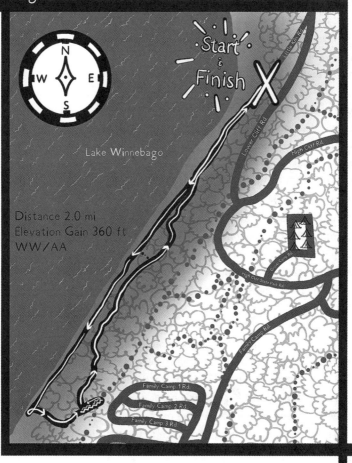

Start & Finish X

Lake Winnebago

Distance 2.0 mi
Elevation Gain 360 ft
WW/AA

Little Kau Rd.
Lower Cliff Rd.
High Cliff Rd.
Group Camp Rd.
High Cliff State Park Rd.
Family Camp Rd.
Family Camp 1 Rd.
Family Camp 2 Rd.
Family Camp 3 Rd.

DESIGNATED DOG SWIMMING AREA: The pet beach is north of the people beach and can be accessed via the road to the marina, though there isn't an actual parking lot on the south side of the marina. Parking is allowed on the south side of the road, and we'd recommend parking along the road rather than any of the parking lots. From the end of the marina road, the pet beach is a short walk and can be accessed via an opening in the tree line.

This is one of the most isolated pet beaches we've encountered at a Wisconsin state park, and I mean that in a good way. Trees and shrubbery provide a barrier between the beach and adjacent picnic areas. The people swim area can be seen down the shoreline from the pet beach, but again, vegetation provides a distinct and impenetrable barrier between these two beaches. In this secluded area, there is a wide and long swatch of grass, a thin strip of sand and debris, and then the lake. The grassy area is large enough for many dog owners to settle in with picnic blankets, beach chairs, coolers, and other gear for an afternoon. The thin strip of sand is littered with branches, other natural debris, and a decent amount of trash (which is my only complaint about this beach). The water is shallow far into the lake. Dog owners can be seen standing in waist-deep water some distance offshore, calling their dogs out to join them in the lake.

Because of how sheltered the pet beach is from the rest of the park, I didn't feel the same expectation to immediately leash Lucky the second his paws left the water. He and another dog chased each other down the length of the beach, as owners watched without worrying someone would complain, because there is no reason for any sans-doggo groups to be in this area. To get to this location, you must deliberately seek it out and enter it. There's no way someone could accidently stumble into the pet beach.

There's also a canoe/kayak launch in the pet picnic area on the north side of the marina where dogs can dip their toes, but considering how awesome this pet beach is, I wouldn't bother with the canoe/kayak launch.

DESIGNATED DOG PICNIC AREA: There are three different pet picnic areas at High Cliff. The most scenic pet picnic area is on the north

Dog swimming area at High Cliff State Park (Danielle St. Louis)

side of the marina. It offers views of the boats coming in and going out of the marina, the breakwater, and the lake beyond. This picnic area comes equipped with a couple of picnic tables, several benches looking out over the water, and a campsite fire pit with grate. A couple of trees provide shade, and flush toilets and a concession stand aren't far away. The area also hosts a canoe/kayak launch where your dog can take a dip to cool off, but we recommend going to the pet beach for extended swim time.

The second pet picnic area is on the south side of the marina. It can be accessed via the road to the marina, though there isn't an actual parking lot on the south side of the marina. Parking is allowed on the south side of the road, and we'd recommend parking along the road rather than any of the parking lots if possible. This pet picnic area offers views similar to the one on the north side of the marina, but doesn't feel as cohesive. It comes equipped with a couple of picnic tables, a park grill, and is closer to the water spigot along the road. It is also closer to the pet beach.

The third pet picnic area is on top of the escarpment. To access this pet picnic area, take the park road up the hill to the T-intersection and take a left. The parking lot and picnic area is the first one on the left. This picnic area comes equipped with picnic tables, a park grill, and vault toilets. The area is wooded and offers shade, but there aren't any views, as the area is too far from the edge of the escarpment.

The pet beach could function as another pet picnic area, though there are no picnic tables or grills. BYO picnic blanket or camp chairs, and you're all set!

WORTH A MENTION: High Cliff has plenty of options for recreational ramblers. The Butterfly Pond Trail, an interpretive trail that offers two paved loops, both less than a mile long, is a great option and does allow dogs. Red Bird and Indian Mound trails are flat and wide; a great option for the less adventurous or the less fit. These trails offer lots of room for passing other groups without even having to pull off to the side of the trail, and connections to other trails and the roads make it possible to create a custom loop of whatever distance you're looking for.

HEADS-UP: Because Red Bird runs parallel to the road, campsites, picnic areas, and more, it doesn't have the feeling of secluded wilderness many are looking for in a hike. On Red Bird, you're constantly aware of civilization nearby, so if you're looking for a more technical and secluded hike, stick to the recommended Lime-Kiln Trail.

RECOMMENDED HIKE: Lime-Kiln Trail

DISTANCE AND ELEVATION GAIN: 2 miles, 360 feet

HEADS-UP: The distance and elevation gain include a jaunt up the staircase to Red Bird Trail to check out the top of the escarpment before coming back down to finish Lime-Kiln.

DOG AND HUMAN FITNESS LEVEL: weekend warrior/avid adventurer

TRAIL CONDITIONS/MATERIALS: Lime-Kiln Trail is primarily gravel, dirt, and rocks, with some sections of protruding roots. There are numerous wooden footbridges, a wooden staircase (or two if you go up to the top of the escarpment), and wooden steps. After a heavy rain, be prepared for sections of mud along the lake and slippery conditions, especially on wooden steps and bridges.

The portion of the trail that runs along the lake is flat and wide enough for walking side by side, with plenty of space for stepping aside to let others pass. When the trail turns to go up the escarpment and then traverses along the escarpment, it becomes narrower, and stepping off to the side is more difficult. This portion of the trail can be technically challenging and includes some steep climbs and descents. It's best navigated single file.

TRAIL MARKINGS/EASE OF NAVIGATING: Personally, I think the DNR map for High Cliff is crazy confusing. I'm used to each trail being marked with its own color or having its own dot/dash pattern. In this case, the colors and patterns of dots/dashes relate to uses for the trail. It's possible one trail could be marked with multiple color/dot/dash combinations over its length. The physical trails are marked with colored dots on the trees, but don't confuse the color of dots on the trees with the color of the dots on the map. For example, Red Bird Trail is marked with red dots on the trees, but the red dots on the map aren't specifically indicating Red Bird Trail (though part of Red

Bird trail is marked with red dots/dashes on the map). The technical communicator in me is not a fan of the High Cliff system. Ultimately, we didn't rely too much on the dots on the trees because the trails were relatively obvious and well established. We referenced the map when we reached intersections, but between intersections, it was usually clear where the trail was and where it was not.

Lime-Kiln Trail is a well-established trail and easy to follow. It's marked with blue dots on the trees, there is a sign at the intersection where you decide between the shorter loop or the longer loop, and there are several icons on trees where the trail makes sharper turns.

THE EXPERIENCE: Park at the lot for the Old Kiln Ruins. The trailhead is at the south end of the parking lot and starts as a wide, flat gravel road. As the name suggests, the trail first takes you past the ruins of the old lime kilns, which are on the left, and to the right is a scenic view of the lake. This area is spacious and could accommodate crowds of tourists. Continuing past the ruins, the trail narrows a bit, though it is still wide enough for a vehicle. A guard rail keeps visitors (and vehicles?) on the trail. Next, the trail takes you between the remains of two giant concrete structures, which were likely part of the mine at one time.

The trail crosses a culvert, and just past the culvert on the left is where the Lime-Kiln Trail loop reconnects to this main trail segment. Stay straight, and hike along the lake first to complete the loop counterclockwise. Along the lake, the trail narrows some, but it's still wide enough to walk side by side. Throughout this section of trail, there are several social trails that lead down to the water's edge. We advise using caution on these social trails. During one visit, we gave in to the allure of the social trail and headed for the lake's edge, but because of recent rain and slippery conditions, my traction was compromised by Lucky's momentum. As one foot went forward, the rest of my body, supported by the other foot, went backwards as if unsuccessfully doing the limbo. My quadricep bore the brunt of the slip, and thankfully I wasn't seriously injured (though I did take the rest of the trail tenderly and with some trepidation). Use caution if exploring these areas.

Soon you'll reach an intersection with a bench and a wooden sign indicating your options. Take a left to complete the short loop, otherwise stay straight to complete the long loop, which is our recommendation. The trail remains flat and wide enough for walking side by side, even over the frequent wooden footbridges. In between the footbridges, roots start to protrude into the trail more, and if it's rained recently, this section of trail may be full of puddles and mud. The trail gets really rooty and narrows more just as it reaches the southernmost point before turning left to go up the escarpment.

The climb starts on some uneven wooden stairs, but this is where Lime-Kiln Trail really starts to shine. The trail going up the escarpment is narrow and more technical, and now, in addition to the mixed hardwood forest and undergrowth, the landscape includes rock outcroppings covered in moss. It's quite the scene; Lucky and I have stopped for many pictures of him posing majestically on moss-covered boulders with forest and cliff in the background. Eventually the trail brings you to the face of the escarpment—on the right, an imposing wall of rock flanks you, and straight ahead is a towering rock formation. It's an impressive sight that you can't miss. Between the rock formation and the cliff face is a passageway that leads to the wooden staircase to the top of the escarpment. We suggest checking out the passageway, and if you're feeling up to it, climbing the stairs to the very top of the escarpment. We think it's worth checking out from every vantage point.

Back at the base of the cliff face, stay to the left of the rock formation to continue on Lime-Kiln Trail. At first, the trail weaves through some protruding rocks, but it quickly gets less technical and wider as it traverses the side of the escarpment. The trail's descent is mostly gradual, but it does have some steeper and rockier sections. A wooden staircase takes you down a particularly steep section of the trail, which is followed by an easier and wider segment and a longer wooden footbridge. At the next intersection, continue straight to stay on the higher ground and to finish out the long loop.

The final section of the long loop continues to navigate the side of the escarpment, alternating between rocky technical descents and level easygoing traverses. Eventually, the trail becomes more uniform in width and composition as it goes left and down to connect with the main segment of Lime-Kiln Trail just past the culvert. To complete the hike, take a right to retrace your steps back past the two giant concrete structures and the remnants of the lime kilns to the parking lot.

Lost Dauphin State Park

Many of Wisconsin's state parks have interesting pasts, some with a sprinkle of scandal, but none of the parks can quite match the drama that's at the heart of Lost Dauphin State Park. The central character of this story is Eleazer Williams, whose biography is interesting even without the conspiracy. Williams was raised by Mohawk parents in Canada. He left the tribe to go to school in Massachusetts and was next recruited to spy for the Americans during the War of 1812. After the war, he became a religious leader in New York, naturally, and then led a tribe of Oneida to Christianity and then west to Green Bay. Finally, he married and settled down on this plot of land along the Fox River.

This is when things get really interesting. Around 1840, Williams starts claiming he's the long-lost son of King Louis XVI. Wait. What? Here's a French history refresher. During the French Revolution, King Louis XVI, Queen Marie Antoinette, and their two living children, Louis-Charles and Sophie, were taken captive. The king and queen were executed, and Louis-Charles supposedly remained in captivity until he died of tuberculosis in 1795 at the age of ten. There were rumors that loyalists had smuggled the children out of France, but those were just rumors. That is, until Williams received a visit from the Prince de Joinville, son of the newly restored King of France. According to Williams, he was the lost dauphin (*dauphin* means the eldest son of the king of France, or crown prince). He claimed he had been smuggled out of France as a child, brought to Canada, and raised by his adoptive Native American parents. The prince came to visit him in Green Bay to tell him of his royal roots and to ask him to sign away any claim to the throne for a substantial sum of money.

Apparently, the Prince de Joinville did come to visit Williams, so says the sign at the park, but other reports suggest the prince was in Green Bay and may have just bumped into Williams on a steamboat. Either way, I imagine things in Wisconsin were just getting boring for our man Eleazer, so he fabricated this story to spice things up. He did so to moderate success. A guy named John Hanson wrote a book about him called *The Lost Prince*, and he got more than the average fifteen minutes of fame. But Williams wasn't alone. Many other people also came forward claiming to be the long-lost son of King Louis XVI, and eventually Williams's fifteen minutes were over.

At the time of Williams's claim, DNA testing wasn't a thing. Fast-forward to the year 2000, and DNA tests of a shriveled-up chunk of heart confirm that the real heir to the throne did in fact die in France. But the story of this chunk of heart is equally astonishing. Evidently, the heart was removed during the autopsy of the young boy who died in 1795, and then smuggled out of the prison. It was preserved in booze, until the booze evaporated, and then it dried out and bounced around from one place to another. At one point it was donated to an archbishop, and then plundered from a palace, put in a crystal urn, passed on as an inheritance from one generation to another, and finally interred in the royal family's necropolis. Crazy, right?

Lost Dauphin might be a small park, but the story alone makes it worth a visit.

WATER AVAILABILITY: None. BYOW.

BATHROOM AVAILABILITY: At the time of our last visit, there was a "Jim's John" port-a-potty by the main picnic area.

TRASHCAN AVAILABILITY: There is a trashcan next to the picnic shelter.

DESIGNATED DOG SWIMMING AREA: None, as there are no bodies of water in this park.

DESIGNATED DOG PICNIC AREA: At the time of our last visit, there was no designated pet picnic area. I normally recommend checking with park staff when you visit in case designations have changed, but it's unlikely there will be someone there for you to ask. The main picnic area is spacious and offers nice views of the Fox River. We say go for it!

RECOMMENDED HIKE: The gravel trail

DISTANCE AND ELEVATION GAIN: 0.7 miles, 28 feet

HEADS-UP: The distance and elevation gain include the walk to and from the parking lot at the bottom of hill, so in earnest, the trail itself is maybe, at most, half a mile.

DOG AND HUMAN FITNESS LEVEL: recreational rambler

TRAIL CONDITIONS/MATERIALS: The trail is gravel and mostly flat, with some rolling undulations that barely register as elevation changes. It's well maintained, though at the time of our last visit there were some signs of erosion from heavy rainfall on the downward slopping portions of the undulations. The trail is wide and can accommodate walking side by side. There is plenty of room for passing other hikers and dogs.

TRAIL MARKINGS/EASE OF NAVIGATING: The trail is well established and easy to follow. There are no trail maps or markers, but there really is no need. The trail is one loop through the woods, with one short trail connecting the park to the nearby subdivision.

THE EXPERIENCE: Park at the entrance, in front of the Lost Dauphin Park sign. There is room in this area for several cars to park. There is a gate across the road that leads into the park, and at the end of that road is another larger parking lot; however, it's unclear when/if the public can use this lot. We're guessing the gate is only opened and the parking lot used when the picnic shelter is reserved for parties. Otherwise, vehicles are restricted to the small area at the main entrance. At the time of our last visit, there was a "no motor vehicles" sign laying on the ground near the entrance. It looked like it may have had a run in with a motor vehicle.

The hike begins with a walk up the driveway to the picnic area. It's a short walk up a gradual hill on a gravel road that leads to the larger parking lot and the picnic area. The picnic shelter, a few benches, and a swing set are to the right. This portion of the park offers a nice view overlooking the Fox River. To get to the trail, walk through the parking lot and head to the left. There are two entrances, but they both lead to the same trail. We recommend heading into the woods the first chance you get, naturally. The trail is on the other side of a small grass clearing, and it dips down as it enters the woods. This first rolling hill leads to a Y-intersection. Stay to the left and continue to follow the gravel trail as it passes along a small gully. A few more undulations, and the trail divides around a small stand of trees. The left branch of the trail leads to the adjacent subdivision, so at this intersection, stay to the right.

The trail crosses to the other side of the gully and has fewer undulations on the return trip. The final intersection presents you with the option of continuing straight and coming out of the forest at the second entrance to the trail or taking a right and looping back to the first entrance into the forest—the one you came in on. Both are fine options and eventually get you back to the parking lot by the picnic area. We recommend taking in the views and reading about the history of Lost Dauphin Park before heading back down the gravel driveway to the park entrance.

Newport State Park

Newport State Park is a formally designated wilderness park, a designation that locals fought hard for and obtained in 1974. To be a wilderness park, Newport can't be developed to increase day use; it must be kept in its most natural state. Trails are maintained for safety and invasive species are controlled, but you won't find a golf course, tennis court, or volleyball net at Newport. You also won't find any RVs or car camping—only rustic hike-in campsites are available. The wilderness park designation was locals' way of keeping their sliver of paradise from turning into a tourist trap.

Considering its current rustic state, it's surprising to think that Newport was once a bustling village with a colorful history. In 1881, Hans Johnson became Newport's first private owner. Hans served as the town's treasurer until 1905, when he drank up all $2,250 of the town's funds. Disgraced, Hans spent the rest of his life on a farm in Newport that he no longer owned, and he eventually died of tuberculosis. Peter Knudson became part-owner of the town in 1892. He fared well, building a sawmill and, it seems from historical records, cutting down almost every tree on the Door County Peninsula.

Meanwhile, a German immigrant in Chicago named Ferdinand Hotz was amassing a fortune selling gems and designing custom jewelry. Business took Ferdinand across the United States and Europe, and then in 1905, the fine jewelry business brought him to Marinette, Wisconsin, naturally. Ferdinand caught feelings for Door County during a day trip to Fish Creek, and multiple visits and six years later, he started purchasing Door County land left and right.

Ferdinand was a preservationist—an early adopter of "leave no trace"—and generously allowed public use of his land in Newport until that use started to leave a mark. His conservation mentality was instilled in his children and grandchildren, who decided against further developing the land and sold off portions of the property to the state of Wisconsin in 1966 and 1978. That land is now Newport State Park and, as the land has been allowed to return to wilderness, it's almost impossible to tell that a town once existed in this location, save a few vestiges from the Hotz's homestead.

Ferdinand's story is an interesting and inspiring one, and he would likely be proud of the park's wilderness designation. So Lucky and I encourage you and your dog to tread lightly while hiking at Newport in respect of Ferdinand's legacy.

WORTH A MENTION: It's dark out here. Newport has also been designated as a Dark Sky Park by the International Dark-Sky Association. It's one of 23 places in the United States and one of a handful of parks in the Midwest to receive this designation. So, if you're out at Newport at night, don't forget to look up.

WATER AVAILABILITY: Water is available at the park office and at the main picnic area by parking lot 3.

BATHROOM AVAILABILITY: Flush toilets are available at the park office, and vault toilets are available near parking lots 2 and 3. If visiting the vault toilets at parking lot 2, be prepared to hike a short distance to the bathrooms, located about halfway between the parking lot and the beach.

TRASHCAN AVAILABILITY: No trashcans on site; plan on carry-in/carry-out.

DESIGNATED DOG SWIMMING AREA: Pets are allowed on the northern stretch of beach at Newport Bay. Park at lot 3 and take the paved sidewalk toward the lake. Once you reach the beach, there is a sign to the left indicating that dogs are allowed in the section of beach past the sign. The people beach is close by, just on the other side of this invisible line, which means dog owners should be especially careful to keep their dogs on leash when not in the water. But it also means this

Newport State Park

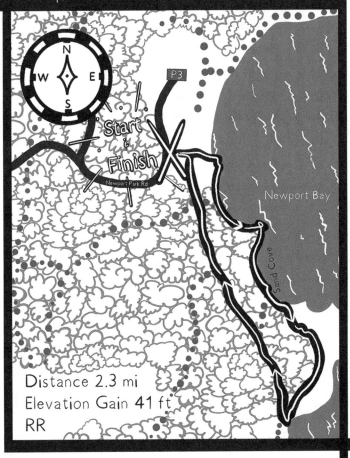

N
W · E
S

P3

Start
&
Finish

Newport Park Rd

Newport Bay

Sand Cove

Distance 2.3 mi
Elevation Gain 41 ft
RR

beach is legit. Some parks designate a stretch of shoreline for dogs only when that real estate is undesirable for people. This stretch of shoreline is nice enough to be a people beach but has been graciously bestowed upon pets and their owners.

There is a second beach on the southern section of Newport Bay that can be accessed from parking lot 2. This beach isn't designated as a pet beach, but at the time of our last visit the park superintendent implied that dog restrictions weren't strictly enforced in off-peak months (it was September). She seemed rather unconcerned with where I took Lucky as long as I kept him on leash and picked up his poop. Done and done. But as always, check with park staff when you visit in case designations have changed.

DESIGNATED DOG PICNIC AREA: At the time of our last visit, there was no designated pet picnic area, but every time we visit, dogs and their owners are enjoying their lunches at the picnic area by parking lot 3. As always, check with park staff when you visit in case designations have changed.

WORTH A MENTION: It was difficult to pick a recommended trail because there are a lot of great options at Newport. If you love ferns, like I do, and are at the park during the summer, make sure to check out Fern Trail. It's an accessible trail, so it's wide and flat and alternates between boardwalk sections and dirt trail. More important, it's bordered on both sides by loads of ostrich ferns that thrive in this microhabitat. Lynd Point Trail and Rowley's Bay are also nice options, as segments of these trails run parallel to the shoreline, but they don't offer the same beachy experience as the recommended hike.

RECOMMENDED HIKE: Sand Cove/Duck Bay + Newport Trail

HEADS-UP: Technically, there is no trail named Sand Cove/Duck Bay trail, but there is an unnamed trail that follows the shoreline, making stops at Sand Cove and Duck Bay. So that's what I'm going to call this trail.

DISTANCE AND ELEVATION GAIN: 2.3 miles, 41 feet

DOG AND HUMAN FITNESS LEVEL: recreational rambler

TRAIL CONDITIONS/MATERIALS: These trails are mostly dirt with some rocks and roots, as well as sand along the shoreline. This route is flat, and, for most of Sand Cove/Duck Bay trail, narrow. Hiking is easiest single file until coming back on Newport Trail, which is wider and can accommodate walking side by side. Passing others on the trail is possible throughout the hike but is easiest on Newport Trail.

TRAIL MARKINGS/EASE OF NAVIGATING: The trail is well established and easy to follow. There aren't markers tacked to trees along Sand Cove Trail, but there are wooden signs at intersections with Newport Trail indicating which trails go in which directions and distances to parking lots. Some intersections even include a trail map with a blue "you are here" dot. Honestly, the number of signs along Newport is impressive and reassuring, especially when someone in your hiking party is counting down the tenths of a mile to the bathrooms (clearly, not Lucky).

THE EXPERIENCE: Park at lot 2 and find the entrance to the trail on the east side of the parking lot. The dirt trail is wide as it heads into the woods and takes you east toward the lake. On its way to the beach, this connector trail crosses Newport Trail. Continue straight, past the vault toilets on the left, until you reach the beach. This isn't the official pet beach, but dogs are allowed on leash. Depending on the time of year, you might also be able to let your dog swim at this beach, but check with park staff before doing so. This is also a nice spot to have lunch on a picnic blanket if the picnic area near lot 3 is crowded.

There is no sign indicating the trail, but if you're looking at the lake, there is a path in the sand to the right. The trail is separated from the beach by a plot of beach grass.

This sand path starts out wide and then quickly narrows as it progresses down the shoreline. The trail through the sand dead-ends at a little cove—not *the* Sand Cove, but a little blip of a cove before you get to the real deal. On some of our visits, this spot has been like a mini private beach where I let Lucky enjoy some water time, but on other visits, it's been a quagmire of ew. So, if it's nice, stop. And if it's not, take a right and head up into the woods. This transition from the beach to the woods can be mildly confusing, especially since trail maintenance is minimal. The trail might not be immediately obvious,

Sand Cove/Duck Bay trail at Newport State Park (Danielle St. Louis)

and you may have to navigate over the weathered remains of a fallen tree and through some overgrowth. Also, it's a slight uphill to get to the cedar forest.

Once you're in the cedar forest, the trail widens a bit as it navigates around roots and rocks protruding out of the ground. Lucky and I enjoy this section of the trail because we're partial to cedar forests, ferns, and rocks covered in vibrant moss. Plus, it continues to run parallel to the lake for a bit, so you can still see and at times access the water on your left. There are at least two spots along this section of trail where Lucky and I like to swing out and sit on the rocks and take in views of the lake. Eventually, the trail departs the shoreline and narrows as it cuts through stands of saplings and understory. When the trail arrives at a brown park sign indicating directions for Newport Trail, Sand Cove, and Duck Bay, take a left and head down the narrow, sandy trail to Sand Cove. Sand Cove is a narrower and shorter stretch of beach than the beaches near lots 2 and 3, but it's a great spot to stop for a snack, a swim, and a selfie.

When you're ready, backtrack on the narrow sandy trail to the brown park sign and take a left to keep going southeast on Sand Cove Trail toward Duck Bay. This section of Sand Cove Trail is less interesting than the previous segments as it departs the water and heads into the deciduous forest. The next intersection is where Sand Cove Trail meets Newport Trail. Here, you can gauge how much gas you and your dog still have in the tank. If you have a lot of gas left, heading south on Newport Trail will provide you with additional options for extending your hike. You could continue to the next intersection with Ridge Trail or go even farther and loop back on Rowley's Bay/Newport or go even farther and loop back on Rowley's Bay. Be advised though, these loops are lengthy and would take this hike solidly into the weekend warrior category. To complete the recommended hike (2.3 miles), take a right onto Newport Trail and head north. Once on Newport Trail, the scenery is still deciduous forest, but the dirt trail widens, making walking side by side and passing others much easier.

As you progress along Newport Trail, you'll come to several intersections marked with brown wooden signs. Continue straight through each intersection until you arrive back to the very first intersection on this hike. You should recognize the Toilets/Beach/ Picnic Area and Newport Trail signs. When you reach this intersection, take a left to backtrack on the connector trail to the parking lot to finish this hike.

WHILE YOU'RE IN THE AREA: You should also visit Peninsula, Rock Island, Potawatomi, and Whitefish Dunes state parks. Al Johnson's Stabbur Beer Garden is the perfect place for a post-hike beer. The establishment and staff are super dog friendly; they have dog bowls and water for your pup and the bartenders dole out sizable dog biscuits.

Peninsula State Park

Peninsula State Park is Wisconsin's most popular camping destination, and its popularity is in part due to the assortment of activities available here, including swimming, fishing, kayaking, canoeing, boating, biking, volleyball, tennis(ish), playgrounds, and an 18-hole golf course. The golf course is home to two additional attractions: a Memorial Pole and the grave of Chief Simon Onanghuisse Kahquados.

The golf course was established in 1921, and the Memorial Pole was erected between the first and ninth fairways in 1927. The pole serves to commemorate the Potawatomi and other native groups who used to inhabit the area until the US government "relocated" them outside of Door County. A putt away from the Memorial Pole is the grave of Chief Simon Onanghuisse Kahquados, the last Potawatomi chief living in Wisconsin, who was buried here when he died in 1930. While these commemorative actions may have been performed with the best of intentions, the idea of honoring the Native peoples who were kicked off their land by deeding a tiny piece of real estate on a golf course to a memorial pole and burying the last Wisconsin Potawatomi chief nearby seem wholly inadequate. Adding insult to injury, park visitors can only go see the pole and grave during nonplay hours of the golf course, which leaves them dusk until dawn May through October, and the off-season months of November through April.

The injustice is further underscored by the juxtaposition of how Native Americans were evicted from the land with how European squatters were granted permission to live in the park. When the park was established in 1910, campers who had been squatting in Nicolet Bay

were granted "life leases." The park manager even delivered them gro-
ceries and mail. These semi-permanent communities were around until
the 1960s when the last life-leaser passed away.

Lightening the mood, did you know that Peninsula State Park first
used computers to schedule camping reservations in 1982?

More enduring than recreational facilities (just ask the park's tennis
court), and undoubtedly the main reason for the park's popularity, is the
convergence of water, earth, flora, and fauna that happens here. Among
the remarkable habitats in Peninsula State Park is a portion of the Niagara Escarpment, the long cliff that stretches all the way to New York. The
escarpment is home to a vertical forest of northern white cedar trees
that hug the bluffs, and hugging those trees is a globally rare species of
snail. From the large features of Green Bay and the Niagara Escarpment
to the small details of warblers and black-eyed Susans, one can understand why Peninsula State Park has been dubbed Wisconsin's most
complete park.

HEADS-UP: Peninsula State Park is the Door County equivalent of
    Devil's Lake State Park, and by that I mean it's a tourist trap.
    Peninsula State Park has seen more than one million visitors a year
    since at least 2002, which is as far back as I could locate attendance
    data. Peninsula is often the second or third most-visited state
    property, always behind Devil's Lake State Park and sometimes third
    to the Kettle Moraine South Unit.

WORTH A MENTION: Driving down Shore Road through the park, just
    north of the intersection for Mengelberg Lane, there is a sign on the
    east side of the road that says "Tennis Court" and an arrow points
    into the woods. There is no road to the court, only the beginning of
    Skyline Trail. A short hike gets you to the destination, but there, in the
    middle of the woods, is no tennis court. This paved and fenced plot
    of forest is half low-security prison yard, half Chernobyl tennis club.
    The cracked blacktop and leaves piling up at the foot of the net mock
    the "1 Hr limit when others are waiting" signs. The space feels
    haunted by ghosts of tennis pros past. Even if you stay long enough
    to take some eerie photos in the ruins of this bygone recreational
    space, you'll still be well within your one-hour time limit.

HEADS-UP: The last time Lucky and I visited Peninsula State Park, we camped for a weekend in Tennison Bay. When I checked in at the office, the park attendant asked if I had any dogs. I said yes, and she stapled a bright pink square of paper solidly to the bottom of my campsite permit. The permit then gets clipped to the post at the entrance to your site. I'm used to the campsite permit routine. It's possibly the one protocol that is consistent throughout all of Wisconsin's state parks. But the pink square was new. When she handed me the permit, I saw that the pink portion included the park's dog rules and in bold the instruction "Keep this notice affixed to camping permit." I couldn't help but feel like I had just been handed my scarlet letter.

I dutifully affixed the permit to my post, pink paper and all. Now, in addition to notifying park staff that I'm at the correct campsite and the dates of my reservation, the permit also alerts park staff and other visitors that I have a dog that may need to be policed. Ugh. As I walked through the campsite, I noticed a lot of other dogs, but saw only one other group with the pink paper affixed to their permit. As much as I disliked this new aspect of the campsite permit protocol, I was even more disheartened to see dog owners not complying. As more people take their dogs to state parks, it becomes even more important for owners to be respectful of rules and other visitors' experiences. If not, the rules concerning dogs may become more restrictive. It's a pink paper now, but if we don't adhere to the rules, it's only a matter of time until dogs aren't allowed in campgrounds at all. I encourage you and your dog to be exemplary ambassadors for dogs in Wisconsin's state parks by following the rules, even if the rules seem Puritanical.

WATER AVAILABILITY: Water is available at the park office, Nicolet Beach, and Weborg Point.

BATHROOM AVAILABILITY: Flush toilets are available at the park office, Nicolet Beach, and Weborg Point. Vault toilets are available at Fish Creek, Nelson Point, Welcker's Point, and Eagle Terrace.

TRASHCAN AVAILABILITY: Trashcans are available at Nicolet Beach. There's a dog poop bag dispenser at the pet picnic area, between the Nicolet Beach parking lot and the overflow parking lot.

Peninsula State Park

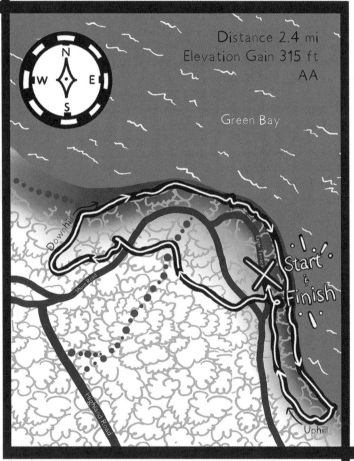

Distance 2.4 mi
Elevation Gain 315 ft
AA

Green Bay

Downhill

Shore Road

Highland Road

Eagle Terrace

Start & Finish

Uphill

DESIGNATED DOG SWIMMING AREA: At the time of our last visit, there was no designated pet swim area. Dogs are not allowed anywhere north of the parking lot at Nicolet Beach. You can access a rocky stretch of Nicolet Bay shoreline from the Minnehaha Trail and there are a few points of access to the water along Eagle Trail, but these are also very rocky. As always, check with park staff when you visit in case designations have changed.

DESIGNATED DOG PICNIC AREA: The Pines area at Nicolet Beach is the designated pet picnic area. The area is the wooded section between the main Nicolet Beach parking lot and the overflow parking lot. A sign at the back of the main lot points in the direction of the overflow lot and has a dog poop bag dispenser on it, as well as a sign that says, "Leashed Pets Permitted." There are picnic tables and a charcoal park grill or two scattered throughout this wooded area.

To get to the designated pet picnic area from the park headquarters, take Shore Road through the park past the Tennison Bay campground. At the intersection with Bluff Road, take a right and head past the Nature Center and the firewood station. When Bluff Road dead-ends at Shore Road, take a left onto Shore Road. Then, either take a right to park in the lot for Nicolet Beach or take a left to park in the overflow parking lot. The picnic area is between Shore Road and the Nicolet Beach parking lot.

RECOMMENDED HIKE: Eagle Trail

DISTANCE AND ELEVATION GAIN: 2.4 miles, 315 feet

DOG AND HUMAN FITNESS LEVEL: avid adventurer

TRAIL CONDITIONS/MATERIALS: During one of our visits, Lucky and I encountered several hikers using trekking poles to help them navigate the terrain. When we came upon them, they stopped and asked if Lucky would be able to handle the rocky hike. I laughed and assured them that if they needed to worry about anyone, it was me—Lucky is part mountain goat, after all. They looked at me confused, as if they were honestly wondering if I thought dogs and goats could reproduce, and then they trudged past us.

The trail is 50 percent rocks, 50 percent roots, and 100 percent fun. When I say rocks, I mean the big ones that erupt out of the ground at all angles. Someone like me could easily twist an ankle on this trail—I have peculiarly weak ankles. Between the rocks is dirt, and in some stretches of trail, the ratio of dirt to rock swings in dirt's favor. But that's usually where the roots start protruding from the ground in tangled knots. While hiking most of Eagle Trail, my eyeballs are glued to the ground in front of me, and I have to stop so I can look around without taking a tumble. The trail also has sections that include stone stairs of varying heights/widths as well as some swampy sections outfitted with wooden planks to walk along.

The trail's width fluctuates constantly. Some segments are wide enough to walk side by side with your dog and allow for easy passing. Other sections are narrow and only allow for single-file walking, though there is still the option of stepping aside to let others pass. And in other areas, like the sections of wooden planks and some sections by the sea caves, passing could be a real challenge.

TRAIL MARKINGS/EASE OF NAVIGATING: The trail is well established and mostly easy to follow. There are signs at the trailhead and at major intersections and landmarks that include trail maps and an array of icons. Over the length of the trail there are a collection of Eagle Trail, blue hiker, blue arrow, and brown arrow icons nailed to trees. Markers are posted more frequently where the trail is less obvious, which is mostly on the climb back up to Eagle Terrace.

THE EXPERIENCE: The parking lot at Eagle Panorama is small and fills up quickly, so we suggest parking at one of the lots along the drive to Eagle Terrace. There is one parking area right by the Terrace, but there are a handful of additional parking lots and picnic areas along the road.

Lucky and I recommend saving Eagle Terrace for the end of the hike because the view is even more impressive when you've become familiar with the world between the terrace and the water of the bay below. So, begin the hike at the trailhead on the west side of the main Terrace parking lot. The trail starts out especially rooty and goes through a short section of forest before crossing Shore Road. The trail continues through the forest on the other side of Shore Road. Next, Eagle Trail intersects with Sentinel Trail. Keep going straight (west) on Eagle Trail toward Eagle Panorama. The trail crosses Shore Road again at the parking lot for Eagle Panorama. Travel Wisconsin has one of their #scenicwisconsin selfie stations at Eagle Panorama, so you can get a picture of you and your pooch at the panorama even if no one is around to take it (though the popularity of this spot makes it unlikely you'd be alone here).

After taking in the views of Horseshoe Island and the expanse of Green Bay from the panorama, return to the parking lot and jump back on Eagle Trail going clockwise. As the sign at the trailhead in the parking lot suggests, this is where things start to get more difficult. A short flight of stone stairs begins the descent down the Niagara Escarpment. The trail seems like a straightforward gradual descent at first, but it gets a bit more technical further down. Eventually, the trail turns to an inconsistent combination of dirt and rocks and more stone stairs appear, but the deliberateness of their positioning is uncertain.

Another sign reiterates the difficulty level of Eagle Trail where it intersects with Minnehaha Trail. At this intersection, take a right to continue on Eagle Trail. The trail is again predominantly rocks, and you can't see the water through the trees just yet. The lack of view is for the best, since focusing on foot placement is important through this section. Eventually, the trail runs parallel to the edge of the bluff, but views of Green Bay are still obstructed by the northern white cedars growing out of and up the side of the escarpment. The white cedars add a different texture to the trail, which is now blanketed with leaves and crisscrossed by roots, but the rocks eventually reemerge as the predominant trail material.

A little less than a mile into the hike, the trail gets closer to the bottom of the escarpment and several segments are lined with wooden planks to preserve the trail and keep hikers out of the mud that is quick to get sloppy in wet conditions. After walking the planks, the trail finally reaches the rocky shoreline and offers your dog a place to dip his toes in the water. This first water access point is marked with yellow number 5 signs on posts: one just off the trail and one closer to and facing the water. I'm assuming these are markers for kayakers. On this stretch of Eagle Trail, there are blue hiker icons affixed to trees signaling the trail and there will be four more kayak landings marked with numbered signs. These kayak landings are good spots for taking in views of the lake, but they're not great for sitting down for a picnic or for wading in the water. Just after passing kayak landing 4, there it is.

When you first look up at the exposed escarpment from below, it's easy to get excited. You've arrived at the coolest segment of this hike. Now the trail traverses the side of the 150-foot cliffs, offering you a front-row experience of the Niagara Escarpment and the ancient sea caves that were carved into it ages ago but have now been left high and dry. And man, is one of them really high! You might just miss the most impressive cave if you don't remember to look up.

The trail along this stretch of escarpment is narrow and rocky, with a couple more mildly treacherous social trails down to the water's edge, before reaching the end of the exposed escarpment. Passing other hikers along this stretch could be challenging because it's rocky and technical, but you can always wait in one of the sea caves as others pass. Then, the trail takes you past some impressively gnarly trees as it turns inland. An especially narrow section through thick understory and saplings opens to a community of elderly northern white cedars. Besides exploring the sea caves, navigating this section of trail between kayak landings 2 and 1 is my favorite. These trees, some of which are more than five hundred years old, emote wisdom and honesty—characteristics I had never attributed to trees until I encountered this crowd. The trail through the cedar stand is wide and accommodating, complimentary to the trees' demeanor, and though it's easy going by comparison to the rest of the trail, Lucky and I recommend you take your time through this gathering. Eventually, an Eagle Trail marker nailed to one of the ancient trees reminds hikers that they are in fact on a mediated trail, despite feeling like the trees have parted to accommodate you of their own friendly accord. The trail says farewell to these elderly cedars and takes one more dip down to the water's edge at kayak landing 1. And then, without much ado, a small brown arrow points into the woods and to your gradual ascent back up the escarpment.

As you ascend the escarpment, follow the blue arrow and hiker icons through the maze of rocks and roots that form crude stairs up the side of the bluff. Occasionally, a series of stones appear in the form of stairs that are less haphazard than the rocks and roots. The trail reaches an outcropping of the escarpment—a miniature version of the bluffs seen from below but too far from the water to have sea cave features. The trail scrambles up the right side of the outcropping, switches back to the left, and continues up, up, up. Momentarily, the trail gets flat and wide as it backtracks the distance you walked along the shore at the bottom of the escarpment, before narrowing again and continuing the vertical push to the top. Throughout this section, trail markers are more frequent as the narrow trail navigates over rocks and through trees and understory. You'll begin to see swatches of blue water through the branches and leaves on your right just before reaching a sign pointing left for Eagle Terrace Overlook and right for Eagle Trail.

Follow the trail to the left to get to the Eagle Terrace Overlook. The first small overlook offers some nice views of the lake, but this is not *the* Eagle Terrace. Follow the stone wall and railing to the sizable staircase carved into the escarpment. At the bottom of the stairs is Eagle Terrace, an impressive overlook with varying levels and expansive views of Eagle Harbor. It's a short walk back up the staircase and along the trail to the Eagle Terrace parking lot, completing this recommended hike.

WHILE YOU'RE IN THE AREA: You should also visit Rock Island, Newport Beach, Potawatomi, and Whitefish Dunes state parks. Al Johnson's Stabbur Beer Garden is the perfect place for a post-hike beer. The establishment and staff are super dog friendly; they have dog bowls and water for your pup and the bartenders dole out sizable dog biscuits.

Potawatomi State Park

Based on DNR attendance estimates, Potawatomi State Park is the second most visited state park of the five in Door County. But it's not a close second. Annually, Potawatomi receives fewer than a quarter of the number of visitors that go to Peninsula State Park. At the time I'm writing this, there's around 1,000-plus #potawatomistatepark posts on Instagram, and around 14,000 #peninsulastatepark posts. And frankly, I don't understand why. Potawatomi offers an authentic Door County experience without pretense. It has similar features to Door County's most popular park, including a stretch of the Niagara Escarpment, its own length of shoreline along Sturgeon Bay, and its own rotting observation tower that's only a foot shy of Peninsula's former Eagle Tower. Peninsula's tower was taken down in 2016, and Potawatomi's was closed in 2019 due to wood decay.

Dogs weren't allowed up the Observation Tower anyway, so we recommend the view at the Old Ski Hill Overlook, which provides a similar and still impressive view of the surrounding area. At max fall foliage, this would be an amazing spot to take in the patchwork quilt of trees blanketing the landscape all the way to the horizon. In my opinion, Potawatomi is one of the most underrated parks in the state, and I prefer it to other more ostentatious parks (ahem, Peninsula).

WORTH A MENTION: Potawatomi State Park is home to the eastern terminus of the Ice Age Trail.

WATER AVAILABILITY: Water is available at both picnic shelters and at the boat launch.

Potawatomi State Park

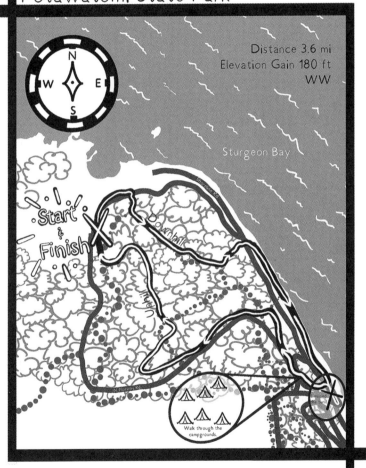

Distance 3.6 mi
Elevation Gain 180 ft
WW

Sturgeon Bay

Start & Finish

Downhill

River

Shoreline Rd.

N. Norway Rd.

Walk through the
campgrounds.

I missed
the turn.

BATHROOM AVAILABILITY: Flush toilets are available at the entrance to the south camp area. Vault toilets are available at the boat launch, by the Observation Tower, and both picnic areas.

TRASHCAN AVAILABILITY: Standard state park policy says trashcans and recycling are available for campers only. Day use visitors should plan on carry-in/carry-out. However, Tower Trail takes you through the north camp area near the dumpster and recycling, and there's another dumpster and recycling station across from the park office on your way out. Don't plan on dumping your trash from home here, but I think slinging a bag of poop into one of these cans is probably ok.

DESIGNATED DOG SWIMMING AREA: At the time of our last visit, there was no designated pet swimming area. There are a few points where Tower Trail/Ice Age Trail run along the shoreline that get you close to the water, but these spots are rocky and a bit of a drop to water level. Lucky's not adventurous enough for that—he prefers wading in gradually. The boat launch offers a more gradual entrance into the water, but it's an official area for boats, not dogs, so use discretion if you take your dog over to explore the boat launch. As always, check with park staff when you visit in case designations have changed.

DESIGNATED DOG PICNIC AREA: At the time of our last visit, there was no designated pet picnic area. Since there is no official pet picnic area, we make these recommendations: set up lunch on a picnic blanket at the Old Ski Hill Overlook or pull off while hiking Tower Trail/Ice Age Trail along the shoreline and eat lunch sitting on a rock throne right on the water. As always, check with park staff when you visit in case designations have changed.

RECOMMENDED HIKE: Tower Trail
DISTANCE AND ELEVATION GAIN: 3.6 miles, 180 feet
DOG AND HUMAN FITNESS LEVEL: weekend warrior
TRAIL CONDITIONS/MATERIALS: Tower Trail is a mostly dirt trail with its share of protruding rocks and roots. The stretch of Tower Trail along Sturgeon Bay is especially rocky and rooty. In the fall, the trail

tends to be covered by a considerable amount of leaf litter, which can hide slippery rocks underneath. There are a couple flights of stone stairs on the way down to the shore from the Observation Tower: one long and deliberately engineered flight west of Shoreline Road, and one shorter and less purposeful flight east of Shoreline Road. Most of Tower Trail is wide enough to accommodate you and your dog walking side by side, but Lucky and I were more comfortable single file. There is enough room for passing other hikers and dogs and space to step off the trail if needed.

TRAIL MARKINGS/EASE OF NAVIGATING: The trail is well established and mostly easy to follow. There were two points where Lucky and I had to do a little backtracking—we missed our turn where Tower Trail departs from Ice Age Trail, and at first we couldn't figure out where the trail resumes on the other side of the north campground. Otherwise, the trail is well marked with Tower Trail markers, and the shared segment with Ice Age Trail is well marked with yellow blazes. Brown wooden blocks with white arrows have also been nailed to trees to mark Tower Trail in some places. The segment from Old Ski Hill Overlook to the Observation Tower is marked with blue blazes. There are posts with trail maps at most major intersections. There are also frequent markers indicating which activities are and are not allowed on the trails.

THE EXPERIENCE: From the park entrance, head east on the park road until it dead-ends at S. Norway Road. Take a left onto S. Norway Road. and then at the next Y-intersection take another left onto N. Norway Road. Take the next left to park in the lot for the Old Ski Hill Overlook lot. Walk toward the sign for the Ice Age Trail. Start the recommended hike on this spur trail, which dips into the stand of birch trees and understory behind the sign. The trail is flat and wide and marked with blue blazes and wooden arrows nailed to trees. It cuts through the forest for a little less than a quarter of a mile before arriving at the parking lot to the Observation Tower. Walk past the tower and through the parking lot toward the vault toilets; Tower Trail resumes in the woods just past the vault toilets.

The trail is wide and well-marked with both Tower Trail markers and Ice Age Trail yellow blazes. At the first intersection continue straight on Tower/Ice Age Trail, which is shared with off-road bicycling until you reach the next intersection. At this next intersection, stay left on Tower/Ice Age, which is now just a hiking trail. Slabs of rock start erupting from the otherwise level ground, and the gradual downhill plateaus and then gives way to a long flight of stone stairs that deposit you within sight of Shoreline Road.

On the other side of Shoreline Road, you're ushered into a grove of white cedars. The trail narrows just a bit as it passes through the trees, though there is still plenty of room to step off the trail between the trees if you need to. It continues parallel to but above the shoreline for a short time, and then it turns left down a less deliberately engineered flight of stone stairs. At the bottom of this flight of stairs is your first opportunity to get familiar with the waters of Sturgeon Bay, and at about a mile into the hike, this is a great place to stop for a snack, water, and some photos.

To continue on Tower Trail, take a right at the water and follow the trail markers through the cedar and birch trees. This is where the trail gets especially rooty, but it's consistently wide and flat, so otherwise easygoing. Throughout this section of Tower Trail, the lake is visible on your left and occasionally slabs of Niagara Escarpment are visible on the right. Shoreline Road runs parallel to the trail here, but it's above you and unnoticeable past the escarpment and forest. There's another rocky spot on the water's edge that would make a great picnic and photo spot before you reach an exposed section of trail. This section is short and kind of sad—a scar without a story. The trees between the trail and the water have all been cut down. It looks a tad bleak, but it's a short section, and you're back under the awning of cedars before you know it.

There are a couple additional rocky perches with views of the lake along the trail before it arrives at an intersection marked with a trail map. Here, you can turn right to shorten your hike. Otherwise, continue straight to do the entire length of Tower Trail and complete the recommended hike. Next on Tower Trail you'll reach the navigation aid (you literally can't miss it), at which point the cedars turn into sentinels, taking up their posts in parallel rows on either side of the trail.

At the end of the line of sentinel cedars, Tower Trail departs Ice Age Trail. The first time Lucky and I hiked this route, we missed the right turn. Unlike other trail intersections, there was no trail map. There was a wooden post with a yellow blaze and an Ice Age Trail badge. There was also a brown block of wood with a white arrow nailed to a tree near the Ice Age post. And, obstructed by foliage and not visible from the intersection, there was a Tower Trail marker nailed to a tree, a few feet down the right turn. So, when you reach the wooden post with the Ice Age marker and the random arrow block on the tree pointing to the right, take the right.

The trail narrows and leads gradually up to Shoreline Road. After crossing Shoreline Road, walk through the woods for a second and then cross another road to enter the north campgrounds. This is the only other section of the hike that confused us. The trail literally cuts right through the campground past the water fountain—where there's a trail map and a Tower Trail marker on a tree. Somehow, I still got confused. The trail leaves the campground at the northwestern corner, cutting not very conspicuously through the thick understory and saplings. This transition from the campgrounds back into the forest may not be obvious, but once you get back into the forest, the trail becomes again a wide and well-defined path.

Throughout this segment Tower Trail markers appear at regular intervals. Next, the trail reaches a T-intersection. If you had taken the right earlier to shorten the hike, this where you would have ended up. Take a left to stay on the Tower Trail loop and the recommended hike. This segment of Tower Trail will cross the off-road bicycle trail five times before getting back to the Old Ski Hill Overlook. Additional markers have been added to this stretch of trail to try to clear up any confusion. At each intersection with the bicycle trail, continue straight, following the Tower Trail markers. After crossing the off-road bicycle trail for the fifth time, it's a short distance to the road. Once you emerge from the forest onto the road, use the crosswalk to get to the other side of N. Norway Road and head back to the parking lot to complete this recommended hike.

WHILE YOU'RE IN THE AREA: You should also visit Peninsula, Rock Island, Newport Beach, and Whitefish Dunes state parks. Al Johnson's Stabbur Beer Garden is the perfect place for a post-hike beer. The establishment and staff are super dog friendly; they have dog bowls and water for your pup and the bartenders dole out sizable dog biscuits.

Rock Island State Park

Sometimes the story of the land is interesting, and other times, the story of the guy who owned the land is worth a mention. The guy in this case is Chester H. Thordarson, an Icelandic immigrant and the eponym of the Thordarson Loop Trail. Chester emigrated to America with his family in 1873 when he was around six years old. His first decades in the states were spent in parts of Wisconsin, North Dakota, St. Louis, and Chicago. He was an avid reader and rare book collector, and he started working on electric motors, which lead to a job with a Chicago electric company. At age twenty-seven, he got married, started his own business, and was contracted by Purdue University to make a half-million-volt transformer to be exhibited at the 1904 St. Louis World's Fair. His transformer was a huge success, so he eventually made an even bigger one million volt transformer, because why not?

Unsurprisingly, his electric manufacturing company in Chicago was making loads of money. With those loads of money, Chester purchased his first chunk of Rock Island in 1910 when he was forty-three and purchased the remaining acres over the next few years. Why Rock Island? His wife's relatives lived on Washington Island, and Rock Island seemed like a perfect retreat from city life in Chicago. He spent the rest of his life making improvements on the island, including building the boat house and water tower. Though he made improvements, he didn't develop the island at the expense of the environment. He worked to preserve the natural landscape, native animals, and wildflowers, and for doing so, the University of Wisconsin gave him an Honorary Master of Arts in 1929. He also continued to tinker in his workshop on Rock

Island. Over the course of his life, he developed more than one hundred inventions, most of them patented. Chester accomplished all of this despite having completed only a seventh-grade education—when he was twenty. When he died in 1945, his family continued to live on the island until it was sold to the state in 1965.

Chester's story reminds me of his contemporary, Ferdinand Hotz (see the Newport State Park entry). Both men were immigrants whose industrious and entrepreneurial spirits helped them succeed in business, which made it possible for them to buy chunks of beautiful Door County land, which they then helped preserve for future generations. For that, Lucky and I are incredibly grateful.

As far as the land goes, it doesn't get any more northeast than Rock Island State Park. Given its location at the entrance to Green Bay, the island was an easy target for shipwrecks. So, in 1836 before Wisconsin was even a state, the Pottawatomie Lighthouse was constructed on Rock Island. It was rebuilt in the 1850s, restored in 1910, automated in 1945, added to the National Register of Historic Places in 1979, made solar powered in 1986, and relocated to the steel light tower west of the lighthouse in 1988. Now, the lighthouse is maintained by the Friends of Rock Island and is open daily for tours from 10 am until 4 pm late May through early October.

HEADS-UP: Some Rock Island regulars informed me that biting flies are frequently a problem by the lighthouse and sometimes at the beach. During our first visit, the flies by the lighthouse were so horrible we took a few quick photos and then ran away as fast as possible.

HEADS-UP: Getting out to Rock Island State Park is a little more complicated than going to other state parks, but it's worth it. First, there's a ferry ride out of Northport over to Washington Island, and then you have to get across Washington Island to catch the Karfi Ferry to Rock Island. You are probably going to shell out at least $50 to get to Rock Island, so I'd recommend spending as much time there as possible. Do the whole Thordarson Loop Trail and more if you want the exercise and have the time. If you don't have a lot of time, walk the Sandy Shore Line/Thordarson Loop Trail from the campground to

Rock Island State Park

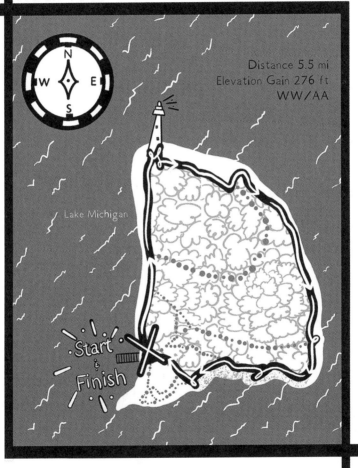

N
W   E
S

Distance 5.5 mi
Elevation Gain 276 ft
WW/AA

Lake Michigan

Start
&
Finish

the A/B hike-in sites. Just make sure you make it back to the dock in time to catch the last Karfi back to Washington Island, otherwise, you're spending the night!

WATER AVAILABILITY: Water is available near the boat house and near the maintenance shed. Water is also available at the park office at the Jackson Harbor Ferry landing on Washington Island.

BATHROOM AVAILABILITY: There is a flush toilet in the lawn area near the boathouse, which I highly recommend. Recently built, it has an industrial meets country style to it—very posh as far as state park toilets go. There is a vault toilet at the Pottawatomie Lighthouse, and flush toilets are available in the park office at the Jackson Harbor Ferry landing on Washington Island.

TRASHCAN AVAILABILITY: There are trash and recycling cans at the boat dock. There's even a pet poop bag dispenser and trashcan by the trash/recycling and another one by the lighthouse.

DESIGNATED DOG SWIMMING AREA: At the time of our last visit, there was no designated pet swim area. There are some beach access points along Thordarson Loop Trail near Rutabaga Field that Lucky and I have explored during the shoulder season. As always, check with park staff when you visit in case designations have changed.

DESIGNATED DOG PICNIC AREA: At the time of our last visit, there was no designated pet picnic area. Lucky and I recommend having your picnic at one of the benches between the boat house and the ranger's residence. There might not be picnic tables, but the view is amazing. Check with park staff in case designations have changed.

RECOMMENDED HIKE: Thordarson Loop Trail

DISTANCE AND ELEVATION GAIN: 5.5 miles, 276 feet

DOG AND HUMAN FITNESS LEVEL: weekend warrior/avid adventurer

TRAIL CONDITIONS/MATERIALS: If you do this whole loop, you'll encounter almost every kind of material possible: gravel, grass, stone, dirt, roots, rocks, pine needles, white cedar leaves, and sand. The trail is predominantly flat, with a few gradual ascents and descents, but nothing especially strenuous. Thordarson Loop Trail is wide enough to accommodate you and your dog walking side by side, except for infrequent sections that narrow to single file. For most of the hike, there is plenty of room for passing and room to step off the trail if you need to give others an even wider berth to pass.

TRAIL MARKINGS/EASE OF NAVIGATING: Thordarson Loop Trail is well established and easy to follow. At trailheads and intersections, wooden signs indicate trails and distances, and there are trail maps at intersections.

THE EXPERIENCE: We normally start experiences by suggesting where to park. In this case, you'll be leaving your car at the Jackson Harbor Ferry landing on Washington Island. The Karfi Ferry drops passengers off at the dock by the boathouse. Here, right by the dock, are the trash and recycling cans as well as a pet waste bag dispenser—so handy in the event you forgot to bring your own. From there, a gravel road leads up to the main lawn, and a brown wooden sign indicates directions and distances to the lighthouse and the beach. Take a left and follow the sign to the lighthouse to get started on the Thordarson Loop trail, going clockwise. Gravel tire tracks parallel the edge of the island toward the ranger's residence. After passing the ranger's residence, the tire tracks disappear into a grass clearing. Keep straight (north) through this clearing until you come to a short wooden "TO LIGHT HOUSE" sign on your right. This sign points to a narrow gravel path with wooden stairs and stones protruding from the ground at irregular intervals. After the initial stairs, the trail levels out but remains narrow. This is one of very few narrow segments on this hike, but it's a relatively short segment and is surrounded by understory. The trail passes another stone building (the water reservoir) before reaching another grassy clearing where a strange-looking wooden structure is fenced off.

It would be helpful if there was a sign here to explain what this contraption is, but there isn't—so I'll tell you. This strange-looking situation is what remains of a gate Chester Thordarson built out of three cedar trees. At one time, it was very ornamental, but over the years the wood rotted, and pieces were removed. In 2015, the whole gate was supposed to be demolished, but the demolition was halted because of public opposition. The hope is to restore the gate, but until that time, the gate is fenced off for public safety.

Walk around the fenced-off gate and follow the wide grassy trail as it enters the woods and transitions back into dirt and then gravel tire tracks. Continue straight on the tire tracks, past the connector trail on the right, toward Fernwood Trail and the lighthouse. When Thordarson Trail intersects with Fernwood Trail, you could take the right, cutting off a significant portion of the loop including the lighthouse, and still get to hike the best parts of Thordarson Loop Trail on the other side of the island. If you want to see the lighthouse or are up for the challenge of hiking the entire perimeter of the island, take the left. Staying to the left, the wide dirt and gravel trail continues through the woods until it reaches the lighthouse.

Near the lighthouse, there's another pet waste bag dispenser and trashcan. There might also be a lot of biting flies. If you stick around the lighthouse to explore, there is a sign for beach access—or almost-beach access on the eastern side of the lighthouse. At the time of our last visit, the wooden staircase down the cliff was closed because it had sustained some structural damage. However, the sign still encouraged visitors to take the stone stairs to the top of the cliff to check out the view. If you do, you'll add about 87 feet of elevation gain to this otherwise flat hike. The stone stairs lead to a dirt trail that, at the time of our last visit, dead-ended at a landing and a lot of caution tape. The view from the landing is partially obstructed by trees but does offer a sliver of unobstructed lake vista. Going back up the stone stairs is probably the most challenging segment on the entire island, and since this detour isn't really part of Thordarson Loop Trail, feel free to skip it if you and your dog aren't down to climb the stairs.

Back at the clearing, find where Thordarson Loop Trail goes back into the woods. There is a wooden sign and trail map to help you identify the trail. Follow the arrow for East Area/Thordarson loop heading east/southeast—or clockwise on the loop. A very short distance back into the woods, the wide trail meets an intersection with a narrow trail, marked with a short wooden sign reading CEMETERY. If you want to add this cemetery pit stop to your journey, take the narrow trail an even shorter distance into the woods to the small fenced cemetery. Without going inside of the fencing, it's hard to make out the inscription on the one intact headstone. Lucky and I didn't dare walk inside the fencing, as there are several crumbling ancient headstones, and we didn't want to inadvertently disrespect someone's eternal resting place. If you find this sort of thing spooky, feel free to bypass this point of interest and keep going on Thordarson Loop.

The next stretch of Thordarson is a wide path with spurts of grass, and it gently curves and undulates through the woods. Most of the scenery is of the hardwood forest, but further along this segment there are some views of the forest canopy on the cliffs below, and beyond the forest the water and then the horizon. One of these views is marked on the map as a scenic overlook, though it isn't obvious which overlook is the "official" one when you are on the trail. Around two miles into this hike, the trail intersects with the other end of Fernwood Trail. Take a left to stay on Thordarson Loop Trail; you'll be heading toward the water and beginning some of the best hiking on the island.

The trail narrows and starts down several widely set wood stairs. Then, the trail narrows even more, and it finally feels like you're on an actual hiking trail rather than a road. Walking single file is appropriate, but there are still opportunities for stepping aside if there happened to be someone else on the trail at the same time as you (though I think this is unlikely). Through this section, the trail is a combination of grass, dirt, and roots, but as it gets closer to the edge of the island, the trail gets rockier and more scenic.

Now, the trail takes you past an overlook of the lake that is one of many great places throughout this next stretch of trail to stop to take in the setting. The narrow and rocky trail widens and goes through a stand of saplings before emerging again along the edge of the cliff. It remains a wide and vast network of roots, separated from the edge of the cliff by a dense line of white cedars. The trail dips into the woods momentarily for a second time and then comes back to the edge of the cliff, only this time the cedars are less organized. The trees have broken ranks, leaving space in between to see down the cliff to the water. More sporadically spaced trees populate the cliff's other levels, and a rock ledge awaits visitors hoping to capture the mystique of this spot. Delightfully, there are plenty of photo opportunities ahead. The trail narrows to super single file and heads through the understory once more before reaching another spot where the tree-speckled cliff sprawls down toward the water. Here, there are social trails down to the edge of the cliff, though Lucky and I didn't explore these offshoots. I was too worried I would roll my ankle, no one would find us, and we'd be stuck on the island overnight—or maybe forever.

Next, Thordarson Loop Trail goes back into the woods. A short distance into this stretch of the trail, a wooden sign nailed to a tree points toward the second cemetery along this hike. Despite our best hurried efforts, Lucky and I weren't able to locate it. While the cemetery might be difficult to find, the trail isn't. A very straight stretch of trail cuts through the trees and leads to a bench positioned at a scenic overlook. The next point of interest, the water tower, is just a short distance down the trail.

The water tower is a modest stone structure that I wouldn't consider an "attraction." Right after the water tower, the trail turns into the widest of grass paths, which deposits travelers into a large clearing. At the center of the clearing are signs indicating trails and distances, as well as a trail map and a weathered interpretive sign describing the Hidden Village. From this point, you can shorten the hike 0.8 of a mile by taking Havamal Trail back to the boat dock, but if you do so, you'll completely miss out on the beaches of Rock Island. So, we recommend taking the path through the prairie grass out to the cliff's edge for another view of the lake and then continuing clockwise on Thordarson Loop Trail. Thordarson is straight across the clearing from where it emerged from the water tower, and it continues to parallel the edge of the island, though the next section doesn't include any water views.

The next section of trail is as basic as it gets. It continues through the woods before reaching the vault toilet for hike-in campsites E, D, and C. The section of trail between sites E, D, and C and sites B and A is much the same: wide, grassy, and uneventful. But, as you approach sites B and A, the forest starts to transition from young mixed hardwoods to older unorganized white cedars. Eventually those unorganized cedars transition to towering cedars positioned equidistant from each other in neat orderly rows. Clearly this stand of trees was engineered—and we can't help but love it. It's a strange thing to see nature conforming in this uniform way, but unlike the trees along the cliff's edge that are fighting for sunlight and real estate on an eroding cliff face, the engineering allowed these trees to grow to their full potential. And man, are they tall!

Hike-in campsites B and A are accessed through these ranks of trees, and if there aren't campers currently occupying the sites, we think it's worth hiking out to see one. The trail to campsite A is bordered with white rocks. Following the rocks through the tall and imposing trees feels like the beginning of a Grimm brothers' fairy tale, and the twisted cedar on the edge of the cliff at the campsite could very well be mystical.

Back to Thordarson Loop Trail. After passing by the access points for the hike-in campsites, the trail turns back into grass and leaves the neatly engineered stand of trees to take a jaunt through a prairie. A trail map indicating you're almost to Rutabaga Field stands on a post near where the grass trail begins to turn to sand. To the left, the sand carves a narrow trail through the prairie grass and following it takes you out to the first of a few spots to access the beach. The beach here is full of rocks and debris and may not be very wide depending on the tide, but it's a great spot to let your dog take a dip. Don't worry if you get sand in your hiking boots, since the next section of Thordarson Loop Trail is 100 percent sand. Continue following the sand trail as it tracks parallel to the water. Additional social trails lead down to the beach and the water—we recommend exploring any or all of these access points to take pictures, sit down for a snack, or take a dip in the waters of Lake Michigan if it's not too cold.

The sand trail rather abruptly transitions back to grass and cuts through Rutabaga Field. Rutabaga Field is much larger than the previous clearing by the Hidden Village remains. To the left is another beach access point and to the right is access to Blueberry Trail, which is an option to get back to the boat dock if you've had your fill of the beach. Otherwise, continue straight across the field on Thordarson. Back in the woods, the trail turns back into a wide dirt-and-grass path marred by tire tracks. When you start seeing sand again, it means you're getting close to the main beach access point. Narrow sandy social trails climb up the dune, rolling down the other side onto the beach. The trail passes the changing stalls; this is where we recommend departing from Thordarson Trail and suggest taking Michigan Avenue back to the boat dock instead. Taking Michigan Avenue cuts off a little distance, and by now, you might be ready to get back to the boat dock and take a load off.

It's a straight shot back to the boathouse on Michigan Avenue. Once you're back and have confirmed that you haven't missed the last ferry back to Washington Island, we recommend checking out the ramp down to the water on the south side of the boat house. Lucky and I think it's a great spot to have a snack while you wait for the Karfi.

WHILE YOU'RE IN THE AREA: You should also visit Peninsula, Newport Beach, Potawatomi, and Whitefish Dunes state parks. If you're killing time on Washington Island, the Schoolhouse Beach is cool, but dogs aren't allowed on the beach or in the picnic areas. Al Johnson's Stabbur Beer Garden is the perfect place for a post-hike beer. The establishment and staff are super dog friendly; they have dog bowls and water for your pup and the bartenders dole out sizable dog biscuits.

Whitefish Dunes State Park

If I weren't such a city girl, my next move would be to the edge of Whitefish Dunes State Park. This park is alluring, and not just because it has the best dog beach of all of Wisconsin's state parks. The composition of plants and sand is a departure from the classic Wisconsin deciduous forest, and the straightforward trails make it easy to look around at the fascinating flora while hiking. The park preserves the largest sand dunes in Wisconsin, including Old Baldy, which is the tallest dune in the park at 93 feet above lake level.

The park also has a rich anthropological history, but that should be no surprise. Even the earliest peoples recognized that Whitefish Dunes was an amazing piece of real estate. Archeological digs of the area have revealed its progression of inhabitants, for which the site is listed on the National Register of Historical Places. Artifacts under the soil speak to the ancient history of the land, while artifacts offshore speak to the less ancient history of the water. As trade expanded so did the number of ships voyaging on Lake Michigan and consequently the number of shipwrecks. Several shipwrecks happened off the coast of Whitefish Dunes starting in 1869, claiming the schooners *Grey Eagle, Hungarian, D. A. Van Valkenburg, James Garrett, Otter, Success,* and *C. Harrison,* as well as the steamer *Australasia* in 1896. Most of these ships were casualties of bad weather and broke up on shore, but fragments of the *Australasia* and *Success* remain intact offshore under water and sand.

WATER AVAILABILITY: Water is available at the park office/Nature Center, near the walkway to the first beach access point, and at the picnic area.

Whitefish Dunes State Park

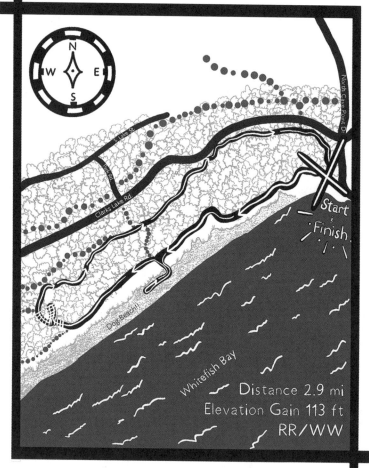

North Cave Point Dr.

Clark's Lake St.

Park Rd.

Clarks Lake Rd.

Dog Beach!

Start

Finish

Whitefish Bay

Distance 2.9 mi
Elevation Gain 113 ft
RR/WW

BATHROOM AVAILABILITY: Flush toilets are available at the park office/Nature Center. Vault toilets are available near the picnic area and each beach access point. If hiking the Red Trail, you'll pass the vault toilets at the second and third beach access points. If you're hiking any other color trail, go before you get started.

TRASHCAN AVAILABILITY: There's a pet poop bag dispenser and trashcan by the third beach access point and another a short way down the Black Trail.

DESIGNATED DOG SWIMMING AREA: Dogs are allowed on the southernmost section of beach. To get to the dog beach, take the Red Trail from the Nature Center about 0.75 mile to the third access point, which is marked with signs indicating pets are allowed.

If I were to pick the best Wisconsin state park dog beach, this would be it. Not only is it specifically allocated for dogs to use, but it's also actually a beach! It's not a sad narrow strip of water-adjacent land that's been given over to dogs because it's been rejected by people. It's a wide, soft sandy swath that gradually meets the waters of Whitefish Bay. It is a little bit of a hike to get to, but the Red Trail there and back is mostly flat and wide. It's well worth the walk.

During our first visit, there were a couple of other dogs on the beach, and Lucky chased after a dog chasing after a stick until his humping tendencies kicked in. Apologizing for his embarrassing behavior, I separated his bucking pelvis from the other dog and took him further down the beach. Once further removed from the temptation of dominating other dogs, Lucky was content to wade in the water and sniff the sand. My point in sharing? There is so much beach that multiple dogs and owners can enjoy it simultaneously with plenty of space in between.

I have heard that park rangers strictly enforce the "back on leash as soon as paws are out of the water" rule. While there were no park rangers at the pet beach during our visits, this doesn't surprise me. Whitefish Dunes has some of the most thorough dog rules signage, yet I imagine there are still plenty of people who disregard the rules, which results in stricter enforcement. So, follow the rules and be cool.

Dog swimming area at Whitefish Dunes State Park (Danielle St. Louis)

DESIGNATED DOG PICNIC AREA: There is a picnic table at the third beach access point (aka dog beach) on the Red Trail side of the dune, but one picnic table hardly constitutes a picnic area. Especially when compared to the park's beautiful main picnic area where dogs are not allowed. I recommend enjoying lunch by the water—but be on the lookout for other dogs who might try to sneak a snack from your picnic basket. Another great option is to take your dog and picnic down the road to Cave Point County Park, which does allow dogs in the picnic area and gives you another cool option for hiking/exploring after lunch. As always, check with park staff when you visit in case designations have changed.

HEADS-UP: Dune ecosystems are fragile. Interference from one human or dog can set a dune's development back years, just by walking or digging on it. Always stay on designated trails at Whitefish Dunes.

RECOMMENDED HIKE: Red + Yellow + Yellow/Green

HEADS-UP: The length of the Red Trail from the Nature Center to where Red dead-ends past the boardwalk to Old Baldy is also a bike trail. Keep a look out for cyclists ahead and behind.

DISTANCE AND ELEVATION GAIN: 2.9 miles, 113 feet

DOG AND HUMAN FITNESS LEVEL: recreational rambler/weekend warrior

TRAIL CONDITIONS/MATERIALS: Red Trail is composed of gravel, dirt, sand, leaf litter, grass, and weeds in various ratios. The trail is mostly flat with several rolling undulations. To get to the pet beach, you have to go up and over the sand dune, which is a little steeper. The most strenuous section is the boardwalk and stairs up to the top of Old Baldy. The observation platform at the top of Old Baldy is large enough to accommodate a handful of adults and a dog comfortably. On our first visit to Whitefish Dunes, there was family with three rambunctious children on the observation platform, so Lucky and I waited on the boardwalk for our turn. Most of the boardwalk treads are well embedded in the sand below and most are spaced at regular intervals, but there are sections where the spacing is inconsistent. The wooden stairs are consistent in their spacing and appear well maintained. The boardwalk section is narrower and best traveled single file. Passing other hikers and dogs may be difficult in this section; hikers are reminded to stay on the trail to preserve the fragile landscape. Red, Yellow, and Yellow/Green trails are wide enough for walking side by side and for passing other hikers and dogs with greater ease.

TRAIL MARKINGS/EASE OF NAVIGATING: The trail is well established and easy to follow. There are a lot of things to like about Whitefish Dunes, and thorough signage is one of them. There are brown posts frequently along the trails, adorned with a combination of color-coded arrows, rectangles, activity markers, trail maps, and assorted wooden signs indicating bathrooms and other points of interest. There are also signs indicating closed and protected areas, and each beach access point has a large sign listing prohibited beach activities and the pet rules. Additional signs at the beach access points remind visitors there are no lifeguards on duty and indicate whether dogs are allowed at that access point or not. There is no shortage of signs.

HEADS-UP: At the time of our last visit, there was a discrepancy between how the trails were labeled on the DNR's map and how they were labeled IRL with markers and on the trail maps at the intersections. I mention this for your information, but it shouldn't be an issue when navigating the recommended hike.

THE EXPERIENCE: After parking, head toward the Nature Center. The trailhead for the Red Trail is just to the right of the Nature Center and is marked with plenty of signage. Follow the pointing dog silhouette around the side of the Nature Center to begin a clockwise loop of the recommended hike. The trail is wide and flat as it takes you into the woods. A low wooden fence lines the trail on the right, and beyond the wooden fence are replica wigwams, summer lodges, hide racks, and other staples of an Oneota and a Late Woodland village. Interpretive signs explain the progression of native peoples that occurred in this area and the lifestyles they led. Past the replica villages, the trail begins a long gradual ascent. During one of our visits, I saw a snake cross the trail in this area. Thankfully, Lucky didn't see it, but be aware there could be snakes slithering around. Once the trail levels out again, the uniqueness of the dune's ecosystem becomes more apparent—and not just because of the retaining wall on the right holding the sand dune back from swallowing up the trail. This is where you might start noticing some less familiar flora, like a shrubby conifer called Canadian yew, growing out of the sandy backside of the dune.

Just past the retaining wall is the second beach access. No pets are allowed at the beach here, which is made clear by the NO PETS ALLOWED signs. So, keep heading down the Red Trail. A short distance past the second beach access are the vault toilets. After the vault toilets, it's another half-mile to the third beach access. Between the second and third beach accesses, the Red Trail goes through the Whitefish Dunes State Natural Area. This is a great trail for looking around at the different trees and groundcover. On the left is the backside of the dune, which is sparsely populated with tall white birches, thick balsam firs, and twisty white cedars. On the right, this group of cohorts is joined by sugar maple, large-tooth aspen, eastern hemlock and American beech.

When you arrive at the third beach access point, aka the dog beach, there's a picnic table, a bench and a convenient pet waste bag dispenser and trash bin at the access point, and of course, a sign reminding visitors of prohibited beach activities and the pet rules. The trail up and over the dune to the pet beach is much narrower than the Red Trail. There isn't room for stepping off the trail, so if you can tell others are coming, it is best to wait and take turns going over the dune. The moment you reach the apex of the dune, the change in environment is arresting. I'm always amazed by natural borders, and the borders on the lakeside fore dune are stark. The trees concede to the beach grass and then the beach grass to the sand and water of Whitefish Bay. Closer to the water there is a sign to the left (northeast) that indicates no pets are allowed on that portion of the beach, but everything to the right is fair game. There is a lot of beach for exploring, but you'll eventually need to return to the access point to get back up and over the dune and back on the Red Trail.

When you return to the backside of the dune, take a left to continue down the Red Trail toward Old Baldy. Unlike at most observation towers and some park attractions, dogs are allowed on top of Old Baldy (all covered in sand), so we suggest taking advantage of the access and hiking up to see the view. When the Red Trail reaches the beginning of the boardwalk, take a right onto the boardwalk and remember to stay on the trail in order to preserve the fragile landscape. Passing other hikers and dogs may be difficult in this section because the boardwalk is narrow. This section is the most technical, strenuous, and entertaining of the whole hike. Following the boardwalk as it curves around, up, and down the dune feels as if you're in an M. C. Escher drawing.

Where the boardwalk eventually forks, take the right fork and continue up the stairs to the observation platform. The platform is large enough to accommodate a handful of adults and a dog comfortably. If the platform is occupied, you can wait on the landing for your turn. After taking in the views from up top, backtrack down the stairs and boardwalk to the fork and take a right. The boardwalk gradually descends the dune, eventually ends, and the sand/dirt trail resumes. The sand trail forks, and once again, stay to the right to continue on the Red/Yellow Trail. This stretch of trail along the backside of Old Baldy is another great opportunity to take in the unique composition of the sand dune ecosystem and look for plants like the Canadian yew and other funky-looking groundcovers.

For the remainder of the hike, the trail is marked with posts with colored arrows and rectangles. Continue to follow the red arrows and rectangles through the forested old dune, with its mix of white pine, hemlock, and beech-maple. Since this stretch of trail is groomed for cross-country skiing in the winter, it's wide and mostly flat, with an occasional rolling undulation. The rest of this hike is straight forward though several intersections that are all marked with trail maps and colored arrows. Continue straight through each intersection until you reach a Y-intersection with the Brachiopod Trail. Take the right branch, which is now Red/Yellow/Green/Brachiopod trail. The Nature Center is only a short distance past this last intersection.

HEADS-UP: If you're looking for a shorter hike or aren't interested in going up/around Old Baldy, after the dog beach you can head back the way you came on the Red Trail or take the bike trail/Green connection to do a shorter loop, returning to the Nature Center on Red/Yellow/Green. For a longer hike, rather than taking a right on the backside of Old Baldy, stay straight/left to add on some or all the Yellow Trail. Or take Red Trail along the backside of Old Baldy to the Green Trail connector. Use the connector to get to the other side of Clark Lake Road and head back to the Nature Center on the northern segment of Green/Yellow. There are lots of options here!

WHILE YOU'RE IN THE AREA: You should also visit Peninsula, Rock Island, Newport Beach, and Potawatomi state parks. Another great, super close option that's not a state park: Cave Point County Park. This park is two minutes (seriously, TWO minutes) down the road from Whitefish Dunes State Park, dogs are allowed in the picnic areas, and it's a super scenic spot with views of the cliffs and the lake.

THE SOUTHEASTERN REGION

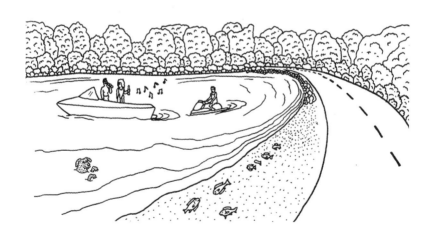

Big Foot Beach State Park

Let me begin with a point of clarification. If you go to Big Foot Beach State Park, you'll be in the city of Lake Geneva, but the lake is called Geneva Lake. Both the city and lake were named after Geneva, New York, because of the striking resemblance between the two areas. If you'd like to hike more than the 6.5 miles of trails in the park, there is a 26-mile-long shore path that goes all the way around Geneva Lake. The shore path follows the route of the Potawatomi Indians and was declared public domain by early European settlers. To this day, the path remains open to the public, and pets are allowed on leash.

And here are some words of warning. No alcohol is allowed anywhere in Big Foot Beach State Park. However, anchoring party boats off the rocky portion of the park's beach and drinking alcohol onboard appears to be permitted—the Wisconsin equivalent of international waters. A less raucous activity that is popular at this park is fishing in the Ceylon Lagoon. If you happen to forget your bait and tackle at home, don't fret. There's an on-site vending machine ready to dispense live bait and tackle 24 hours a day. Make sure to watch out for discarded daily catches along the trail; Lucky has sniffed out and eaten several dead fish while hiking at Big Foot Beach.

WATER AVAILABILITY: Water is available by the flush toilets by the Ceylon Lagoon and by the people picnic areas.

BATHROOM AVAILABILITY: Flush toilets are located by the Ceylon Lagoon. Vault toilets can be found by the shelter picnic area.

Big Foot Beach State Park

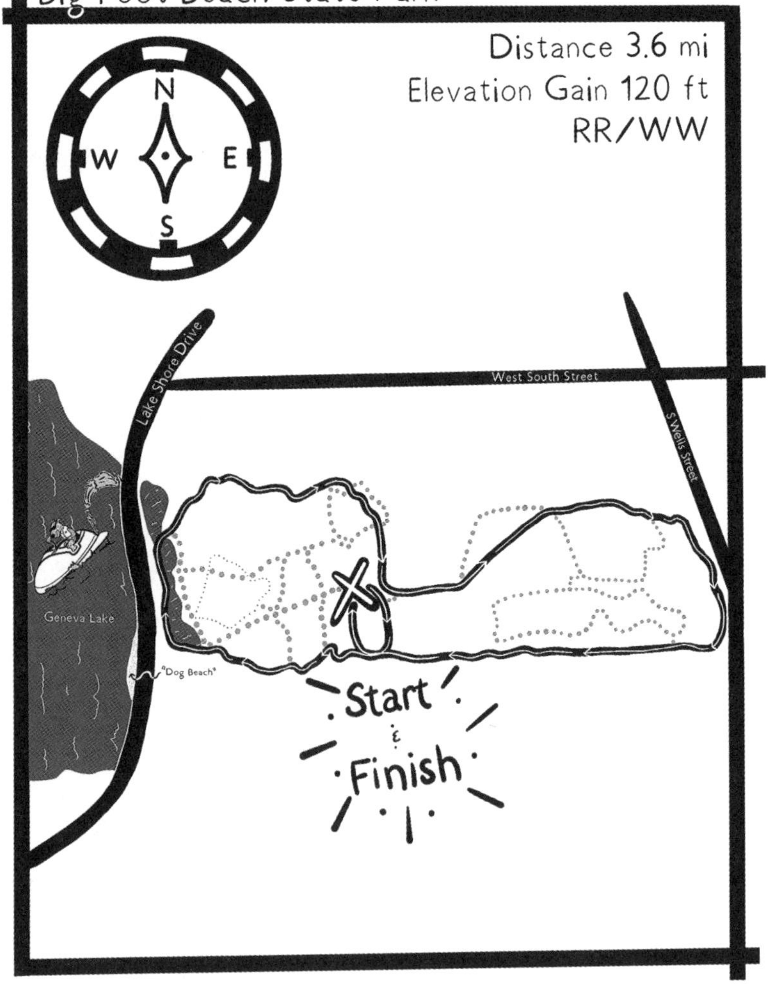

Distance 3.6 mi
Elevation Gain 120 ft
RR/WW
N
W
E
S
Lake Shore Drive
West South Street
S Wells Street
Geneva Lake
"Dog Beach"
Start
&
Finish

TRASHCAN AVAILABILITY: There is a row of dumpsters alongside the building that houses the flush toilets near the Ceylon Lagoon.

DESIGNATED DOG SWIMMING AREA: While the park "boasts" 900 feet of shoreline, a little less than half of that shoreline is actual beach. The people beach is the southernmost section of the shoreline, and the swimming area is a distinctly marked off 100-foot section. At the time of our last visit, there was no designated dog swimming area, but I was told I could let Lucky in the water north of the people beach. The area north of the people beach is a short section of shoreline that loosely resembles a very narrow beach, but it quickly transitions to a blunder of boulders. Be prepared to share these waters with boaters and jet skiers who are coming to drop anchor and hang out. Also, this short narrow beachy section of shoreline is only a stone's throw from the busy S. Lakeshore Drive. And as always, check with park staff when you visit in case designations have changed.

DESIGNATED DOG PICNIC AREA: The designated pet picnic area is on the right as you enter the park, just past the main parking lot and across the road from the RV Dump Station. Rather than picnicking with a view of people unloading their RV toilets, Lucky and I recommend going into the city of Lake Geneva and finding a restaurant with a pet-friendly patio or eating your picnic at one of the other city parks that allow dogs.

RECOMMENDED HIKE: Green Loop

HEADS-UP: Hiking at Big Foot Beach is a choose-your-own-adventure story. Trails overlap and intersect frequently, so you can easily tailor your experience to your, and your dog's, fitness level. Attempting to make one giant loop around the park, we cobbled together this recommended route, which goes past the major water attractions (Ceylon Lagoon and Geneva Lake) and through each of the different ecosystems within the park.

DISTANCE AND ELEVATION GAIN: 3.6 miles, 120 feet

DOG AND HUMAN FITNESS LEVEL: recreational rambler/weekend warrior

Dog swimming area at Big Foot Beach State Park (Danielle St. Louis)

TRAIL CONDITIONS/MATERIALS: The trails are grass and dirt, with the exception of crossing or walking along the paved road. There are also two wooden bridges over the Ceylon Lagoon, which account for most of the elevation gain along this route. The trails are flat and wide enough to allow for walking side by side and easy passing.

TRAIL MARKINGS/EASE OF NAVIGATING: The color naming conventions used at Big Foot Beach may seem confusing, as trails often overlap. But the trails are wide, well established, and well marked, making navigation mostly easy. The only potentially confusing sections are where trails cross through or run alongside the road, parking lots, or picnic areas.

THE EXPERIENCE: Park in the second lot on the right, near the picnic shelter, to start a clockwise hike around the perimeter of the park. Begin hiking along the road heading south and pick up the Green Trail. The Green Trail runs alongside the road and then skirts on the back edge of a parking lot, which is where it becomes Green/Yellow and dips back into the hardwood forest. You may notice what appears to be an abandoned picnic area on the right before reaching a clearing and the Ceylon Lagoon. Walk around the left side of the lagoon and toward the road and chain-link fence, and then turn right to continue walking around the lagoon. Go past the first bridge to the second one. Cross the lagoon using this second, northernmost bridge, and then take a left to continue on the Green/Yellow trail. From here, the trail takes you back into the hardwood forest and along the perimeter of the park.

At the next Y-intersection, take the left branch to stay on the Green Trail. When you reach the road, cross it and continue straight along the west (right) side of the tree line. You'll be walking through a large clearing past the picnic areas where the trail isn't as discernable, but if you stay close to the tree line, you'll soon see the trail entrance back into the forest. Take a left into the entrance and onto the Green/Black Trail, which goes through a mixed forest with plenty of shade. Then, the forest parts like the Biblical Red Sea and the trail turns into a double-wide mowed grass path with no shade. At the next Y-intersection where the Green and Black trails split, you can take either route. If it's hot and sunny out, Lucky and I recommend taking the right branch onto Black, so you can get through this section faster. Otherwise, take the left branch to stay on Green. The branches rejoin on the other side of the mowed service road.

The Green and Black trails rejoin at a four-way intersection along with the Purple Trail. If you took the Black Trail to get here, continue straight. If you took the Green Trail to get here, take a left. Now the trail is Green/Black/Purple as it follows along the perimeter of the park. At times along this section of trail, Badger High School is visible through the trees, which are once again providing some shade. The next Y-intersection is where Purple departs from Green and Black. Take the left branch to keep heading clockwise around the park on Green and Black. This section of trail runs alongside a road, but the trees provide a partial sight and sound barrier. When the trail turns back to the west, the final stretch takes you through a restored prairie.

Once again there is little shade along this section of the trail, but a couple of wooden benches along the way offer a place to rest, drink some water, and enjoy the views.

Green/Black eventually intersects with the paved service road, and you can either take a left to continue along Green, which runs alongside the road, or go straight across the service road and take Black back to the picnic area and parking lot. For simplicity's sake, we recommend taking Green along the service road to the main road and back to the parking lot, completing the recommended hike.

Harrington Beach State Park

I hadn't done much research prior to our first visit to Harrington Beach State Park. Considering Harrington is on Lake Michigan and the word *beach* is in its name, I was expecting the lake and beach to be the main attractions. But there's an impressive point of interest that I didn't expect—a hole in the ground filled with water, better known as Quarry Lake.

The quarry was first opened by David Whittaker and his son George in 1894. However, the Whittakers couldn't dig themselves out of debt, so they ended up selling in 1901 to the Lake Shore Stone Company, an operation backed by some big investors, including Charles Pfister. Lake Shore Stone Company developed and ran the quarry successfully for almost twenty years until limestone stopped being the material of choice for building roadbeds. The quarry shut down around 1925, the company houses were destroyed or moved, the forest grew back in, and the quarry gradually filled with water. The resulting lake is striking; the water is crystal clear and reflects the cobalt blue sky and vibrant greens of the forest. The trail around the lake offers many opportunities to get right to the water's edge and to even stand at the mouth of a tiny waterfall as it descends into the lake below. Because of its charm, we selected Quarry Lake Trail as the recommended hike.

While the quarry's story is one of industry and capitalism, the park honors the story of a famous Wisconsin conservationist. The park is named for Cornelius Louis "Neal" Harrington, who was largely responsible for establishing the Flambeau River, Kettle Moraine, and Black River state forests. He was a pretty cool dude and kept a neat photo collection.

You can check it out by visiting www.wisconsinhistory.org and searching for "C. L. Harrington."

HEADS-UP: When you grow up outside of Milwaukee, the phrase "cooler by the lake" is a common expression, and for good reason. It's always a smart idea to pack extra layers when heading to a park on Lake Michigan, even on warm days.

HEADS-UP: At the time of our last visit, the park office was equipped with pre-highlighted maps indicating where dogs are and are not allowed. They take their dog rules seriously at Harrington, and so should you while you're visiting with your dog.

WATER AVAILABILITY: Water is available by the park office, by the Welcome Center, and by most of the picnic areas. There is no water available in the pet picnic area.

BATHROOM AVAILABILITY: Vault toilets are available near Puckett's Pond, the Welcome Center, Quarry Lake, and the South Picnic Area.

TRASHCAN AVAILABILITY: Noncampers should plan on carry-in/carry-out. To assist you in this effort, many of the park signs have trash bag dispensers attached.

DESIGNATED DOG SWIMMING AREA: Dogs can swim at the South Beach. To get to the South Beach, walk down the shuttle bus road from the Ansay Welcome Center parking lot. Cross through the South Picnic Area, which is not the pet picnic area, and go down the hill to the water. From the point of access, the pet beach area goes on to the south (right) for about a quarter of a mile.

The South Beach is narrow, with no space for picnicking, sunbathing, or doing much of anything other than walking. The water is shallow, making it nice for wading, but to swim, a dog would have to get much further away from the shore. Also, consider checking water quality before you go. The beach is sometimes temporarily closed due to unhealthy water conditions.

DESIGNATED DOG PICNIC AREA: There is a designated pet picnic area along the shuttle bus road, between the North and South beaches. It's a large clearing with a few benches and picnic tables and views of the lake below. There's a trash bag dispenser attached to the Pet

Dog swimming area at Harrington Beach State Park (Danielle St. Louis)

Picnic Area sign. There is also a metal staircase that can take you down to the water, but we would not recommend using this route to access the pet beach. The staircase is relatively steep and ends in an inhospitable section of barely beach and murky water. For another scenic option, consider picnicking somewhere along Quarry Lake Trail.

RECOMMENDED HIKE: Quarry Lake Trail

DISTANCE AND ELEVATION GAIN: 1 mile, 59 feet

HEADS-UP: While Quarry Lake Trail is about a mile long, if you walk from the Welcome Center parking lot, down the shuttle bus road, do the Quarry Lake Trail loop, walk down to the pet beach, and then back to the parking lot, you'll get in a total of about 2.8 miles of walking.

DOG AND HUMAN FITNESS LEVEL: recreational rambler

TRAIL CONDITIONS/MATERIALS: The official trail is made up of crushed limestone. In many places, you can hike along the edge of Quarry Lake on dirt and stone social trails but watch out for exposed roots. This trail is flat and wide enough to walk side by side with easy passing. There is one wooden bridge to cross.

TRAIL MARKINGS/EASE OF NAVIGATING: Quarry Lake Trail is well established and easy to follow; it's a path of crushed limestone that loops around Quarry Lake. There are a few opportunities along the trail to pick up other trails and to get back out to the shuttle bus road. These intersections are marked with wooden signs.

THE EXPERIENCE: The Quarry Lake Trail is a one-mile loop, but you'll have to do some walking to get to it. Start at the Welcome Center parking lot, walk down the shuttle bus road, and pick up the Quarry Lake Trail by the shuttle bus stop and vault toilets. Take a right off the road by the toilets and follow the crushed limestone trail the short distance to the lake. A fishing platform and picnic area sit right on the water's edge, and this is a great spot to stop and take in the view. Continuing clockwise around the lake, you'll cross a short wooden bridge. Because the water is so clear, as you cross the bridge you can see the remains of quarry structures in the water below.

There's another fishing platform just past the bridge, and then the trail jogs to the left, putting more distance between you and the lake.

The lake is still visible from the official crushed limestone trail, but to get the best views while you hike, dip back down to the water's edge where dirt and stone social trails weave through the white cedars and pines that surround the lake. When you reach the intersection with the Whitetail Trail (J), take a right and then stay to the right to continue on Quarry Lake Trail. Just past this intersection with J, dip back down to the edge of the lake to stand at the mouth of a small waterfall as it descends into the lake below. Back on the official trail, you'll be back to the start of the loop in no time. Once you're back to the beginning, you might go out to the shuttle bus road and head down to the dog beach and the dynamism of Lake Michigan. Or you might just take another lap to enjoy the tranquility of this smaller lake instead.

WHILE YOU'RE IN THE AREA: You should also visit Kohler-Andrae State Park and Fischer Creek State Natural Area.

Kohler-Andrae State Park

The hyphen in Kohler-Andrae signifies the union of two separate state parks that now operate as one entity, though it's unclear why Kohler gets first billing in the hyphenate. Andrae would come first alphabetically and historically. Terry Andrae State Park was established thirty-eight years before John Michael Kohler State Park. One possibility is that Kohler gets top billing due to sheer name recognition. But it could also be because the Kohler Company donated 158 more acres to the state than Elsbeth Andrae, suggesting that when it comes to state parks, size does matter.

Frank Theodore (Terry) Andrae bought the property along Lake Michigan back in 1924, but it was his wife, Elsbeth, who invested in reforesting the land and who donated 122 acres of the pine-dunes lakefront property to the state when her husband died in 1927. Poor Terry didn't really get to enjoy the land for very long, but thanks to Elsbeth, Wisconsinites have gotten to enjoy the land for more than ninety years.

Thirty-eight years after Terry Andrae State Park was established, along came the hyphenate. In 1966, the Kohler Company donated 280 acres north of Andrae State Park to the state in honor of the company's founder, John Michael Kohler. Kohler was born in Austria in 1844 and emigrated to America with his family when he was ten. He settled in Sheboygan, got married, and started living the American dream. The Kohler name is recognized the world over, most notably known for its plumbing products (who hasn't sat on a Kohler?). The state of Wisconsin eventually purchased 600 more acres from the Kohler Company, bringing the combined acreage for the parks to nearly 1,000. While the

Kohler-Andrae State Park

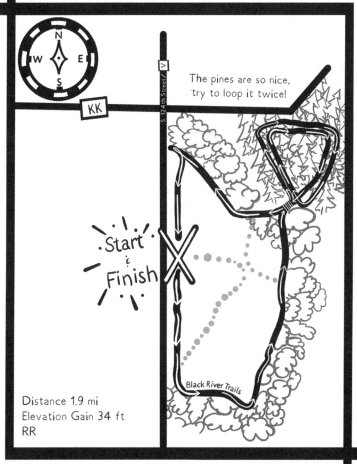

N
W   E
S

KK

S. 124th Street / V

The pines are so nice,
try to loop it twice!

Start
&
Finish

Black River Trails

Distance 1.9 mi
Elevation Gain 34 ft
RR

two parks are managed together, they are still considered two separate properties, though there's only one entrance, one park office, and you have to drive through Kohler to get into Andrae State Park.

HEADS-UP: When you grow up outside of Milwaukee, the phrase "cooler by the lake" is a common expression and for good reason. It's always a smart idea to pack extra layers when heading to a park on Lake Michigan, even on warm days.

HEADS-UP: Kohler-Andrae has particularly well-defined guidelines for dogs in the park. In addition to the regular park map, they also have a pet-specific map, which shows you where your dog can and cannot go. They take their dog rules seriously at Kohler-Andrae and so should you while you're visiting with your dog.

HEADS-UP: Dune ecosystems are fragile. Interference from one human or dog can set a dune's development back years, just by walking or digging on it, which likely explains why dogs are not allowed on Creeping Juniper Nature Trail or Woodland Dunes Nature Trail.

WATER AVAILABILITY: Water is available in the park office, and an additional water fountain with side dog fountain is available at the bathrooms next to the pet picnic area.

BATHROOM AVAILABILITY: A flush toilet is available in the park office. Vault toilets are available next to the pet picnic area.

TRASHCAN AVAILABILITY: A poop bag dispenser and trashcan are available at the Black River Trailhead. Poop bags, but no trashcan, are available at the pet picnic area.

DESIGNATED DOG SWIMMING AREA: The dog beach is north of the Sanderling Nature Center. After entering the park, take the first sharp left and head north to parking lot 2. There are a couple of different access points to the beach from this parking lot. The dog-friendly section of the beach extends north from the main access point at parking lot 2. As far as beaches go, this one is alright. It's a narrow strip of sand between shrubby dunes and the water. At times the beach gradually eases into the lake, while at other times it drops off abruptly. But the sand is soft, and the lake is huge. If it's crowded, walk further north to find some space to call your own.

Dog swimming area at Kohler-Andrae State Park (Danielle St. Louis)

DESIGNATED DOG PICNIC AREA: The pet picnic area is also accessed from parking lot 2. After entering the park, take the first sharp left and head north to parking lot 2. This grassy knoll feels cozy, with some shade and a couple of picnic tables and charcoal park grills. The picnic area can comfortably accommodate a couple of groups, but with the lake just steps away, I'd recommend having your picnic on the beach.

RECOMMENDED HIKE: Black River Trails

HEADS-UP: The Black River Trails are also open to horses and mountain bikers.

WORTH A MENTION: I didn't suggest the Dunes Cordwalk as the recommended hike because with a dog your only options are out-and-backs. If you start at parking lot 2, you can walk on the Cordwalk south until you reach Sanderling Lane and the Sanderling Nature Center. Then you'll have to turn around and head back the way you came because dogs are not allowed on the Creeping Juniper Nature Trail Loop. Similarly, if you start at parking lot 5, you can take the Dunes Cordwalk north until you reach the Creeping Juniper Nature Trail Loop. At that point, you must turn around and head back to parking lot 5. You'll want to check out part of the Cordwalk so you can experience the dunes' unique ecosystem, but we just recommend hiking Black River Trails first.

DISTANCE AND ELEVATION GAIN: 1.9 miles, 34 feet

DOG AND HUMAN FITNESS LEVEL: recreational rambler

TRAIL CONDITIONS/MATERIALS: The trail is mostly grass with some dirt and sand. After a heavy rain, be prepared for some mud. The trail is flat and wide enough to accommodate you and your dog walking side by side. There is enough room for passing other hikers and dogs and space to step off the trail if needed.

TRAIL MARKINGS/EASE OF NAVIGATING: The Black River Trails are the only trails in this section of the park. The set consists of a large loop with two tangents that intersect in the middle and a smaller loop. So there are plenty of choose-your-own-adventure ways to hike this trail. There are some trail markers along the way, but they only mark that you are on the trail and don't include maps with "You Are

Here" dots. I'd make sure to bring a park map with you, so you can keep track of which loop and/or tangent you are on. Until you get the lay of the land, it might be a bit confusing.

THE EXPERIENCE: You don't have to go into the park to get to the trailhead for Black River Trails, although a state park pass is still required. The trailhead is along Country Road V, south of Country Road KK. There is a parking lot on the east side of the road. At the parking lot there's an information kiosk with trail maps, a poop bag dispenser, and a trashcan. The main loop starts right from the parking lot. If you're at the information kiosk facing the trailhead, look right and left—you'll see the main loop. Lucky and I overestimated how far into the prairie we needed to go to pick up the loop and ended up taking a tangent and then backtracking on the other tangent. We became very familiar with the tangents.

Take a right onto the trail from the parking lot to begin counterclockwise on the large loop. At the next two intersections with the tangent trails, continue straight to stay on the outer loop. The open prairie eventually transitions to a hardwood forest, where you'll be sheltered from any lake-effect breezes. When the trail reaches the next four-way intersection, take a right and cross over the footbridge, which connects the large loop to the small loop. On the other side of the footbridge is a bench and a sign that explains the magical area you are about to enter. This section of the trail loops through a stand of giant pines, where the sun splinters through the trees creating a mosaic of light and shadow on the pine needle path. We'll often repeat this loop in the pines because we just love the aura of this section of the trail.

After completing one or more small loops, cross back over the footbridge and take a right to continue on the large loop. The trail emerges from the hardwood forest into the prairie, where you can enjoy some sunshine as you complete the final segment of this hike which runs south parallel to the road all the way back to the parking lot.

WHILE YOU'RE IN THE AREA: You should also visit Harrington Beach State Park and Fischer Creek State Recreation Area.

Lakeshore State Park

Lakeshore is Wisconsin's youngest state park, having just opened in 2007, which explains why I was completely unaware it existed despite many visits as a young adult to the lakefront and Summerfest grounds. Lakeshore State Park is a perfect urban oasis and a great option for dogs and humans in the Milwaukee area who can't make it out to other more rural state parks. It's also good for beginners, since the trail is completely paved, and the terrain is flat. Plus, a state park pass isn't needed, making the park even more accessible to city dwellers. With views of Lake Michigan, the Hoan Bridge, downtown Milwaukee, the Discovery World Museum, and even the Milwaukee Art Museum in the distance, this park offers very different views from any other state park. Though the trail is short, there's plenty to take in during your stroll.

Not only is the park new, but the land it's on is relatively "new" as well. Lake Michigan's original shoreline used to be about 1,000 feet inland, and the land along the shoreline all the way west to Miller Park (now American Family Field) used to be wetlands. But in the 1800s, as people settled in the area, they needed easy access to rivers and ships needed safe places to harbor, so the wetlands were filled in with all sorts of junk—soil, waste, pretty much whatever they could find. Wildlife habitats were destroyed in the name of progress, which is sadly still too often the case.

In 1927, Maitland Field opened in the area now occupied by the Summerfest grounds. It was one of the first downtown airports in the country, but wind conditions on the lake weren't reliable for on-time departures. In 1956 the US Army moved in and opened a Nike missile base, which housed rockets until the land was turned into the Summerfest grounds in the 1970s, replacing rockets with rockers.

The piece of land the state park sits on was created in the 1980s with limestone debris deposited in the lake courtesy of the Milwaukee Metropolitan Sewerage District's (MMSD) Deep Tunnel Project. The Deep Tunnel is essentially the overflow tank for holding excess sanitary and storm water until it can be processed by a water reclamation facility. I suppose dumping tunneling debris into the lake and creating an island for recreational activities is better than dumping untreated wastewater into the lake. The Deep Tunnel was a step in the right direction for MMSD, and after the cryptosporidiosis outbreak of 1993, they really got their act together. The MMSD has captured and cleaned 98.5 percent of all the water and wastewater from the region since 1994.

All this talk about water quality has me thinking about what I can do to help keep our planet's water healthy. Did you know picking up your dog's poop is actually good for our planet's water? By picking up your dog's poop, you prevent the poop (and the bacteria in the poop) from running off into storm drains and water supplies. That's just one more compelling reason to pick up your dog's poop.

WORTH A MENTION: If the mile loop within the park isn't enough to tire your dog out, you can continue south on the Hank Aaron State Trail or head north on the Oak Leaf Trail that runs along Lake Michigan.

HEADS-UP: When you grow up outside of Milwaukee, the phrase "cooler by the lake" is a common expression and for good reason. It's always a smart idea to pack extra layers when heading to a park on Lake Michigan, even on warm days.

HEADS-UP: For many people, driving and parking in cities can be a stressful, so it's a good idea to know what your options are for parking before leaving the house. There are two entrances to the park: the north entrance and the south entrance. If you are driving to Lakeshore State Park, Lucky and I recommend parking at the south entrance.

The parking options at the north entrance include a limited number of street-level metered spots, the parking ramp at Discovery

World, or the O'Donnell parking ramp across Lincoln Memorial Drive. The first time we visited Lakeshore, I opted for the north entrance because I am more familiar with navigating that area of the lakefront. There were no metered street parking spots available, so I parked in the Discovery World parking garage. However, there is no pedestrian exit from the parking garage to the outside—after parking, museum visitors use the elevators or stairs to go directly up into the museum lobby. Seeing no other option, I brought Lucky onto the elevator, through the Discovery World lobby, and then outside. No one seemed to mind or even look surprised to see him/us there, but I'd rather not inadvertently be somewhere we aren't meant to be.

Rather than deal with the limited parking/parking ramp situation, we recommend parking at the south entrance. It might be a little tricky to get to—even the DNR site suggests "visitors from outside the city may wish to view a map of the area to better understand the written directions." But once you get there, actually parking and getting into the park are easy and straightforward.

HEADS-UP: If you visit the park in the fall, be prepared for lots of birds (both geese and seagulls), which could overwhelm some dogs. And where there are lots of birds, there is usually lots of bird poop. This can make for a complicated hike for humans trying to not step on goose poop land mines while trying to prevent doggos from eating all the goose poop noms. This is where "leave it" and, if needed, "drop it!" come in handy if your dog is anything like my very special boy Lucky.

WATER AVAILABILITY: None.

BATHROOM AVAILABILITY: None.

TRASHCAN AVAILABILITY: We found one trashcan by the north entrance to the park.

DESIGNATED DOG SWIMMING AREA: At the time of our last visit, there was no designated pet swim area. As always, check with park staff when you visit in case designations have changed—if you can find park staff at Lakeshore.

DESIGNATED DOG PICNIC AREA: At the time of our last visit, there was no designated pet picnic area. But there are plenty of places to picnic outside of the park along the lakefront.

RECOMMENDED HIKE: Multiuse trail
DISTANCE AND ELEVATION GAIN: 1 mile, 40 feet
DOG AND HUMAN FITNESS LEVEL: recreational rambler
TRAIL CONDITIONS/MATERIALS: The trail is a paved, flat multiuse trail. It is wide enough for walking side by side and for easy passing. Keep an eye out for cyclists and skaters.
TRAIL MARKINGS/EASE OF NAVIGATING: The trail is well established and easy to follow.
THE EXPERIENCE: Park along the road to the south entrance and walk north along the Hank Aaron State Trail. The entrance to the state park is just past the BMO Harris Pavilion. Once you enter the park, you can proceed clockwise or counterclockwise around the multiuse trail. Lucky and I recommend taking the path clockwise, starting along the inlet side of the park and finishing on the lakeshore side of the park. The trail meanders through a prairie and past a decent beach, a fishing pier and numerous benches. At the north end of the park, you can cross over the bridge to explore the mainland and continue on the Hank Aaron Trail to connect to the Oak Leaf Trail. Staying in the park, the multiuse trail passes the marina before looping back along the lakeshore. The shoreline is comprised of giant boulders, which are great for getting photos of your dog posing as a mountain goat. Throughout this hike, Lucky and I suggest stopping to take a million photos and to enjoy the views before returning to the south entrance and heading back to your car.

THE SOUTH-CENTRAL REGION

Aztalan State Park

Even before Lucky and I had ever visited Aztalan State Park, the name sounded familiar. This could have been because I'd driven past the Aztalan Cycle Club sign on I-94 a hundred times, but I'm pretty sure it sounded familiar because it reminded me of Aslan from *The Chronicles of Narnia*. In many ways, that association is fitting. In *The Chronicles of Narnia*, Aslan is dignified and so is Aztalan State Park.

The name *Aztalan* was bestowed upon the area by early settlers who thought the native inhabitants were related to the Aztecs of Mexico, but it turns out they were really from the very exotic locale of southern Illinois. The Native Americans who migrated to this spot along the Crawfish River from their home on the Mississippi constructed a town complete with three earthen mounds and a stockade wall fortifying the town from external threats. What once was a thriving civilization is now a premiere archaeological site and national historic landmark.

Driving into the park is much like being transported to another world—no magical wardrobe needed. Two of the mounds and portions of the stockade wall have been restored, and even though the logs aren't the originals, their stature captures the imagination. The portentous line of logs and the sacred mounds construct a solemn scene full of reverence and ritual. The park's footprint of 172 acres with two miles of hiking trails belies the breadth of experience one is likely to have while exploring this park. And your dog will likely be thrilled to have so many posts to pee on.

HEADS-UP: Dogs are not allowed on the portion of trail from the south parking lot down to the canoe launch. There is a "No Pet Area" sign on a post in the center of the trail from the parking lot, but if you are coming from the north on the trail, there are no signs near the boat launch directing dogs to use an alternate path.

WATER AVAILABILITY: Water is available near the picnic shelter and near the main picnic area at the end of the park road.

BATHROOM AVAILABILITY: Vault toilets are available near the picnic shelter and near the main picnic area at the end of the park road.

TRASHCAN AVAILABILITY: No trashcans on site; plan on carry-in/carry-out.

DESIGNATED DOG SWIMMING AREA: At the time of our last visit, there was no designated pet swim area. Given the "No Pet Area" sign at the top of the path leading to the canoe launch, I'm assuming dogs aren't supposed to be at the canoe launch. But just north of the current canoe launch are the remains of a previous launch site. Our last visit was on a really hot day in August. The entire time we walked along the trail that parallels the Crawfish River, Lucky kept looking in its direction longingly. I could tell he was hoping for a social trail that would lead him down to the water. I think he had almost given up hope when we found a narrow detour off the main trail that took us down to the old canoe launch site. Despite the water looking less than fresh, I let Lucky take a dip in the Crawfish River. It was really hot. If park staff are present when you visit, check with them in case designations have changed.

DESIGNATED DOG PICNIC AREA: There are a couple of "Pet Area. Keep Pets On Leash" signs in the vicinity of the picnic area just inside the park. Park at the first lot on the left. There are a few picnic tables and park grills near the information and self-registration station.

RECOMMENDED HIKE: Park trail

DISTANCE AND ELEVATION GAIN: 1.8 miles, 134 feet

DOG AND HUMAN FITNESS LEVEL: recreational rambler

TRAIL CONDITIONS/MATERIALS: The park trail is mostly a wide swath of mowed grass, with a couple of sections coated with woodchips and a segment or two where the grass is sparse, making the trail mostly dirt. The trail is predominantly flat and wide enough to accommodate you and your dog walking side by side. There is room enough to step aside in the event you need to let other groups pass.

TRAIL MARKINGS/EASE OF NAVIGATING: The trail is well established and easy to follow. There are no trail markers, but there really is no need. The trail is essentially two loops: one in the northern part of the park that goes through prairie, woods, and past the marker mounds, and one in the southern part of the park that runs parallel to the stockade wall and the riverbank.

THE EXPERIENCE: Park in the lot immediately to your left after entering the park. The information and self-registration station are conveniently located in this lot, and the picnic area at this lot is pet friendly. Start walking toward the stockade wall on the mowed grass path accessible from the east side of the parking lot. The path starts out with a barely perceptible descent through the prairie directly to the stockade. At the corner of the stockade, stay to the left and continue east along the outside of the log wall. The path widens and narrows with the wall's protrusions—at its most narrow, you may need to walk single file between the forest on your left and the stockade on your right.

When the path reaches the river and a T-intersection, take a right, passing through the wall, to continue south along the river. The path parallels the river for a little less than a half of a mile, and as it goes along, it gets further from the river and deeper into the understory. It's possible to catch glimpses of the river on the left between the trees and shrubbery and distant views of the mounds on the right. The path again runs directly into a small portion of restored stockade wall. This segment marks the corner of where the original wall may have been, providing visitors a visual cue for imagining the entire perimeter. Get skinny and pass through the wall, or walk around it, and then take a right to head west toward the parking lot and picnic area.

Follow the path from the corner of the stockade up to the picnic area. Water and vault toilets are available at this picnic area in case you're in need of either of those amenities. Pass the first mowed path, opting instead for the one at the northwest corner of the picnic area. This path is a direct shot up to the stockade and the southern mound. Stay to the right of the wall, explore the different levels of the mound, and enjoy the views of the surrounding area from this vantage point before heading north along the stockade. When the wall ends, continue on the extra-wide mowed path to the other mound. After spending some time at the northern mound, you can either head back to the parking lot via the same segment of trail the hike started on, or, to complete the recommended hike, head back toward the river, this time on the inside of the stockade.

When the path reaches the river, take a left, pass through the wall again, and continue north through the woods. The path eventually splits when it turns west and into the prairie. Stay to the right for both the bit of shade the trees provide and for the chance to see the marker mounds. At the marker mounds, take a left and head back to the parking lot, walking between the prairie on the left and the marker mounds on the right.

Belmont Mound State Park

Not to be confused with a Native American mound, Belmont Mound State Park is a monadnock surrounded by a peneplain; or in other words, a high point made up of erosion-resistant rock surrounded by a flat area formed by erosion. The reason Belmont Mound survived the erosion of the surrounding area is because it's capped with Niagara dolomite—yup, the same mineral that makes up the Niagara Escarpment. In western New York, the Niagara Escarpment is the massive cliff Niagara Falls plummets over; in northeastern Wisconsin, the Niagara Escarpment carves through High Cliff, Peninsula, and Potawatomi state parks; and in southwestern Wisconsin, all that's left of the Niagara dolomite are the hard caps of Blue, Platte, Belmont, and Sinsinawa mounds. If it weren't for its Niagara dolomite cap, Belmont wouldn't be a mound at all. But it is a mound, and at 1,400 feet, it's taller than some "mountains" in Wisconsin (ahem, Wildcat Mountain). I always roll my eyes at the idea of mountains in Wisconsin, so I appreciate it when something is called what it is—a mound. But really, the joke is on me, since Belmont comes from the French *belle mont* meaning "beautiful mountain." So, it turns out that, for good measure, this hill was named Beautiful Mountain Mound. Good grief.

On a nongeological note, the first capital of the Territory of Wisconsin is a half-mile west of the park. It was at this historic council house that the territorial legislature selected Madison from nineteen other towns to be Wisconsin's permanent capital city. Sorry Cassville, we can't all be winners (see Nelson Dewey State Park entry).

WORTH A MENTION: Belmont Mound's trails aren't groomed for cross-country skiing, so this park is an option for winter hiking with your dog.

HEADS-UP: At the time of our last visit, the observation tower was closed. This is why I'm not recommending the hiking trail that goes up the mound. Without the observation tower, there are no views from the top of the mound. All you see around you is deciduous forest. But if you did want to add on a trip up to the top of the mound, the loop up, around the top, and back down is about 0.6 miles with 144 feet of elevation gain.

HEADS-UP: In general, I don't recommend this park as a vacation destination, but it's fine as a stop on your way to somewhere else.

WATER AVAILABILITY: Water is seasonally available near the picnic shelter.

BATHROOM AVAILABILITY: There is a vault toilet near the picnic area.

TRASHCAN AVAILABILITY: No trashcans on site; plan on carry-in/carry-out.

DESIGNATED DOG SWIMMING AREA: None, as there are no bodies of water at this park.

DESIGNATED DOG PICNIC AREA: At the time of our last visit, there was no designated pet picnic area.

RECOMMENDED HIKE: X-C Ski, Mt. Bike, Hiking Trail

DISTANCE AND ELEVATION GAIN: 1.1 miles, 51 feet

DOG AND HUMAN FITNESS LEVEL: recreational rambler

TRAIL CONDITIONS/MATERIALS: The trail is mostly dirt, grass, and weeds. It is minimally maintained, so you may encounter downed trees or other obstacles. In the fall, watch out for black walnuts on the trail; one could easily twist an ankle and black walnuts are toxic to dogs. The trail isn't too narrow, as it accommodates cross-country skiers in the winter, but we found it was still easiest to navigate single file. Also, it's possible to step off the trail to let others pass, but in our experience there haven't been many hikers on the trails at Belmont.

TRAIL MARKINGS/EASE OF NAVIGATING: For the most part, the trails are well established and easy to follow. At the time of our last visit, there weren't trail maps at the park entrance, so I took a screenshot of the map on the DNR website to reference while we were out on the trail. The X-C Ski, Mt. Bike, Hiking Trail is marked with wooden posts with hiker, biker, and skier icons on them as well as an indicator of the level of difficulty of the ski route.

THE EXPERIENCE: Park in the lot by the picnic area. You can begin this loop by hiking on the road and then picking up the trail on the left of the road just past the gate. The trail is in the woods but follows the curvature of the road for about the first quarter of a mile. Then, the trail departs from the road's curve and delves deeper into the woods. At the first intersection, stay to the right and follow the trail as it heads south. This segment of trail traverses along the edge of the woods, and you can see farm fields distinctly on the left. Then the trail turns to the west and heads back through the woods to the playground and picnic area. Once you reach the picnic area, you are done with the recommended hike. If you and your pup still have energy to burn, you can also add on the hiking trail that goes up and around the top of the mound. This trail is on your right as you approach the picnic area from the X-C Ski, Mt. Bike, Hiking Trail.

Blue Mound State Park

Blue Mound State Park is in Wisconsin's Driftless Area—a moniker that has always confused me a little. What does it mean that this area is without drift? In layman's terms, it means this area didn't get steamrolled by glaciers. We know this, in part, because the area lacks all the rocks, sand, and other junk that glaciers transport into an area and then leave there when they melt. So, this area is without the junk, aka drift. And because the glaciers didn't steamroll this area, we can enjoy the remaining mound. Just like Belmont Mound, Blue Mound isn't a Native American mound; it's also a monadnock surrounded by a peneplain thanks to its erosion-resistant cap of Niagara dolomite. In fact, thanks to that cap, Blue Mound is the highest point in southern Wisconsin. The 360-degree views of the forest, Lower Wisconsin Riverway, and Baraboo Bluffs from the park's observation towers are popular photo opportunities.

On your way to the East Observation Tower, you might notice a memorial marker that has been placed near the road to honor four soldiers who lost their lives in Blue Mound State Park. Thanksgiving weekend in 1944, a US Army cargo plane was flying from Chicago to Minneapolis and got caught in a winter storm. Ice was building up on the plane, so they tried to turn around to go back to Chicago, but they never made it. The plane crashed in Blue Mound, and the four passengers died: Captain Allen L. Swinton of Minneapolis, Minnesota; 2nd Lt. John A. Oppreicht of Lynxville, Wisconsin; Pfc. John B. Nolan of East St. Louis, Illinois; and Pvt. Stanley A. Schlesinger of Richmond Hills, New York.

Now, I don't put much stock in the supernatural, but during one already spooky visit to Blue Mound, on a particularly secluded trail, Lucky started freaking out. It was as though he spotted something in the woods—a deer maybe—and felt the need to bark and whine like crazy. It wasn't an excited bark. It was an anxious bark. I couldn't see or hear anything out of the ordinary. I told myself it was nothing. Lucky is just a spaz. But we started hiking a bit faster. Eventually Lucky calmed down, but we had to return along the same stretch of trail. As we backtracked through that section of forest, he got agitated again and started to bark and whine. I still couldn't see anything, so we just hiked though it as fast as we could, me doling out treats the whole way to keep Lucky from going bonkers. After I blogged about our experience, a reader reached out to let me know her dog also freaked out at that SAME SPOT. Could it be that our dogs were sensing something paranormal?

HEADS-UP: Dogs are not allowed on the observation towers, so if you want to see the views from above, bring a friend and take turns climbing up the towers.

WORTH A MENTION: In the winter many of the trails at Blue Mound are groomed for cross-country skiing, which means you can't hike on them with your dog. But what you can do is hike/snowshoe the single-track mountain bike trails. Exercise caution when going out into the parks in the winter—it's wild out there after all!

WATER AVAILABILITY: Water is available at the park office, near the Friends Shelter, and at the picnic areas and observation towers.

BATHROOM AVAILABILITY: Flush toilets are available at the park office and swimming pool. Vault toilets are available in the picnic areas.

TRASHCAN AVAILABILITY: No trashcans on site; plan on carry-in/carry-out.

DESIGNATED DOG SWIMMING AREA: None, as there are no bodies of water at this park other than the park pool, and, of course, dogs are not allowed in the pool.

DESIGNATED DOG PICNIC AREA: At the time of our last visit, there was no designated pet picnic area. As always, check with park staff when you visit in case designations have changed.

RECOMMENDED HIKE: Indian Marker Tree Trail

HEADS-UP: While you're hiking, keep an eye out for an oak tree that Native Americans felled over one hundred years ago and pointed in the direction of a natural spring. Lucky and I always get so caught up in the scenery of this trail and checking out the rock outcroppings that we forget to look for the oak tree. This trail has everything we love: ferns, rock outcroppings, moss, an oak tree we can't locate/ identify (aka mystery). So, it's easily our favorite, even if it is shorter than other trails in the park.

DISTANCE AND ELEVATION GAIN: 1.1 miles, 165 feet

DOG AND HUMAN FITNESS LEVEL: recreational rambler

TRAIL CONDITIONS/MATERIALS: Indian Marker Tree Trail is primarily dirt with some gravel, lots of rocks, and occasional protruding roots. There is a wooden footbridge along the trail and a flight of wooden stairs that lead up to the East Observation Tower. The trail is consistently narrow, except for the stairs, which are wider. It's best to navigate the trail single file. Stepping off to the side to let others pass is possible but may be difficult at times. The trail can be waterlogged if it has rained recently. Indian Marker Tree Trail is more technically challenging than other trails in the park that double as cross-country ski trails, which is probably another reason why it's our favorite hiking trail in the park.

TRAIL MARKINGS/EASE OF NAVIGATING: The trail is well worn and easy to navigate. There is a sign on a post at the trailhead from the park road, and there is another sign and a worn-out trail map where Indian Marker Tree Trail intersects with the Flint Rock Nature Trail. Where the trail dead-ends at the wooden stairs, there's another sign on a post indicating that Indian Marker Tree Trail continues up the stairs.

THE EXPERIENCE: Park in the third pull-off parking area along the park road after the parking lot for the East Tower. The trailhead is marked with a signpost pointing toward the woods, at the north end of the suggested parking area. Relatively soon after entering the woods, the trail passes by the first of many rock outcroppings. Continue to follow the narrow footpath as it meanders through the woods along the north face of the mound and past a second spectacular rock outcropping. I say "spectacular" because we really like rock outcroppings. The trail continues to meander through the woods, between rocks and trees and among ferns—our other favorite! Then the trail crosses a wooden footbridge before continuing to meander past rock outcroppings both big and small.

Next the trail intersects with the Flint Rock Nature Trail. Continue straight on Indian Marker Tree Trail. The narrow trail weaves through dense thickets of ferns that transition to general understory and past more moss-drenched rock outcroppings. There's more meandering among trees, underbrush, and rocks, and then the trail is interrupted by the tiniest of tributaries. Depending on the amount of recent rain, this little waterway may be dried up to barely a dribble, but either way, you'll step over its path as you continue on the trail. There's another step over a mini-stream, more rocks and rock outcroppings, and then the trail dead-ends at a T-intersection with a long flight of wooden riser stairs.

Take a right to head up the flight of stairs. This long and gradual flight of wooden stairs is the most strenuous segment of the hike, and it may seem to go on forever. But it only seems that way: the regularly spaced stairs transition to more sporadically spaced treads, then a segment of trail sans treads, then a few more sporadically spaced treads, then another lengthy segment of uniformly spaced stairs, then trail with sporadic treads, and then observation tower! When you reach the observation tower, you've reached the end of this climb, unless you want to get in even more climbing and decide to go up to the top of the observation tower (reminder: no dogs allowed up the tower). The views from the picnic area by the tower are also excellent. You're already technically at the highest point in southern Wisconsin at 1,719 feet of elevation.

From the observation tower, you have several options for completing your hike. You can shorten the hike by heading back to your car via the park road, or there are numerous options for extending your hike. To extend your hike, you can go back down the stairs, take a left onto Indian Marker Tree Trail and then hike the Flint

Rock Nature Trail counterclockwise to the West Tower. Or you could venture even further by taking Flint Rock to Willow Spring Trail or the Basalt and Pepper mountain bike trail. To complete the hike as recommended, head back down the flight of wooden stairs to the intersection with Indian Marker Tree Trail. Take a left to jump back on Indian Marker Tree Trail and retrace your way through the ferns and rock outcroppings until you reach the trailhead and the parking area.

WHILE YOU'RE IN THE AREA: You should also visit Governor Dodge State Park.

Cross Plains State Park

The first time I went to this park, I made sure to go with a friend who had been there before. I am generally familiar with the area, since it's in the Madison metro, and apparently my cycling routes have taken me right past the park many times. But if you don't know it's there, you will most certainly miss it. There is no state park sign heralding the entrance. There is no parking lot or self-service pay station. And there are no trail maps.

The Ice Age Complex at Cross Plains is a patchwork of properties, some owned by the Wisconsin DNR, some by Dane County, some the US Fish and Wildlife Service, and some the National Park Service. And in between these parcels are chunks of privately owned land. It's not the easiest area to make sense of. That first time we visited, we hiked around the main National Park Service portion, which felt a lot like walking around the perimeter of a farm field—because that's exactly what it is. But I've been told on a clear day you can see Blue Mound from the bench on the top of the hill. Since then, we've explored the other properties that make up the Ice Age Complex and are pretty confident that the Wisconsin DNR portion is the most enjoyable hiking.

WORTH A MENTION: Despite the lack of information about this park, it's a nice urban oasis option for Madisonians, and you don't need a state park sticker to visit, so at least there's that.

HEADS-UP: Finding the trailhead can be tricky. Don't use 8075 Old Sauk Pass Road as the address in your GPS. Instead, try 8107 Old Sauk Pass Road, which should get you right to the entrance drive to the

Cross Plains State Park

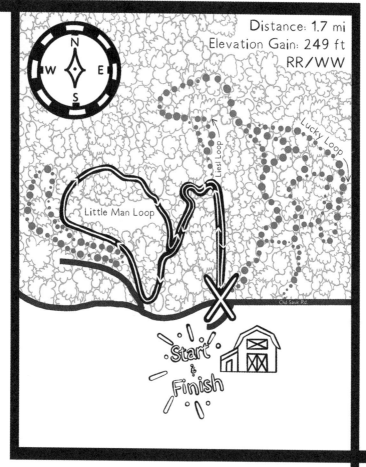

Distance: 1.7 mi
Elevation Gain: 249 ft
RR/WW

N
W · E
S

Liesl Loop

Lucky Loop

Little Man Loop

Old Sauk Rd.

Start & Finish

former Wilkie Farm (red barn). There's room for a few cars to park on the side of the road across from the entrance to the Wilkie Farm, and the entrance to the recommended hike is on the north side of the road, on either side of the gate.

WATER AVAILABILITY: None.

BATHROOM AVAILABILITY: None.

TRASHCAN AVAILABILITY: No trashcans on site; plan on carry-in/carry-out.

DESIGNATED DOG SWIMMING AREA: None, as there are no bodies of water at this park.

DESIGNATED DOG PICNIC AREA: At the time of our last visit, there was no designated pet picnic area. I don't think there's even a people picnic area. If park staff are present when you visit, check with them in case designations have changed.

RECOMMENDED HIKE: Since these trails don't have names, I'm going to take the liberty of naming them. Rather than be clever or descriptive, I'm going to name them after dogs. The first route we hiked on this parcel was with our German Shepherd friend Liesl, so that route is going to be the Liesl Loop. And Little Man joined us during another visit, so I hereby dub the route we hiked that day the Little Man Loop. And of course, there has to be a Lucky trail too. In his memory and honor, I'm going to recommend the Little Man Loop.

DISTANCE AND ELEVATION GAIN: 1.7 miles, 249 feet

DOG AND HUMAN FITNESS LEVEL: recreational rambler/weekend warrior

TRAIL CONDITIONS/MATERIALS: The Little Man Loop is a combination of wide stretches of trail through prairies and narrow stretches of trail through woods and dense understory. The prairie segments are mostly grass and weeds, which are mowed semi-regularly, so the length of the grass and weeds varies. The segments in the woods are mostly dirt with frequent rock protrusions that can be challenging for weak ankles like mine. Take care when navigating these rockier portions. While the prairie segments are wider, most of the Little Man Loop is best hiked single file. It may be challenging to pass others on the trail, especially while in the woods, but the trails have always been quiet when we've visited. You can easily gauge how busy the trails are by how many cars are parked along the road. Ours is often the only car.

TRAIL MARKINGS/EASE OF NAVIGATING: The trails are well established and easy to follow, but there are no official trail markers or maps. We hope the map we've provided here is helpful.

THE EXPERIENCE: Park along the north side of Old Sauk Pass Road, just west of the old Wilke Farm. The trailhead for the Liesl and Little Man Loops is located at the gate on the north side of the road. A couple of brown signs on posts let you know your pet is welcome in the area if it is always on leash and picked up after. So, here's a friendly reminder to not get lackadaisical about leashing your dog here just because this park isn't very busy. Both loops start at this entrance to the DNR parcel, and we typically pick up the trail on whichever side of the gate is least overgrown with prairie grass.

If you access the trail on the left side of the gate, go straight. If you access the trail on the right side of the gate, make sure to stay to the left when the trail forks right away. Staying to the left gets you started on both loops. Both the left and right entrances converge just down the slope from the road. Follow the trail into the prairie. On the left is a portion of prairie and a line of trees, and on the right the prairie extends farther with trees in the distance. Soon the trail jogs left and heads into the trees where it gets narrower and turns into a dirt footpath bordered by weeds, undergrowth, and forest. You can sense the gully on the left and can catch occasional views of it through the trees. At the first intersection, which I'm calling Decision-Making Time, take a left onto the grassy/weedy trail to complete the Little Man Loop.

After taking the left, the trail continues west for a little bit and eventually transitions from grass and weeds to dirt and rocks. Then, the trail swings back to head south as you traverse along the edge of the gully. Throughout this traverse, the trail is extra-narrow, with vegetation encroaching on both sides. When the trail reaches the bottom of the gully, there's another split, which I'm calling Prairie Intersection. Take the trail straight as it continues further south through the woods and then climbs up to traverse along the top of the other side of the gully. Next, the trail turns back to the north/northwest and traverses along the western ridge of the gully, gradually descending through the woods over, under, and between trees until it emerges from the woods into the prairie.

The view as you enter the prairie is striking in a "wow, I can't believe we're just outside of Madison" kind of way; it's like entering an enchanted valley of modest proportions. The trail, now a bit wider and much grassier, meanders through the northeastern side of the prairie, the tree line not too far off on the left. After skipping over a small creek, the trail returns to the woods and meets back up at Prairie Intersection. From here, take a left to backtrack along the side of the gully, up and around to Decision-Making Time. Once back at Decision-Making Time, take a right to finish the recommended Little Man Loop by backtracking through the prairie to Old Sauk Pass Road. Or, if you'd like to get in another mile, take a right at Decision-Making Time to tack on the Liesl Loop. If you want to explore even more, take Liesl Loop to Lucky Trail.

WHILE YOU'RE IN THE AREA: You might also visit Capital Brewery's dog-friendly beer garden.

Devil's Lake State Park

I once had an internationally traveled Air B&B guest visiting from San Francisco stay with me, and the main event on his Madison itinerary was hiking at Devil's Lake State Park. To say Devil's Lake is a popular park is a major understatement. Devil's Lake is Wisconsin's most visited state park, boasting more annual visitors than even Peninsula State Park in Door County. Devil's Lake's annual attendance reached over one million visitors in 1952, and now hovers between 2.5 to 2.7 million a year. That's more visitors a year than 85 percent of the National Park Service's individual properties combined! Devil's Lake is not only Wisconsin's most visited state park, it's also the state's largest state park, and it's over one hundred years old. Founded in 1911, it was Wisconsin's third state park (Interstate was the first and Peninsula was the second).

Even before it was a state park, Devil's Lake was a popular vacation destination. The train tracks that run through the park to this day started bringing visitors to the area in the late 1800s. Hotels were built along the south shore of Devil's Lake and other amenities followed: a grocery store, barber shop, billiard hall, and a bowling alley. There was a golf course in the park from 1922 until 1961 (now the Quartzite Campground), at one point there was a zoo, and apparently people raced horses across the frozen lake in the winter. In the 1930s a Civilian Conservation Corps camp was formed in the park, and much of the park's infrastructure is thanks to the CCC workers. Among the state park's lore are stories of a dog bitten by a rattlesnake and the Ringling Brothers' elephants bathing in the lake. Famous visitors to the park include Ulysses S. Grant and Mary Todd Lincoln.

It's understandable why this park was so popular then and still is now. Its bluffs are part of the Baraboo Range, which, at 1.6 billion years old, is one of the most ancient rock outcrops in North America. Devil's Lake's bluffs include some impressive rock formations like Balanced Rock and Devil's Doorway, and the park is a popular destination for rock climbing. The park has 29 miles of hiking trails, striking vistas, and the lake and beaches. Plus, it's close to Madison. But at a couple million–plus visitors a year, the park is less popular with Lucky and me. If we go, we try to go early in the mornings or during the off-peak season—and even so, there are always plenty of other visitors. The only time we've had the trail all to ourselves was a blustery and frigid day in February. The worst day of winter is the best day to go to Devil's Lake if you don't want to deal with crowds. So, with so many other great options just as close to us as Devil's Lake, we tend to venture elsewhere and leave Devil's Lake to the tourists.

HEADS-UP: Dogs aren't allowed at Parfrey's Glen State Natural Area, a popular spot within Devil's Lake State Park and Wisconsin's first state natural area. The Glen is a fragile area, which is why dogs aren't allowed. If you do visit it sans pup, be sure to stay on designated trails and leave no trace, so future generations will be able to enjoy this cool spot too.

HEADS-UP: Get your state park pass before visiting Devil's Lake State Park. During the summer, the left lane into the park gets backed up with people needing to purchase day passes. You can cruise by the line using the right-hand lane if you already have your annual park pass.

WATER AVAILABILITY: Water is available at the north shore headquarters and Visitor Center. In the summer, water is available at the picnic shelters and near many parking lots. There are also winterized water taps in the Quartzite Campground and near the CCC parking lot in the south shore Group Camp.

BATHROOM AVAILABILITY: Year-round flush toilets are available at the north shore headquarters and Visitor Center. Vault toilets are available near the picnic shelters with a year-round toilet available at the Red Cedar Shelter on the south shore.

TRASHCAN AVAILABILITY: The DNR must recognize how unrealistic it is to expect 2.5 million people a year to carry-in/carry-out. Garbage and recycling are available throughout the park, including near the park headquarters, on either end of the main parking lot on the north shore, at the South Shore Concessions and boat rental parking lot, and at the Red Cedar and Red Oak picnic shelters on the south shore.

DESIGNATED DOG SWIMMING AREA: Devil's Lake has an official off-leash pet swimming area at the South Shore boat launch, but it's really one side of a boat launch that's been designated for launching dogs instead of boats. The left side of the dock is still used operationally by boaters, while dogs can swim on the right side of the dock. On land to the right side of the dock is one picnic table and a tiny patch of sand in between some thick vegetation. There's the paved ramp leading into the water, or one can access the water from the tiny patch of sand. For as large and popular as Devil's Lake State Park is, this is

The concrete ramp into the water at the Devil's Lake State Park dog swimming area (Danielle St. Louis)

a very small area for dogs and their owners. It can quickly get crowded; however, this is one of the few dog swimming areas where I would actually go into the water with Lucky. The water is clear, calm, and hospitable for both dogs and people. If leashed swimming is your dog's thing, you can also take your dog swimming on leash near the north shore boat landing and adjacent to the south shore boardwalk.

DESIGNATED DOG PICNIC AREA: The designated pet picnic area is the picnic area east of the railroad tracks on the north end of the lake. After entering the park via the main entrance on County Road DL, go straight past the main entrance station and visitor center, past the main parking lots and across the train tracks. Then take a right, following the signs for additional parking and the East Bluff attractions. Park in the first lot on the right if there is a spot; the pet picnic area is on your right. Overall, this designated pet picnic area is decent. There is a water fountain and vault toilets nearby and if you loosely interpret the boundaries of the "Pet Picnic Area" sign, there are numerous picnic tables, park grills, and plenty of space.

RECOMMENDED HIKE: East Bluff Trail + East Bluff Woods Trail

HEADS-UP: We've hiked at so many state parks where we didn't see another person or dog the entire time we were on trail, but that is never the case at Devil's Lake. Not seeing another person or dog is rare. The East Bluff Trail offers some fun, technical hiking and amazing views, but the narrow trail is not ideal for hiking with dogs, especially reactive dogs passing other dogs. So, we recommend doing this hike early in the morning before the trails become crowded. If you are hiking later in the morning or in the afternoon, we recommend doing an out-and-back on East Bluff Woods trail. Once you get to the top of the East Bluff Woods Trail, you can venture on a portion of East Bluff Trail to take in some views of the lake from the bluffs before heading back down the way you came. This out-and-back option gives you a chance to see some of the views but avoid most of the narrow and challenging parts of East Bluff Trail. Doing the out-and-back on East Woods Bluff Trail is also a great option if you know your dog would just do better on a wider trail with more room for passing other groups.

Portion of East Bluff Trail, Devil's Lake State Park, where passing is impossible (Danielle St. Louis)

DISTANCE AND ELEVATION GAIN: 2.8 miles, 540 feet

DOG AND HUMAN FITNESS LEVEL: weekend warrior/avid adventurer

TRAIL CONDITIONS/MATERIALS: East Bluff Trail is predominantly asphalt and stone. This trail is technical with many flights of stone stairs and rocks to navigate. East Bluff Trail is narrow and is best hiked single file. Stepping off the trail is required to pass others along most of this trail, and in a couple segments, there is no option to step off the trail to pass. In these instances, you may have to hike back to a more open area to pass. In contrast, East Bluff Woods Trail is mostly gravel and dirt. The trail is wide enough for walking side by side, and there's plenty of room for passing other groups.

TRAIL MARKINGS/EASE OF NAVIGATING: The trails are well established and easy to follow. There are trail markers and trail maps along the route as well as wooden posts with the names of trails and trail icons with directional arrows. East Bluff Trail is especially easy to follow because of the asphalt used along the trail.

THE EXPERIENCE: Park in one of the lots near the East Bluff Trailhead. Walk east, across the park road, toward the trailhead and information kiosk. The wide gravel and dirt trail heads into the woods and quickly reaches an intersection. If you're game for the more technical narrow trail, take the right. If you'd rather complete the out-and-back on East Bluff Woods, go straight.

After taking a right, the trail becomes noticeably narrower and the materials change to asphalt with embedded stone stairs. The long and gradual-for-now hike up to the top of the bluff begins. The trail is easy to navigate through the forest because of the asphalt and stairs, but it's still a physically challenging ascent. The trail finally levels off, and there's a rock outcropping on the right. The right edge of the trail is lined with tree trunks; this is possibly a strategy to signal to visitors to stay on the trail rather than departing for the rock outcroppings. Continue to follow the official asphalt trail, which bends to the left and remains flat as it passes by another rock outcropping.

Next, the flat segment of the asphalt trail transitions to a series of narrow stone stairs that head up, into, and around a crag. After the first series of stairs, there is a landing and just ahead is what looks like the entrance to a cave. This is Elephant Cave, a landmark worth examining before following the brown arrow icon to the right and up more stone stairs. This brings you to the first official vista on East Bluff Trail. The trail traverses the side of the bluff, offering visitors opportunities to venture as close to the edge as feels comfortable to take in the view and to take photos.

The next segment of East Bluff Trail is one of the most narrow and difficult to navigate. Below your feet is the asphalt trail, but on your left is a wall of rock and on your right are some trees, shrubbery, and most important, a tumble down the side of a cliff. There is nowhere to go if you need to pass other groups along this stretch of trail. We have, on multiple occasions, had to turn around and return to the vista to let others through before trying again. This narrow segment is followed by another narrow segment that ascends more stone stairs and has few, if any, options for passing other groups. Eventually, you'll reach the top of the ascent, where a wooden post with an East Bluff Trail marker points to the left. Following the trail to the left finally brings you back onto a more level and "spacious" segment of trail. While the trail is still ascending to the top of the bluff, it's a more gradual climb up the asphalt trail and there is at least room to step off to the side of the trail to let others pass.

The remainder of East Bluff Trail continues in much the same fashion. The asphalt trail climbs through the woods along the edge of the bluff, frequent stone stairs head up, into, and around a crag, and occasional views of the lake and surrounding countryside make for an enjoyable jaunt. Though the trail remains narrow, there aren't any more impossible passes, though an East Bluff Trail marker reminds visitors to "Please stay on trail." It's a good reminder to only step off the trail when you absolutely have to. You'll reach a final vista, this one equipped with tourist binoculars, and then just a bit further along the trail, East Bluff Trail intersects with the Ice Age Trail and East Bluff Woods Trail. Take a left at this intersection onto East Bluff Woods Trail. A short segment of narrow and flat asphalt trail leads further into the woods and opens into a clearing. Stay to the left on the main branch of East Bluff Woods Trail, which takes you back down to the parking lot.

East Bluff Woods Trail is noticeably wider than East Bluff Trail and is predominantly gravel and dirt. Its extra-wide course through the woods is a straightforward and gradual descent down the back side of the bluff. Toward the bottom of the descent, the trail runs alongside a stream, which adds to the tranquility of this stretch of trail. You'll arrive at the main intersection, where East Bluff Trail begins, and then it's just an easy stroll back to the trailhead and parking lot.

WHILE YOU'RE IN THE AREA: You might also visit Natural Bridge State Park or Mirror Lake State Park.

Governor Dodge State Park

Governor Dodge State Park is one of my favorite Wisconsin state parks, partly because of its proximity to Madison but also because of its charm. It's another park in Wisconsin's Driftless Area—aka the area that didn't get steamrolled by glaciers—so it boasts exceptional geological features, like 450-million-year-old sandstone bluffs. The park also has a popular water feature, Stephens Falls, and some caves, though these aren't super easy to get to and you have to time your visit around the bats' naps. It has one dog beach, one dog cliff jumping area, and nearly 40 miles of trails.

Because of my personal affection for this park, I was excited to learn more about its history, but I was a little disappointed to discover the park's past is somewhat unremarkable. Yeah, yeah, the feat of four glaciers somehow all missing this swath of land; sure, that's pretty crazy, but it's not a history unique to this park. The anthropological history is also relatively standard: earliest man found shelter among the bluffs after long days of hunting bison; Fox, Sauk and Ho-Chunk peoples mined the lead ore until they were forced out by enterprising colonists. Hm, now here's something. The 1827 conflict, known as the Winnebago War, is where the park's eponym makes his debut into the story.

Henry Dodge was the first child born to parents from the colonies in what is now Indiana. His father was from Connecticut and his mother from Kentucky—everyone else in Indiana at the time was either Native American or French-Canadian. So that's interesting, kind of. More interesting? Wait for it . . . Dodge was recruited by Aaron Burr in 1806 to be part of the Burr Conspiracy, Burr's attempt to create a new country in the southwest. Apparently, Dodge thought this might be his shot, so he went to the rally point. But when he found out Thomas Jefferson declared Burr's plan treasonous, he went home. I guess Dodge didn't want to be Burr's right-hand man that badly. Dodge was indicted for conspiracy, but according to some accounts, the charges were dropped because Dodge whipped members of the grand jury. It's not clear if this account came from someone who was in the room where it happened.

Twenty-odd years and a bunch of militia service later, Dodge moved from Missouri to what's now Dodgeville, Wisconsin, staked a mining claim, and commanded US militias against the Ho-Chunk in the Winnebago War. Long story short, promises were made to the Ho-Chunk that the US government would investigate and evict American miners, including Dodge, who were trespassing on Ho-Chunk lands. But this never happened. Dodge and the rest were never evicted, and the Ho-Chunk ended up having to sell the land to the US government. Dodge went on to be appointed the first Territorial Governor of the Wisconsin Territory in 1836 and was renamed Territorial Governor in 1845. Then, when Wisconsin became a state, he was elected as one of its first senators. To his contemporaries, Dodge was a hero, but the eye of history sees his greatest accomplishments in a different light. He may have been "instrumental in establishing peace in the area" but it was a peace that only prospered the European miners (Dodge included) and ultimately came at the expense of the Ho-Chunk people.

HEADS-UP: Every trail at Governor Dodge is open to hiking in nonwinter months, but many of the trails are multiuse. Be conscientious when hiking on trails, as you may be sharing them with mountain bikers, horses, or mountain bikers *and* horses.

WORTH A MENTION: I always try to stop by Stephens Falls when we visit Governor Dodge, but because it's a popular spot, there are often a lot of people, children, and other dogs in the area. It can get especially crowded at the base of the falls. Stephens Falls Trail is my favorite, and, minus the steeper and semi-technical descent down to the falls from the parking lot, it's a great recreational rambler trail. It's lush with tons of ferns and vibrant green moss-covered rock outcroppings. The trail follows the stream through the gully, and it's just dreamy.

WATER AVAILABILITY: Water is available at the park office and at the picnic areas, including both pet picnic areas and the Enee Point Picnic Area.

BATHROOM AVAILABILITY: Flush toilets are available at the park office and people beaches. Vault toilets are available at the picnic areas.

TRASHCAN AVAILABILITY: There are no trashcans on site for day use; plan on carry-in/carry-out.

DESIGNATED DOG SWIMMING AREA: There are two dog swimming areas at Governor Dodge State Park: one at Cox Hollow Lake and one at Twin Valley Lake. The swimming area at Cox Hollow is far superior to the Twin Valley option. The Cox Hollow dog beach can legitimately be described as a beach because there's a sandy area that gradually leads into the water—you know, like a beach. The beach isn't huge, but the water is easily accessible to dogs and calm (only electric motorboats are allowed on the lake), there are a few picnic tables and a park grill in the grassy area adjacent to the beach, and the people swimming area is far enough away that you don't have to worry about potentially crossing a "no dogs" boundary. The park road does run past the Cox Hollow dog beach, and there is a pull-off for cars to stop and unload canoes and kayaks, which can be launched from the dog beach. The road and pull-off are not as close to the beach as the road at Big Foot Beach State Park is to its pet swimming area, but just be aware of activity on the road or in the pull-off that might catch your dog's attention. To access the Cox Hollow dog beach, park in the lot for the Cox Hollow people beach and picnic shelter. If possible, park in the first, northernmost section of the parking lot as you enter, as you have to backtrack on the road west, past the people beach to the dog beach.

The dog swimming area at Twin Valley Lake can't be called a beach because there's no sand and no gradual incline into the water. There are places where the shoreline, which is a couple of feet above the water, has eroded, making it possible for the most athletic and adventurous dogs to access the water. Calling it a dog cliff-diving area is probably hyperbolic, but it's the best way I can think to describe the way most dogs would have to jump from the shore into the water below. Like the dog swimming area at Cox Hollow, this spot is far enough removed from the people beach that you don't have to worry about potentially encroaching on a "no dogs" area, but you might have to worry about your dog's ability to get into and out of the water. To access the Twin Valley dog swimming area, park in the lot for the Twin Valley people beach and picnic shelter. If possible, park in the first section of the parking lot as you enter, as the dog swimming area is to the south/southeast. Head toward the lake, staying to the left. As you approach the lake, continue left along the shoreline to the dog "swimming" area.

DESIGNATED DOG PICNIC AREA: There are two designated pet picnic areas, one near each of the pet swimming areas. To access the Cox Hollow pet picnic area, park in the lot for the Cox Hollow people beach and picnic shelter. The pet picnic area is just north of the road

The dog swimming area at Cox Hollow Lake (Danielle St. Louis)

into the parking lot. There are several picnic tables, a park grill, and a water fountain/spigot in the area. A couple of posts with "human walking dog" icons identify the boundary of the pet picnic area. There are also a few picnic tables and a park grill in the grassy area adjacent to the Cox Hollow dog beach, which is relatively spacious and very segregated from the people picnic area, but I'm not a huge fan of its proximity to the road.

For this reason, I prefer the pet picnic area at Twin Valley Lake. While the pet swimming area at Twin Valley Lake leaves a lot to be desired, the pet picnic area is spacious, shaded, has several picnic tables, park grills, and a water fountain, and is further removed from the road and parking lot; it is closer in proximity to the people picnic area, though. For those with reactive pups, you may need to choose between proximity to a road versus proximity to other picnicking families. Park in the lot for the Twin Valley people beach and picnic shelter. The pet picnic area is to the south/southeastern side of the larger picnic area. A line of posts with "human walking dog" icons identify the boundary of the pet picnic area.

RECOMMENDED HIKE: Pine Cliff Trail

HEADS-UP: There is more to Pine Cliff Trail than the hike we are recommending. We like this lollipop route: out on Pine Cliff from the Enee Point picnic area, then a loop that goes up to the top of the cliffs, drops back down the shoreline, and then heads back up the hillside to complete the loop before backtracking to Enee. If you hike the rest of Pine Cliff around the southern part of Cox Hollow Lake, here are some things to keep in mind. There is a small portion of Pine Cliff that overlaps with the horse trail, so if your dog doesn't like horses, you may want to avoid a potential encounter. Also, if you keep going on Pine Cliff, there's no great way to make a larger loop of the hike. You can connect to Lakeview Trail for more mileage, but ultimately you are either going to end up doing a lot of backtracking on Lakeview and Pine Cliff or you'll have to complete the loop back to Enee by walking on the road, which I don't recommend. Drivers aren't necessarily paying attention to their speed or looking for hikers along the side of the road.

DISTANCE AND ELEVATION GAIN: 2 miles, 444 feet

DOG AND HUMAN FITNESS LEVEL: weekend warrior

TRAIL CONDITIONS/MATERIALS: Pine Cliff Trail is primarily dirt with some gravel, rocks, sand, and occasional protruding roots. There are several wooden footbridges and stairs along the trail, and there's a longer and steeper flight of wooden stairs that leads up to a wooden bridge across a gully. The trail is consistently narrow, except for the stairs, which are wider. It's best to navigate the trail single file. Stepping off to the side to let others pass is possible for most of the hike but there are some exceptions where it may be more difficult. Pine Cliff Trail is more technical than other trails in the park that double as cross-country ski trails; that's probably why it's our favorite for logging some miles.

TRAIL MARKINGS/EASE OF NAVIGATING: The trail is well established and easy to follow. There are no regularly posted signs on longer stretches of the trail, especially on the segment from the Enee Point picnic area to the first intersection, but there are signs at major intersections and turns. The signs are a combination of brown wooden signs with white text and arrows and posts with small dark green tags and brown arrows. Additionally, there's a park map and signs that indicate what traffic is allowed in each direction at the intersection just before Pine Cliff overlaps with the horse trail.

THE EXPERIENCE: Park in the lot for the Enee Point picnic area that is on the west side of the park road. The trailhead is located to the right of the picnic shelter. A wooden footbridge takes you from the picnic area across a creek to the start of the trail. Across the footbridge, the trail turns to the left and navigates between the creek and moss-covered rock outcroppings. The rock outcroppings recede, replaced with a forested hillside sloping up on the right, but the creek remains on the left. A wooden footbridge takes you across the creek and then just a short distance later the trail turns to the right and up the hillside via the first steep flight of wooden stairs. Halfway to the top, there's a landing with a bench where you and your dog can sit to catch your breath before embarking on the second flight of steep wooden stairs. There isn't another bench at the very top of the stairs, but there is at least a railing to lean on as you take in the views of the gully and the rock formation the bridge crosses over. Across the bridge, the narrow trail continues up, but at a less aggressive grade and with natural elements, like tree roots, to assist in your progress. At the first intersection, stay to the left toward Pine Cliffs. This portion of the trail includes interpretive signs explaining the plant life and the history of the area. The trail continues through the woods, and eventually, you may be able to catch glimpses of the lake down to the left.

Next, you'll descend several catawampus railroad-tie-type stairs. The lake is more visible to the left through the trees, and you'll arrive at a magnificent rock outcropping. This spot is our favorite along this route and the tops of the Pine Cliffs are worth some careful exploration. The initial approach is easy to navigate for humans and dogs but getting to the very top of the rock outcroppings is more challenging and may not be for everyone. Once on top, the terrain is level and there's a beautiful, albeit partially obstructed panoramic view of Cox Hollow Lake. It's a nice spot to take a rest, eat a snack, and take some photos, but be careful and make sure to leave no trace.

From the rock outcropping, take a right to follow the trail through the woods as it gradually descends to the lake. The trail begins to run parallel to the shoreline, and there is a short social trail on the left that leads to the lake's edge. This is a nice spot to let your dog take a dip in the quiet waters of Cox Hollow Lake. The trail continues to run parallel to the shoreline at a modulating distance, and the next interpretive sign explains how the lakes were formed. As the trail turns inland and up the hillside for a moment, it gets especially narrow. The trail remains narrow, runs parallel to the lake again for a bit, though at a greater distance, and then turns inland again. The flora throughout this portion of the hike includes bushy little tufts of grass and various types of ground cover and understory, with trees at a distance from the trail. The trail is super narrow throughout this portion, but you could step off to the side easily if you needed to let others pass.

This portion of the trail is marked with brown posts with green Pine Cliff Trail tags and brown arrows. I imagine the markers are because the area surrounding the trail throughout this section is more open, though the dirt trail is still well defined. The trail starts to gradually ascend the hillside, and then it reaches the next intersection where signs indicate what traffic (horses, snowmobiles, etc.) is allowed in each direction. Take a right to stay on the recommended hike and start the rest of the ascent back up the hillside.

Throughout this section, it may be less easy to step aside to let others pass, since the trail is especially narrow and is traversing up the hillside; the terrain rises steeply up on one side and drops steeply down on the other. It wouldn't be impossible to step off the trail, but I would be extra cautious doing so. As a reminder, downhill traffic is supposed to yield to uphill traffic, though we recommend visitors with dogs always yield to visitors without dogs, no matter which direction they're going. Finally, the trail levels out, and there's an interpretive sign that says, "Farming the Flats," which feels like a bit of a joke considering how steep the hike was to get to this point. If you read further, the sign says flat ridgetops were valuable farmland in the hilly terrain, which validates any huffing and puffing you did to get to this point. It might be flat, but you had to hike up the ridge to get here! Eventually, the trail arrives back at the very first intersection on this hike. Take a left to backtrack on Pine Cliff toward Enee Point and to the parking lot. Even though you've already hiked this segment of the trail, the experience may be different heading in the other direction. At the very least, it'll be easier since it's downhill. Once you're back at the picnic area, make sure to grab a selfie with the billion-year-old sandstone bluffs in the background.

Governor Nelson State Park

This park is named after Gaylord Anton Nelson, Wisconsin's thirty-fifth governor—but he was so much more than that. Nelson was originally from Clear Lake, Wisconsin. For some context, Clear Lake is about 30 miles south of Straight Lake State Park, 30 miles southeast of Interstate State Park, and 35 miles northeast of Willow River State Park. Growing up, he spent a lot of time in the Wisconsin wilderness, which made a significant impression on him. The poverty and pollution he witnessed in his hometown made an equally significant impression, and Nelson couldn't help but draw connections between environmental, economic, and social issues. His path into politics started with an economics degree from San José State University followed by a law degree from UW–Madison. After law school, he was drafted into the US Army and served in World War II.

Nelson launched his political career when he returned to Wisconsin after the war, but, running as a progressive Republican, he lost his first attempt to represent Clear Lake in the state assembly to his conservative counterpart. In related Wisconsin political history, it was this same 1946 election in which Joseph McCarthy won his Senate seat. Yay, Wisconsin. Two years later, Nelson succeeded in getting elected to the Wisconsin State Senate, where he served from 1948 to 1958. He was then elected governor in 1958 and served two two-year terms before being elected to the US Senate in 1962. He served in the US Senate from 1963 to 1981. And now that I've touched on his background and listed the offices he held, it's time to get down to a selection of his most significant accomplishments.

Nelson's environmental agenda focused on protection and preservation. During his four years as Wisconsin's governor, he put $50 million toward his Outdoor Recreation Action Program, which purchased thousands of acres of Wisconsin wilderness for preservation and public use. As a senator, he secured protection of Wisconsin's St. Croix, Namekagon, and Wolf rivers as well as federal protection of the Appalachian Trail. He established the Apostle Islands National Lakeshore and, oh yeah, he's the founder of Earth Day.

When Nelson got into politics, the environment wasn't on anyone else's radar, but he was convinced that immediate action needed to be taken in order to prevent irreversible damage to our planet. He also believed having a healthy environment was a basic human right. But he had to get others on board. In 1963, he convinced President John F. Kennedy to do a speaking tour addressing conservation issues, but even so, these issues struggled to get noticed on the national stage—especially since they were competing with the Cold War for the public's attention. Taking a cue from student-led demonstrations opposing the Vietnam War, Nelson suggested students lead a day of activism and awareness for the environment. Nelson suspected that if the student-led efforts could be coordinated on the same day, Washington politicians might take notice. On April 22, 1970, approximately 20 million Americans participated in the first Earth Day, and the event did get Washington's attention.

The success of Earth Day and the resulting interest in environmental issues made it possible for Nelson to make headway passing legislation to protect the environment. He called for government regulations on pesticides, emissions, dumping waste in oceans, and more. His amendment to the Clean Air Act of 1970 set a deadline for equipping cars with emission-reducing technologies. He added protections for predators and marine mammals to the Endangered Species Act of 1973 and preserved 100 million acres of land in Alaska.

In 1995, on the twenty-fifth anniversary of Earth Day, President Clinton awarded Nelson the Presidential Medal of Freedom. Upon receiving the medal, Nelson expressed a sense of urgency but also hope for the future, saying, "The opportunity for a gradual but complete break with our destructive environmental history and a new beginning is at hand. . . .

I am optimistic that this generation will have the foresight and the will to begin the task of forging a sustainable society." Nelson died in 2005, and it seems we've yet to fully realize the potential he saw.

In addition to his environmental agenda, Nelson also worked on consumer rights issues such as side-effect disclosures for pharmaceutical drugs. He specifically took up this issue in the case of oral contraception in 1970, and due to his efforts, the Pill was the first pharmaceutical drug to have a side-effect disclosure insert. On a semi-related note, Nelson was also concerned about overpopulation. After retiring from public office, he continued to pressure the US to limit immigration and to help other countries establish population controls. His position was criticized for being ignorant on numerous fronts, and rightly so. No one's perfect, not even Gaylord Nelson, but he sure is deserving of admiration for most of his legacy, of which I've only skimmed the surface.

There's plenty more I could mention about Nelson, but I'll wrap up the intro to his state park with this tidbit: apparently Vince Lombardi had a beef with Gaylord Nelson. As the story goes, Lombardi (R) said some nice words about Nelson (D) during a banquet. Nelson's campaign then used the sound bite in TV and radio commercials during Nelson's 1968 reelection campaign. The implied endorsement drew the ire of Lombardi and his wife. The Green Bay Packers may have bipartisan support, but Gaylord Nelson wasn't as universally backed.

WORTH A MENTION: In the winter, most of the trails at Governor Nelson are groomed for cross-country skiing. Only the Morningside Trail is available to hikers with dogs when there's snow on the ground.

WATER AVAILABILITY: Water is available at the park office and at the beach picnic area.

BATHROOM AVAILABILITY: There are flush toilets at the park office, at the picnic area by the boat landing and fish cleaning station, and by the Indianola Beach playground and picnic area. There are vault toilets at the Wakanda Parking Area and Trailhead as well as along Morningside Trail near the pet beach.

TRASHCAN AVAILABILITY: There are several poop bag dispensers and trashcans at this park. There is one on the right of the park road just past the main entrance, one just as you get to the pet swim area, and one at the trailhead for Woodland Trail. There is also a dumpster in the Olbrich Picnic and Play Area parking lot.

DESIGNATED DOG SWIMMING AREA: There is a designated pet swim area that can be accessed via Morningside Trail. Park at the Olbrich Picnic and Play Area parking lot and head east, past the dumpster, and onto the paved road. Continue until you reach the intersection with Morningside Trail. Take the left onto Morningside and then follow the signs for the Pet Swim Area. Morningside is primarily a mulch and dirt trail. It's also very wide, which is nice because it's common to encounter other dogs coming and going from the pet swim area. The trail transitions from mulch to grass and there is a poop bag dispenser and waste bin on the right. From here, the pet swim area is to the right.

It would be misleading to call this pet swim area a "dog beach." There are two water access points, and in between these two access points is a pile of rocks. The access points were maybe kayak or canoe launches at one time, but now instead of boats they're used to launch dogs into the water. One dog launch is defined by railroad ties and looks more official, while the other side hasn't been engineered by anyone other than nature. There's not much room for dogs to hang out onshore besides on the pile of rocks between the two launches, and it could get crowded with more than a couple dogs at one time. As a reminder, dogs are supposed to be back on leash as soon as they are out of the water.

Governor Nelson is one of the more convenient places near Madison to take your dog for a dip in a lake, so despite the pet swim area not being super fabulous, it's a pretty popular spot. Consider going at off-peak hours to avoid crowds. Also, make sure you check water conditions before letting your dog in the water. Blue-green algae blooms can be toxic to dogs if they drink or swim in contaminated water.

The dog swimming area at Governor Nelson State Park (Danielle St. Louis)

DESIGNATED DOG PICNIC AREA: The designated pet picnic area is by the pet swim area and can be accessed via Morningside Trail. Park at the Olbrich Picnic and Play Area parking lot and head east, past the dumpster, and onto the paved road. Continue until you reach the intersection with Morningside Trail. Take the left onto Morningside and then follow the signs for the Pet Swim Area. Morningside is primarily a mulch and dirt trail. It's also very wide, which is nice because it's common to encounter other dogs coming and going from the pet swim area and picnic area. The trail transitions from mulch to grass and there is a poop bag dispenser and waste bin on the right. From here, the pet picnic area is to the right.

    The pet picnic area is a clearing with several picnic tables and park grills set back from the shoreline. As far as pet picnic areas go, this is one of the most scenic as well as spacious. We appreciate that the picnic tables can be moved around if more space is needed between you and other picnickers.

RECOMMENDED HIKE: Woodland Trail

DISTANCE AND ELEVATION GAIN: 1.3 miles, 76 feet

DOG AND HUMAN FITNESS LEVEL: recreational rambler

TRAIL CONDITIONS/MATERIALS: Woodland Trail consists of wood chips, dirt, grass, and weeds in various proportions. At times, the grass can get long, and there is one sandy segment of trail. The main trail is wide enough for walking side by side, but the short offshoot trail to the Panther Mound is narrow and requires walking single file. Passing others on the offshoot would be challenging. The rest of the trail is wide enough to accommodate passing, though the trailside vegetation is dense at times if you need to step off the trail.

TRAIL MARKINGS/EASE OF NAVIGATING: The trail is well established and easy to follow. The trailhead is obvious—a kiosk labeled "Woodland Trail" stands at the entrance covered with pages of information, alongside a post with numerous markers and a poop bag dispenser and waste bin. There are signs marking the trails to the effigy mounds—Panther Mound and Conical Mounds—and additional interpretive signs and posts with numbers that correspond to other points of interest in the Woodland Nature Trail Guide (available at trailhead). There are occasional posts with Woodland Trail markers guiding the way, but they are few and far between. Despite the lack of signs, markers, and trail maps along the route, the trails are straightforward, and by the time you get to Redtail Hawk Trail, you can see the park road and can select the appropriate route based on your destination.

THE EXPERIENCE: Park in the western end of the lot for the boat landing and fish cleaning station. Walk out the exit of the parking lot to the park road and take a left. Walk along the road until you see the trailhead for Woodland Trail on the right. Take the trail where it begins to the left of the kiosk. As the trail's name suggests, this route takes you through the forest, which we prefer to prairies. Follow the wide trail into and through the woods. The trail transitions back and forth between a combination of mulch and dirt and long grass and weeds. You'll pass a bench on the left that, at the time of our last visit, was starting to be consumed by the vegetation around it.

Next, you'll come to the short offshoot trail to the Panther Mound marked by a sign on the left. If you're curious and want to add on a short detour, take the left to examine the mound. Otherwise, continue straight on Woodland Trail. The offshoot trail to Panther Mound connects back with Woodland Trail where it also intersects with the Conical Mounds. The intersection is marked with an interpretive sign and a post with the number four on it, though it's not easy to see the Mounds given the dense vegetation. Continue straight on Woodland Trail, which continues to be a wide and well-defined trail. You'll pass an additional interpretive sign and the number six on a post.

At the next T-intersection, stay to the right. Eventually, you'll see another post with a Woodland Trail marker and an arrow. Continue on the wide trail, which once again alternates between dirt, gravel, and sand and long grass and weeds. Next, you'll arrive at the scenic overlook. The overlook is a spacious clearing with a couple of trees in the middle that provide nice shade in the summer. There are four benches for visitors to relax on and an interpretive sign, but the overlook itself is mostly of the prairie in the foreground and forest in the background. To continue on the recommended hike, pick Woodland Trail back up on the north side of the clearing.

Much like before, the trail continues to meander through the woods alternating between long grass and dirt until it emerges from the woods and meets the edge of the prairie. At the intersection with Redtail Hawk Trail, stay to the right to take Woodland Trail back toward the trailhead to complete the recommended hike.

HEADS-UP: Lucky and I like the Woodland Trail loop because it's usually cooler than the other trails in the summer. The other trails in the park meander through the prairie and savannah, so there's not as much shade. But if you want a longer hike, there are myriad ways you can add on to this recommended route.

WHILE YOU'RE IN THE AREA: You might also visit Capital Brewery or Octopi Brewery; both have dog-friendly beer gardens. Octopi even lets dogs in the brewery and taproom.

Lake Kegonsa State Park

Ah, Lake Kegonsa, the park that inspired this #wistateparkdogs project. It was an overcast Sunday in July, so naturally Lucky and I decided to pack up the Renegade, pop out the roof panels despite the chance of rain, and head to the beach. A check on Google told us Lake Kegonsa State Park has a dog beach, so off we went.

This was our first visit to any Wisconsin state park together, and to our dismay, the dog beach was roughly the size of a canoe or kayak launch. Lucky didn't seem disappointed, but I was bummed. We had just spent a day at Montrose Dog Beach in Chicago (now *that's* a dog beach!), so my expectations were high. How anyone could use the term *beach* to describe this area confounded me. As we walked back to the car after our short stint at the dog launch, I reflected on whether I would have bothered to come here if I had known what it really was. My answer was "probably not." And in that moment, I recognized a need for state park information from a dog owner's perspective.

Return visits to Lake Kegonsa State Park haven't been especially redeeming. Blue-green algae often closes the dog launch in the summer, and though the park has "more than five miles" of hiking trails, dogs are only permitted on 2.8 miles of trail. And those 2.8 miles aren't particularly inspiring. I guess what I'm trying to say is that, while there is always something to be appreciated when in nature, I wouldn't travel a great distance to visit Lake Kegonsa State Park.

Possibly the most interesting things about Lake Kegonsa State Park are that it was Dane County's first state park, was built with money from a penny-a-pack cigarette tax, and the name *Kegonsa* comes from the

Ho-Chunk and means "lake of many fishes." Fishing is still a popular activity at Lake Kegonsa, but hopefully smoking has become less popular.

WATER AVAILABILITY: Water is available at the park office, at the parking lot/trailhead for Prairie Trail, at the upper picnic area and boat launch picnic area, and near the parking lot for the people beach, though dogs aren't allowed in the picnic areas or at the beach. There is no water available at the pet picnic area or pet swim area.

BATHROOM AVAILABILITY: Flush toilets are available at the park office, people beach, and the parking lot/trailhead for Prairie Trail. Vault toilets are available at the upper picnic area and boat launch picnic area. A port-a-potty was spotted in the pet picnic area at the time of our last visit.

TRASHCAN AVAILABILITY: One thing Lake Kegonsa State Park has going for it is an abundance of poop bag dispensers and trashcans for pet waste. Trash bag dispensers and trash bins are attached to posts at the trailhead for Prairie Trail, at the trailhead for Oak Knoll Trail, and in the pet picnic area.

DESIGNATED DOG SWIMMING AREA: The parking lot for the pet swim area is the fourth right after going under the overpass on the park road. There are two signs on a post pointing to the lot from the road, indicating Pet Hiking Trail and Pet Swim Area. The pet swim area is a short walk through the woods, over a creek, and out to a clearing with a few picnic tables. Just past the clearing is the dog "beach."

The pet swim area is quite small. It's a tiny patch of sand with a pier. On a nice summer weekend, it would be crowded with just a couple of dogs and their owners. Signs are posted when the pet swim area is closed due to blue-green algae. On the bright side, it's a lake that your dog can swim in, it's easy to get to from Madison, and the pet swim area is only a short walk from the parking lot. You can decide for yourself if it's worth the trip, but at least you have a better idea of what you'll be getting into.

DESIGNATED DOG PICNIC AREA: The parking lot for the pet picnic area is the fourth right after going under the overpass on the park road. There are two signs on a post pointing to the lot from the road,

The dog swimming area at Lake Kegonsa State Park (Danielle St. Louis)

indicating Pet Hiking Trail and Pet Swim Area. The pet picnic area is a short walk through the woods, over a creek, and out to a clearing adjacent to the pet swim area. It's a grassy spot with a few picnic tables, park grills, and a trashcan for pet waste. A port-a-potty was spotted in the pet picnic area at the time of our last visit. Also, Lakeshore Trail runs through the pet picnic area, so there may be non–dog related traffic going through the area.

RECOMMENDED HIKE: Prairie Trail
DISTANCE AND ELEVATION GAIN: 1.3 miles, 30 feet
DOG AND HUMAN FITNESS LEVEL: recreational rambler
TRAIL CONDITIONS/MATERIALS: The trail consists of mostly crushed limestone with a couple short sections of grass and weeds. This route is flat, and the trail is wide enough to accommodate you and your dog walking side by side. There is enough room for passing other hikers and dogs.

TRAIL MARKINGS/EASE OF NAVIGATING: The trail is well established and easy to follow. It's marked infrequently with posts with blue markers, but since the trail is made up of crushed limestone, it's easy to distinguish from its surroundings. Where the two loops of Prairie Trail connect, there is a post with two blue arrows attached, pointing in each direction, but there is no trail map at the intersection.

THE EXPERIENCE: To reach the trailhead for Prairie Trail, take an immediate right after passing the park office. The parking lot is the second left, and it comes up quickly. The trailhead is at the northwest side of the parking lot, to the left of the poop bag dispenser and trash bin. (The trail to the right of the poop bag dispenser and trash bin is the White Oak Nature Trail, and dogs are not allowed.) Start out on the crushed limestone trail, which goes through a short, wooded section before arriving at the prairie. Most of the remainder of the trail circumscribes the prairie, with prairie on the left and woods on the right.

Prairie Trail is a figure-eight; two loop trails that overlap on one edge. The first intersection is where the shared edge starts. Stay to the right and hug the woods to begin the southern loop. The southern loop goes through another wooded section near the Group Campgrounds before returning to the open prairie. The next intersection is where this loop meets the other end of the shared trail segment, which is on the left. Continue straight, and you're now back on the northern loop. The trail splits one more time at the road. Stay to the left to complete the northern loop and get back to the parking lot.

WORTH A MENTION: There are signs for the Pet Hiking Trail at the parking lot for the Pet Swim Area and Pet Picnic Area. The Oak Knoll Trail (aka Pet Hiking Trail) consists of two small loops (0.4 and 0.2 miles) in the wooded area north of the pet area parking lot. These trails are an option if you want to add some mileage to your walk for the day. As its name suggests, Oak Knoll Trail is in the woods, so it's more shaded than Prairie Trail. But in our experience, these loops are also buggier and muddier. If you do opt to hike Oak Knoll Trail, here's some info: the trail is wide enough for walking side by side, but the woods are dense around the trail. Passing other hikers with dogs is possible, but you may not want to or be able to step off the trail to do so.

WHILE YOU'RE IN THE AREA: Springers of Lake Kegonsa is three minutes from the state park and has a pet-friendly patio right on the water. Springers was named, in-part, as a tribute to the owner's love for springer spaniels, and an adjacent building is adorned with a mural of two springer spaniels. It's a great spot to grab a bite to eat and a beer with your pooch, whether or not you're visiting Lake Kegonsa State Park.

Mirror Lake State Park

Mirror Lake State Park is a great alternative to Devil's Lake State Park, and it turns out that's exactly what it was intended to be. As Devil's Lake became more popular, the state started considering ways to alleviate the crowds. Around the same time, the I-90 interstate was being constructed, so the state looked for land for additional parks along the interstate and between Devil's Lake and the Dells. Planning for the park started in 1962, but it took until 1966 to open the park because the state had to purchase all of the land. While Mirror Lake was technically established as an "overflow" park, it's hardly a consolation prize to Devil's Lake. Mirror Lake State Park has its own 50-foot sandstone bluffs, a lake with Narcissus-could-drown-in-this water, lush pine and oak forests, and more than eight times fewer people. According to DNR attendance data for 2018, Devil's Lake State Park had 2,674,386 visitors compared to Mirror Lake's 322,110. For that reason alone, Mirror Lake is our preferred day trip from Madison.

Not surprising, the most impressive feature of Mirror Lake State Park is the lake, which was originally formed when Dell Creek was dammed in 1860 to provide power for a mill. The mill changed hands over the years but found a niche making pancake flour before eventually burning down in 1957. Since then, the lake has been used exclusively for recreational activities. If your pooch enjoys kayaking, canoeing, or stand-up paddle boarding, this is the park for you. And while there isn't a dedicated dog swimming area, at least the pet picnic areas have views of the lake and one is in close proximity to the people beach—so while your pup can't take a dip at the same time, you (or your kids) could get in a swim while your dog hangs out nearby (supervised of course).

WORTH A MENTION: You should go see Echo Rock. It's a cool chunk of sandstone that you can walk 360 degrees around, and the trail to get there is nice and easy. You should also go take in the views from the new accessible fishing pier at the boat landing. Even Travel Wisconsin thought the spot was striking, so much so they installed one of their #ScenicWisconsin selfie stations.

HEADS-UP: Lucky and I don't recommend most of Ishnala Trail. For the most part, it is boring and hot. Another hike/ski trail, it's wide and flat. Much of the trail is through prairie, so in the summer there is no shade. A good portion of the trail runs close to the interstate, so there's a lot of car noise and powerlines. We do like one portion of Ishnala Trail—a section that runs along a little tributary at the bottom of the gorge. We think this segment is delightful. So, we'd recommend just doing an out-and-back on this portion of trail. To get to it, start at the parking lot for the Cliffwood Campground. Take the east segment of Echo Rock Trail to the bridge over Mirror Lake Gorge. Cross the bridge and take a left. Follow the paved trail as it gradually descends the side of the bluff and eventually turns into gravel. The trail swings back around to head southeast and goes under the bridge and along the tributary. There's a stream, sandstone rock outcroppings, and lots of ferns; basically, all the things we love. But once the trail turns to grass, we recommend heading back the way you came rather than completing the loop.

WATER AVAILABILITY: Water is available at the park office and near the Bluewater Bay and Beach shelters.

BATHROOM AVAILABILITY: Flush toilets are available at the park office and seasonally near the Bluewater Bay Shelter. Vault toilets are available near the Beach Shelter.

TRASHCAN AVAILABILITY: No trashcans on site; plan on carry-in/carry-out.

DESIGNATED DOG SWIMMING AREA: There is no designated pet swimming area, but at the time of our last visit, the park attendant said it was ok to let your dog take a dip in the water if you're along a trail somewhere. There is a section along the recommended hike, Northwest Trail, that could be a good option for letting your dog swim. As always, make sure your dog is on a leash when not in the water and be respectful of other park visitors if letting your dog go for a swim. And, for good measure, check with park staff when you visit in case designations have changed.

DESIGNATED DOG PICNIC AREA: There are two designated pet picnic areas at Mirror Lake State Park, one on either end of Lakeview Trail. The larger of the two pet picnic areas is by the beach and the beach shelter. To get there, head into the park and take the second left. Park in the first lot, and the pet picnic area is on the north side of the road. It's very clearly marked with many "Pet Area" posts delineating the boundary between the pet area and the no-pet area. There are several picnic tables and park grills. There are vault toilets and a water spigot nearby. As far as pet picnic areas go, it's spacious enough for multiple groups to use the area at the same time, and it's scenic in that the people beach and lake are within sight.

The other pet picnic area is at the other end of Lakeview Trail. To get to this pet picnic area, head into the park and take the third left and then an immediate right to get to the boat launch parking lot. The picnic area is to the left of the boat launch and includes several picnic tables and park grills. While there may be fewer people picnicking in this area, the boat launch sees a lot of activity and the parking lot is often full.

RECOMMENDED HIKE: Northwest Trail

HEADS-UP: Most of the trails south of Fern Dell Road are multiuse trails, which means they are open to hiking, biking, and skiing, depending on the season. You may encounter bicyclists on these trails from May 1 through October 31. Outside of that time frame, you could hike these trails bike free if there's no snow on the ground. Once it snows, these trails are groomed for skiing and are off limits to hikers and dogs. Northwest Trail is an exception—it is not open to bicyclists, which is one of the reasons we like this trail. But as soon as the snow falls, it's also off limits to hiking and dogs.

DISTANCE AND ELEVATION GAIN: 2.5 miles, 207 feet

DOG AND HUMAN FITNESS LEVEL: weekend warrior

TRAIL CONDITIONS/MATERIALS: The trail is a combination of wood chips, grass, and sand. It's one of the few trails we've encountered in our adventures that's been covered in wood chips. Northwest is groomed for cross-country skiing in the winter, so it is a wide trail. You can easily walk side by side and passing others along the trail is possible without having to step off the trail. The DNR website describes this trail as the most difficult in the park with "some steep rolling hills." The route we recommend stays along the "easy" cross-country ski route, avoiding the steepest of the rolling hills, but even on the easy route, you can pick up some momentum going down some of the hills.

TRAIL MARKINGS/EASE OF NAVIGATING: The trails are well established and easy to follow. Northwest Trail is marked with frequent purple plastic posts with Northwest Trail icons (a compass) and arrow icons. There are park maps at most major trail intersections. If you hike the recommended trail clockwise, as we suggest, you'll technically be going the wrong direction according to the cross-country ski markers. Just keep this in mind because the trail signs are oriented for counterclockwise traffic.

THE EXPERIENCE: The trailhead for Northwest Trail is just west of the park office. Park in the lot by the office, and then walk on the path behind the office, past the park mailbox, and across the road. There is a sign at the edge of the woods for Newport Trail and Northwest Trail. This first segment of trail is as wide as a road and eventually reaches a T-intersection. Take a left onto Northwest Trail. Just a short distance down the trail is another intersection, this time with Time Warp Trail, which wasn't on the paper maps available at the park office at the time of our last visit. Stay to the right to keep going on Northwest Trail.

The trail continues to be wide and flat throughout this segment, and it passes by a bench situated with a nice view of an inlet that is often popular with a bunch of mallards. A little way down the trail from the bench is another split in the trail. Continue down the right fork in the path and follow the purple Northwest Trail markers over the short wooden bridge. The next intersection is the split for the loop portion of Northwest Trail. It looks like a three-way fork, but the path on the left reconnects just a moment later with the middle path. One time, we used the left branch as a detour to avoid another hiker passing with dogs. The little bit of trees and shrubbery, in addition to a couple of treats, were enough to keep Lucky from fixating on the other dogs. No matter which route you pick, you'll eventually end up back at this intersection. We like to do the loop clockwise because it saves the best portion of this trail, the segment along the lake, for last.

To start the clockwise loop, go down the middle or left fork and blow right past the "do not enter" sign. The trail is extra wide and sandy throughout this segment. You'll pass an interpretive sign and numbered posts. There's an offshoot trail at the number 9 post but stay straight on the main trail. Just a bit further down the trail after passing the number 9 post, there is another split in the trail. Stay to the left to continue on Northwest Trail.

The trail remains wide as it weaves through the woods, and backwards purple posts continue to guide the way. The terrain starts to roll, and short ascents and descents keep things interesting. You'll arrive at another fork in the trail where it splits into two paths, one on either side of a tree. There are no signs or markers because we're going backwards on this route and the markers are at the "beginning" of this split to indicate the easy path and hard path. Ultimately, they both end up in the same place, but the right branch is the hard one with a steep hill and the left branch is the easy route. Lucky and I stick to the left and take the easy route.

Northwest Trail continues along, consistently wide and swoopy through the woods, and then you'll reach a short segment that feels like you're in a ditch. The terrain raises on either side of the trail, and it reminds me of a bobsled run. After you shoot out of the bobsled run, the trail continues for a short distance before reaching another fork of sorts. There is a trail marker here to help you navigate the turn, since straight is a dead end. If you take the hairpin turn to the right, you'll be backtracking on the steep hill/harder cross-country skill route. Take the hairpin turn to the left. This is where the very first sandstone rock outcroppings will be visible to the right.

After passing the rock outcroppings, the trail keeps on keeping on: consistently wide and swoopy through the woods with purple posts guiding the way. The next landmark is off to the left of the trail. Two posts are on either side of what might have at one point been an access road. Continue to follow the trail as it turns to the right. After another longer stretch of classic Northwest Trail, you'll reach the intersection with Wildwood Pass. Stay to the left to continue on Northwest Trail.

Now, you may start being able to see the water through the trees on your left. The trail runs parallel to the edge of the bluff for a bit before heading back west into the woods and to the next landmark, the remains of a stone wall. I like finds like this; especially when the trail is otherwise a bit monotonous. After the stone wall, Northwest Trail swings back around to run parallel to the edge of the bluff again. There are a couple of bunny hills along this stretch but nothing strenuous. The next intersection is with Ringling Pass. Keep to the left to stay on Northwest Trail, which now runs parallel to the shoreline.

While there are no social trails that we could see leading directly to the water, the shoreline isn't very far from the trail and it's a nice gradual slope from the shore into the water. This might be a good stretch of trail to find a place for your pup to take a dip in the lake. Along this section, you may be able to see the boat launch and the beach on the other side of the lake. Eventually the trail heads west again, away from the water and into the woods to complete the loop portion of Northwest Trail. You'll arrive back at that initial 3-pronged branch that was really two prongs, where you'll start backtracking to finish the hike. Stay to the left and head back toward and across the wooden bridge. Stay to the left again at the intersection with Time Warp Trail and head back toward the bench with the scenic view of the inlet. Again, stay to the left until you reach the intersection with Newport Trail. Finally, take a right to get back out to the road and the park office.

WHILE YOU'RE IN THE AREA: You could also visit Rocky Arbor State Park, Natural Bridge State Park, or, if you absolutely insist, Devil's Lake State Park.

Natural Bridge State Park

Along the northbound lanes of US-12, a bit north of Prairie Du Sac, is a sign for Natural Bridge State Park. It indicates this state park is to the left, and indeed, heading west on County Road C is one means of getting to the park. In my experience, no matter which route I take, I lose my sense of direction on the winding roads and end up feeling lost in the middle of nowhere until, seemingly miraculously, there's the park. There's a smallish sign and a driveway that leads to a parking lot, and then it's a short hike into the woods to the main attraction—the natural bridge. While the world holds larger wonders, the bridge surely makes the cut as one of Wisconsin's top natural wonders. This hunk of sandstone wasn't steamrolled by the glaciers; rather, it was weathered by wind and water until it formed an arch. Just below the arch is a rock shelter that was used by humans more than 10,000 years ago. The site was excavated in 1957, and pieces of charred wood were found that are from between 9000 and 8000 BC. The archeological evidence suggests that the rock shelter was used seasonally at first but later was used as a permanent residence, making it one of the oldest sites for human occupancy in northeastern North America.

While the bridge is a natural wonder, I think contemplating the lowly rock shelter is a more profound experience. I've been to natural history museums, looked at artifacts in exhibits, and read plenty of plaques recounting the histories of prehistoric peoples, but it's difficult to connect those histories to the world I know. Standing in front of the bridge and looking into the rock shelter while the sun shines through the trees around me, I can't help but marvel at the fact that long ago and not so far away from my own suburban home, some of the earliest humans took shelter here. Rather than cows in pastures and turkey vultures in trees, wooly mammoths roamed around, and teratornis birds flew by overhead. And that was just life for these OG Wisconsinites.

HEADS-UP: The arch is very fragile. Climbing or standing on the arch, really any human contact at all, can speed its deterioration. So, don't touch, climb, or walk on it!

WORTH A MENTION: Natural Bridge State Park is a great option for winter hiking. There are only two trails totaling roughly four miles of hiking and neither are groomed for cross-country skiing, which means dogs are permitted year-round. Plus, the bridge looks majestic covered with a dusting of snow.

WATER AVAILABILITY: None.

BATHROOM AVAILABILITY: Vault toilets are located near the parking lot.

TRASHCAN AVAILABILITY: No trashcans on site; plan on carry-in/carry-out.

DESIGNATED DOG SWIMMING AREA: None, as there are no bodies of water at this park.

DESIGNATED DOG PICNIC AREA: At the time of our last visit, there was no designated pet picnic area. If park staff are present when you visit, check with them in case designations have changed.

RECOMMENDED HIKE: Indian Moccasin Nature Trail

DISTANCE AND ELEVATION GAIN: 1.2 miles, 218 feet

DOG AND HUMAN FITNESS LEVEL: recreational rambler

TRAIL CONDITIONS/MATERIALS: The trail is mostly dirt and grass, with some sections of intermittent exposed roots. There's a flight of wooden stairs going up to the overlook. The trail is narrow and best navigated single file. There are times when it may be difficult to step off the trail to let others pass, but in our experience, there aren't many hikers on the trails at Natural Bridge State Park.

TRAIL MARKINGS/EASE OF NAVIGATING: The trail is well established and easy to follow. In two instances when Indian Moccasin Nature Trail splits, there are trail maps on posts in the vicinity of the intersections. It's a small park and the trails are short, so even if you do take a wrong turn, it's only marginally inconvenient.

THE EXPERIENCE: Indian Moccasin Trail departs from the picnic area, which is pretty much the only area in Natural Bridge State Park. Find a spot in the parking lot, and you're at the trailhead. It's a loop trail, but it's easiest to start out on the trail clockwise, as a counterclockwise route means locating the trail into the woods somewhere behind the bathrooms, which is less obvious. Also, a clockwise route offers the most striking reveal of the natural bridge. So, start on the obvious path, which is easily visible just past the self-pay station and information kiosk.

This initial section of trail is a narrow dirt trail through a grassy clearing, but as it enters the woods the trail becomes more established and well defined. It winds through the woods and gets narrower as it goes along, until it leaves the woods and emerges on the edge of a clearing. This is the first instance where Indian Moccasin Trail splits. Stay to the right to head back into the woods and toward the natural bridge. The trail undulates with an easy dip and a few wooden stairs before arriving at its destination.

After taking in the bridge and reading the information about the rock shelter, continue on the trail as it jaunts to the left of the bridge. The trail arrives at a Y-intersection. Take the left branch to head up to the overlook point. Throughout this section the trail is narrow and the surrounding vegetation thick, so passing and stepping off the trail could be challenging. The trail to the overlook point is the most strenuous section of this hike, with a flight of wooden stairs and about 49 feet of elevation gain over about a tenth of a mile (so, like, not hard, but certainly the hardest part of this hike). The trail dead-ends at the overlook point, which is demarcated with a wooden fence and "End of Trail" signs. The view from this point is better in winter when it isn't obscured by the surrounding trees' foliage, but it's still a nice spot and worth climbing the 49 feet to check out, even in the summer.

Backtrack on the trail to the Y-intersection and now take a hard left, which begins the loop back toward the parking lot. The trail continues through the woods and reaches another small clearing, where the trail splits for the final time. If you want to extend the hike, take the trail to the left out to County Road C, where you can either walk along the road back to the park entrance or cut across C to hike the Whitetail Hiking Trail. We recommend taking the trail to the right, which is a more direct route through the woods back to the parking lot. You'll emerge from the woods behind the bathrooms. And then we recommend checking out one of the other great parks in the area, since you'll likely still have a whole day ahead of you and your pup will probably still have energy to burn.

WHILE YOU'RE IN THE AREA: Since there's not a lot of hiking at Natural Bridge State Park, we recommend trying to visit another state park while you are in this area. Some of our favorite combos are Natural Bridge and Rocky Arbor State Parks or Natural Bridge and Mirror Lake State Parks. Devil's Lake State Park is also nearby, but be forewarned, it can get really crowded.

Nelson Dewey State Park

Nelson Dewey State Park is among Wisconsin's parks named for a former governor, but unlike Governor Dodge, Governor Nelson, and Governor Thompson state parks, Dewey's title wasn't incorporated in the name of the park. This omission is likely because when the park was established in 1935, it was assumed Dewey had so much name recognition that including his title was unnecessary. Now, I think having *Governor* in the park's name would be a helpful cue to denizens like me who probably learned about Wisconsin's first governor in fourth grade civics class but have since forgotten his story. So, for anyone out there like me, here's a Nelson Dewey refresher.

Nelson Dewey was born in 1813 and grew up out east, mostly in Butternuts (LOL), New York. He took after his dad, studying law, and moved to Galena, Illinois, in 1836 to work for a firm of New York land speculators. These speculators thought Cassville, Wisconsin, could be the capital of the Wisconsin territory, but as often happens with speculation, they were wrong. Madison was selected as the capital, and while Dewey didn't quit his day job as a land speculator, he did start pursuing a career in public office. He got elected as a register of deeds, as a justice of the peace, and eventually as the district attorney of Grant County. Throughout the process of Territorial Wisconsin becoming the State of Wisconsin, Dewey served in several other positions, and when it came time for Wisconsin's Democratic party to select a candidate for the first gubernatorial race, they chose . . . someone else. In 1847, the state Democratic party was split into two factions who each put up their own candidate, but neither could get enough votes to secure the nomination. So, the

party went looking for a compromise candidate, and they found Nelson
Dewey. In 1848, Dewey beat two other opponents to become the first
governor of the State of Wisconsin—not to be confused with the first
governor of Territorial Wisconsin, Governor Henry Dodge.

Dewey was governor for two terms spanning 1848 to 1852, and during that time he gained admiration for transitioning Wisconsin from a
territorial government to the new state government and developing Wisconsin's infrastructure. But he became less popular over time because
he and a buddy bought up a bunch of lead mines and invested in mining companies. (For more on why affiliations with lead mining would
be detrimental to a reelection campaign, check out the Governor Dodge
State Park entry.) Dewey decided to not run for a third term. He retired
to Lancaster, Wisconsin, but remained civically engaged, serving one
term in the Wisconsin State Senate and multiple terms on the school
board. And he had never given up on the idea of Cassville.

In 1854 Dewey and his wife Catherine Dunn purchased the village
of Cassville, which was in foreclosure. They built a hotel, a three-story
mansion, and eleven miles of stone fence. Dewey's vision was to turn
Cassville into a large city, but few other people shared this vision. The
city wasn't growing, so next he invested in a railroad line to the village,
hoping a train would bring more people to Cassville. It didn't. And then
he had a really bad year. In 1873 his mansion burned down, and North
America experienced a financial crisis. Dewey lost everything; he was
uninsured and over-mortgaged. His personal life began to suffer. He
filed for divorce from Catherine in 1886, and although the divorce was
never finalized, Catherine moved to St. Louis. Dewey went back to practicing law, and in 1889 he had a stroke while in the courtroom. Paralyzed
after the stroke, Dewey spent the last five months of his life bedridden
in the hotel he'd built in Cassville. When he died in July 1889, he was a
far cry from the successful politician and businessman of his glory days.

While Dewey's story has a sad ending, his legacy includes this state
park that was created using land from his Cassville estate. You might
include a visit to what remains of the Stonefield estate during a trip to
Nelson Dewey State Park, since the park is not very big. And though the
park isn't very big, it offers huge views of Cassville, the Mississippi River,

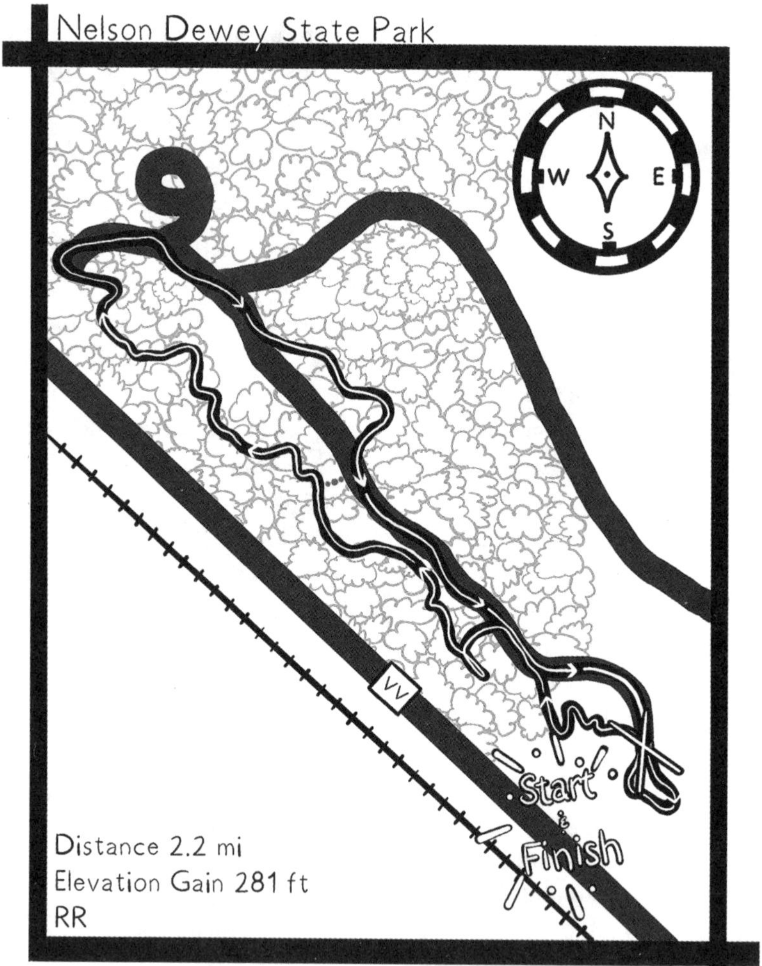
Nelson Dewey State Park
N
W
E
S
VV
Start
&
Finish
Distance 2.2 mi
Elevation Gain 281 ft
RR

and the surrounding area. From the overlook points, it's possible to understand how Dewey could have had such a big vision for this village. And although his speculations for Cassville didn't materialize, I think it's safe to speculate the views from Nelson Dewey State Park are some of the best in the state. The views and this park are certainly among our favorites.

WATER AVAILABILITY: Water is available at the park office, by the Dewey Heights Picnic Shelter, and at the parking area for the Woodbine Nature Trail.

BATHROOM AVAILABILITY: Vault toilets are available at the Prairie Picnic Shelter and at the parking area for the Woodbine Nature Trail.

TRASHCAN AVAILABILITY: Trash and recycling are for campers only. Noncampers should plan on carry-in/carry-out.

DESIGNATED DOG SWIMMING AREA: None, as there are no bodies of water at this park.

DESIGNATED DOG PICNIC AREA: At the time of our last visit, there was no designated pet picnic area. Check with park staff when you visit in case designations have changed.

RECOMMENDED HIKE: Cedar Trail + Prairie Trail + Mound Point Trail + Oakwood Trail (basically all the trails, in order of best views to no views)

DISTANCE AND ELEVATION GAIN: 2.2 miles, 281 feet

DOG AND HUMAN FITNESS LEVEL: recreational rambler

TRAIL CONDITIONS/MATERIALS: Cedar Trail is a mostly flat, narrow dirt and gravel path with sections of exposed Ordovician-age dolomite that goes through prairie and along the edge of the bluff. Passing others on the trail may be challenging because of the proximity to the edge of the bluff and the encroaching prairie. Prairie Trail is also predominantly dirt and intermittent grass with exposed Ordovician-age dolomite, but it's more undulating than Cedar Trail; wooden stairs have been built into the steeper segments of the trail to assist hikers. Prairie Trail is also mostly narrow and should be hiked single file. There are some wider segments where passing others would be possible, but at other points along the trail passing could be challenging. This recommended hike also takes you on the park road. The road is paved, and while I don't normally recommend walking on park roads because they aren't always the safest for pedestrians, the portions of park road on this hike are wide and traffic is typically light.

Mound Point Trail is predominantly grass and dirt. The first half of Mound Point is wider than Cedar and Prairie trails, making walking side by side and passing other dogs and hikers easier. Mount Point runs congruently with the Woodbine Nature Trail for a stretch, so for that portion the trail is paved. After the Woodbine Nature Trail segment, Mount Point Trail is rockier and narrower, making it once again necessary to hike single file and more difficult to pass others. Mound Point Trail from the Woodbine Nature Trail to where it meets the campgrounds has a distinct cadence: down, small footbridge, up, down, small footbridge, up. This trail is probably the most challenging in the park, but its rollercoaster-like bunny hops are manageable for recreational ramblers.

Oakwood Trail is the easiest trail on this recommended hike. The trail is wide, mostly flat, and partially paved. The unpaved portion is mostly dirt and moss, and moss covers much of the paved portion as well. It's possible to hike side by side. There is enough room for passing other hikers and dogs and space to step off the trail if needed.

TRAIL MARKINGS/EASE OF NAVIGATING: There are no trail markers or signs for Cedar Trail, but once you get on the trail, it is well established and easy to follow. There are signs at either end of the other trails (Prairie, Mound, and Oakwood) indicating where the trails start and end, but there are no trail markers along the trails except for a sign where Mound Point departs the Woodbine Nature Trail. The trails are well established and easy to follow. At the time of our last visit, the state park map indicated that Oakwood Trail goes all the way to the Dewey Heights Picnic Shelter, but I don't believe this segment of Oakwood exists anymore. The trail ends at the clearing across from the parking lot for the picnic area and wildlife observation area along Mound Point Trail.

THE EXPERIENCE: After entering the park, drive to the very end of the road and park in the lot at the dead end. There is small picnic area at the south end of the lot and a stone wall just past the slightest of hills. Begin this hike by walking toward the stone wall, and, upon reaching it, take a left. Continue following the wall and dirt path to where the wall ends. Though the wall ends, the trail continues to the right and down a slight grade, passing trees on the left and prairie on the right, until it gets closer to the edge of the cliff. Now, any trees are below or behind you, and you can see for miles. The narrow trail carves through the prairie grass, going slightly downhill before heading back up a slight incline to an outlook with a bench positioned for optimal views of the Stonefield Historic Site and beyond it, the Turkey River and the Turkey River Mounds State Preserve. The trail turns right, continuing to traverse along the edge of the cliff for a few more moments before heading back through the prairie toward the parking lot. The trail emerges on the other end of the stone wall. Walk along the western edge of the parking lot until you reach the entrance to Prairie Trail, which is on the left.

Prairie Trail is a whole 0.2 miles long, but it's an enjoyable jaunt. The first section of Prairie Trail is a rocky scramble down a slight grade and three wooden stairs. The trail descends through the prairie and as it does so, it gets narrower and the prairie transitions to dense understory. As the trail's descent continues, the understory transitions to forest. A bit of that Ordovician-age dolomite protrudes in the middle of the trail, acting as a final step down before the trail begins the ascent back to the top of the bluff. A couple of wooden stairs assist on the climb out of the forest, and just as the foliage transitioned on the way down the bluff, it goes from forest to understory to prairie grass as the trail ascends back to the top of the bluff. After three more wideset wooden stairs, the trail emerges fully into the prairie and along the edge of the bluff. This segment of the trail offers impressive views of the Stonefield Historic Site and surrounding area, and after another small climb, you reach an outlook point with an even more impressive 180-degree view of the Upper Mississippi River National Wildlife and Fish Refuge. After the outlook point, the trail traverses the edge of the bluff for a minute before cutting back through the prairie and heading toward the park road. Now, while the main trail is still a narrow footpath, it is cushioned on either side by some grass and weeds, making this the best section for passing other hikers. The trail finally reaches the main trailhead for Prairie Trail.

From here, take a left and walk on the park road. Normally, I don't like walking on park roads because they are typically not the most scenic or safe for pedestrians. However, the road through this section of the park offers some great views, is wide, and traffic is typically light. The road curves, passing a small parking area and the Dewey Heights picnic area on the right, before reaching a stone wall on the left. The wall is a great spot for taking panoramic photos. An interpretive sign mirrors the view before you and calls out specific points of interest. Continue past the stone wall to the clearing that includes a bench and a Travel Wisconsin selfie station. To the west are more amazing views and to the east is the parking lot for the Prairie Picnic Shelter. Head north from the clearing along the edge of the parking lot and past the picnic shelter to the trailhead for Mound Point Trail.

The entrance to Mound Point Trail begins by passing between two trees. The first section of Mount Point Trail, from the Prairie Picnic Shelter to the wildlife observation area, is wide and grassy with mild undulations and occasional views. The trail comes out of the woods, past a stone structure that resembles a water fountain, and arrives at a clearing with a portion of stone wall, a bench, and semi-obstructed views of the river valley below. Continue north, past the section of stone wall on your right, to where Mound Point goes back into the woods. Here, the trail starts its rollercoaster-like cadence, beginning with a slopy descent. The trail narrows to a single-file footpath and vacillates between dirt and grass. A wooden footbridge marks the bottom of the descent and occasional wooden stairs help with the climb back up to where Mound Point Trail meets the Woodbine Nature Trail. Step over the railroad-tie border of Woodbine and take a left on the paved path, heading toward the edge of the bluff and the river. A bench indicates the ideal spot for taking in the views, and just a bit further down the paved trail, a sign indicates where to cross back over the railroad-tie border of Woodbine to get back onto the dirt trail of Mound Point.

Now, the rollercoaster cadence of Mound Point Trail increases its bunny-hop frequency: down, small footbridge, up, down, small footbridge, up. Though probably the most challenging portion of this recommended hike, it's also rather entertaining. After this final series of undulations, a set of three wooden stairs brings you to the end of Mound Point Trail, in the family campgrounds near the walk-in campsites. You're now at the northernmost end of the park, with a few options for getting back to where this hike started. But, to complete the loop, take a right to head toward the family campground.

Once you reach the campground road, take another right and continue staying to the right, past the bathrooms and past the parking lot for the Woodbine Nature Trail, until you reach the main park road. Once you reach the main park road, you should see the entrance to Oakwood Trail across the road and to the left. Oakwood is wide, flat, paved, and moss-covered. It offers no views of the Mississippi River but is quiet and quaint as it curves through dense woods. It's a storybook kind of trail—I could almost imagine it leading to the cottage of the Seven Dwarfs. And maybe it did at one time. At the time of our last visit, the state park map showed Oakwood Trail going all the way to the Dewey Heights Picnic Shelter, but the trail ended at a clearing across from the picnic and wildlife observation area along Mound Point Trail. There was no option, no turn we missed, to continue south on the trail to the Dewey Heights Picnic Shelter. I don't think that segment of the trail exists any longer, though it may still be on the park map.

After reaching the end of Oakwood Trail, you can take a left on the park road to take it all the way back to the terminus of the road and the parking lot, or you can cross the street and retrace your steps along Mound Point Trail and Prairie Trail to return to the beginning of this recommended hike. Either way, you'll be getting in just a bit over two miles of hiking.

WHILE YOU'RE IN THE AREA: You should also visit Wyalusing State Park and the Wyalusing Public Beach. But if you are visiting in early spring/summer and the Mississippi is still high, some trails at Wyalusing might be closed and the beach might be more muck than sand (but still fun!). We also recommend visiting the Potosi Brewing Company, in Potosi, Wisconsin, which has a dog-friendly patio, yummy food, and refreshing beer.

New Glarus Woods State Park

New Glarus State Park is bordered on the south and east by prairie and on the north and west by the Driftless region. Its position straddling these two geographies is a teachable moment in ecology. When glaciers steamrolled through parts of Wisconsin, they flattened the land in their wake, making it easy for fires to spread. Most trees couldn't survive the frequent fires, but prairie grasses were well suited for this type of environment. This is why most flat areas turned into prairies. Meanwhile, the Driftless Area wasn't flattened by glaciers, and its steep hills and ravines prevented the spread of fires. These areas fostered the growth of dense forests. At one point, the land that is New Glarus Woods State Park was on the edge of a massive forest that people compared to the Black Forest in Germany because it was so dense and had a reputation for being a dangerous wilderness.

Like most of Wisconsin, the land was first inhabited by Paleo-Indians and then Native Americans. The Native Americans established many of the routes through the terrain that the European settlers would eventually begin to traverse as well. One route is worth noting. Originally a Native American trail, it was expanded by European miners to haul oxcarts full of lead, so it was named "Old Lead Road." Today, it's County Highway NN, the main road that intersects the park. The Wisconsin DNR website makes note of some famous folks who traveled Old Lead Road/Highway NN, including Zachary Taylor (twelfth president of the United States) and William S. Hamilton (Alexander Hamilton and Elizabeth Schuyler's sixth kid). These men would have been in the area and traipsing along the Old Lead Road in pursuit of Chief Black Hawk during the Black Hawk War. Jefferson Davis, president of the Confederate States from 1861 to 1865, may have also taken this route while escorting Chief Black Hawk to prison.

For anyone unfamiliar with Chief Black Hawk and the Black Hawk War, here's a quick recap. When lead was discovered in southwestern Wisconsin, European miners took an interest and forced the Sauk from their land east of the Mississippi. While some left, a group stayed on the Illinois side of the river with Black Hawk. They were confronted by the Illinois militia and US Army troops. For sixteen weeks the Sauk tried to elude the troops and get their women and children to safety on the other side of the Mississippi. On a number of occasions, they attempted to surrender, but their attempts were "misinterpreted." On August 1, 1832, the Sauk reached the Mississippi near Bad Axe River, and as they tried to cross to safety, they were indiscriminately slaughtered; a gunboat was waiting in the river and troops fired upon the Sauk from the bluffs behind them. Of the 1,200 Sauk, only about 70 survived. I apologize to any historians out there who take issue with this brief summary of events, but I think it's important to provide some context to why these old "famous" white guys were in this area and using this road.

Additionally, I want to caution park visitors about County Highway NN. There's usually a road within most state parks, but unlike most parks where the road is exclusively used by visitors, County Highway NN is a thoroughfare. Vehicles, including big semitrailer trucks, fly down this road at high speeds. For this reason, I'm not super excited to walk on the side of this road and try to avoid doing so whenever possible.

WORTH A MENTION: New Glarus Woods is a good option for winter hiking and snowshoeing with your dog. While skiing is allowed in the park, the trails aren't groomed, which means they are fair game for you and your dog to use when there is snow on the ground.

HEADS-UP: Hunting is allowed in the portion of the park south of Highway NN. If you are visiting the park between November and January, keep this in mind and be prepared with some blaze orange apparel for you and your dog.

WATER AVAILABILITY: Water is available near the picnic shelter and at the parking lot for the walk-in campsites.

BATHROOM AVAILABILITY: Vault toilets are available at the picnic area.

TRASHCAN AVAILABILITY: Recycling and garbage receptacles are available at a small pull-off on the south side of County NN just west of the parking lot for the picnic area. Technically the receptacles are for registered campers only, but I think it's probably ok to dispose of a poop bag since you don't have to go into the campgrounds to access the bins.

DESIGNATED DOG SWIMMING AREA: None, as there are no bodies of water at this park.

DESIGNATED DOG PICNIC AREA: At the time of our last visit, there was no designated pet picnic area. Check with park staff when you visit in case designations have changed.

RECOMMENDED HIKE: Havenridge Trail + a bit of Basswood Nature Trail

DISTANCE AND ELEVATION GAIN: 3.8 miles, 394 feet

DOG AND HUMAN FITNESS LEVEL: weekend warrior

TRAIL CONDITIONS/MATERIALS: The trails are mostly dirt, grass, weeds, and leaf litter. The grass might be tall in some sections and the path muddy along other sections, depending on recent rainfall. There are several culverts to cross; at the time of our last visit, the ground around one of the culverts had eroded, and the culvert was covered with a pile of branches to, I suppose, aid in crossing. Havenridge is wide enough to accommodate you and your dog walking side by side, and there is plenty of room for letting others pass. The portion of Havenridge north of County Highway NN has some undulating terrain, but no significant elevation gains.

TRAIL MARKINGS/EASE OF NAVIGATING: The trails are well established and easy to follow. There are numbered posts along Havenridge Trail that correspond to points of interest in a guidebook you can pick up at the entrance station. Even if you aren't following along in the guidebook, these numbered posts are helpful for confirming that you are still on Havenridge Trail. Additionally, there are park maps on posts at all trail intersections. There was one instance where the trail seemed to split and there was no map. It turns out the offshoot wasn't really a trail, hence there was no trail map. I mention this intersection in The Experience section and let you know which way to go.

THE EXPERIENCE: Park at the pull-off lot in front of the picnic area along County Highway NN. If you turn onto Highway NN from Highway 69, the parking area is just past the entrance station on NN. Be careful unloading and getting ready for your hike here, as cars and trucks speed through the park on Highway NN. The trailhead for Havenridge Trail is on the south side of the road a bit further west down Highway NN. There is an icon on the trailhead sign showing a person with a dog, so though this trail is called a "nature trail" the sign overrides the general rule and reassures that dogs are allowed on Havenridge Trail.

New Glarus Woods straddles lands steamrolled by glaciers and lands spared the leveling. Havenridge Trail is our choice because it takes you through both sections; the first section of Havenridge on the south side of Highway NN features parts of the land that were steamrolled and are now prairies and meadows. The trail is wide and heads through the woods with a couple of slight undulations before reaching the edge of the woods and entering the prairie. Throughout the prairie sections, the trail is flat and easy going, though you may be able to see and hear traffic on Highway 69. The trail goes on to weave between the woods and the prairie, back and forth, providing points of contrast to contemplate as well as intermittent shade. The trail heads back into the woods and reaches the first intersection with Walnut Trail. At the intersection, stay to the left on Havenridge Trail.

The trail remains wide and flat as it winds through the woods. Next, the trail appears to split like a Y. There is no trail map here because technically, this isn't a legit trail intersection. Stay to the right and in the woods to keep going on Havenridge Trail. Around trail marker number 15, you can easily see through the sparse trees on the left to the meadow that lies past the trees. There's one more short section of woods before the trail turns left and heads into the prairie/

meadow. Here you'll encounter the first culvert. At the time of our last visit, some of the earth around the culvert had eroded, so a branch had been placed along either side of the metal drainage pipe. This crossing was still easy enough to navigate. I was able to basically step over the entire area. Lucky navigated it with a leap, which I think was overkill, but it was the choice he made.

The trail eventually turns back and heads toward the woods again. A fence with private property signs is visible on the left, indicating the park boundary. Just past trail marker number 19 is the second, even jankier culvert crossing. At the time of our last visit, the earth around this culvert had completed eroded away. In its place was a combination of branches and sticks in a crude pile on top of the metal drainpipe. This time, Lucky was right to leap across the pile, and I had to choose my footing carefully. After the janky culvert crossing, the trail gradually goes uphill and skirts along the edge of the forest. Throughout this section there are some mild undulations in the trail, and one particularly low segment of trail that may be washed out/muddy depending on the time of year and any recent rainfall. Next, you'll reach the second intersection with Walnut Trail. Take a left to stay on Havenridge Trail, which intersects with Highway NN in a few moments—you may already be able to hear the cars and trucks speeding down the road.

The trail continues on the other side of the street. This portion of Havenridge Trail on the north side of Highway NN meanders through the segment of the park that did not get steamrolled by glaciers (aka part of Wisconsin's Driftless Area). You may notice the undulations in the trail are steeper and more frequent through this portion of forest. It might be a bit more strenuous than the first half of the hike, but we think this second half of the hike is a lot of fun.

Not long after crossing the road and passing trail marker number 27, you'll reach the first intersection with Fox Trail. Stay to the left on Havenridge Trail. As the trail continues through the woods, it is more variable in terms of elevation but remains consistently wide. The next intersection is with Vista Trail. Keep right, and just a short way down the trail you'll encounter the second intersection with Fox Trail. At this intersection, take a left to complete the final segment of Havenridge Trail. Along this final stretch is the third culvert; thankfully, at the time of our last visit it was in much better shape than the others with little to no erosion and no branch reinforcements.

When you come to the end of Havenridge Trail, there are three options for your return. We recommend taking the left branch of Basswood Nature Trail to head back to the parking lot because it brings you out on the eastern side of the picnic area. Dogs aren't allowed in the picnic area, so it's a less flagrant intrusion if you emerge from the forest on this eastern side and then stay to the left around the outside of the picnic area on your way back to the car. In some parks, I'm more inclined to walk through a picnic area on our way to/from a hike, but as you come to the end of Basswood Trail, there's a post with a "No dogs allowed in picnic area" sign right there. I think New Glarus Woods means business, so we encourage everyone to be the most rule-abiding, dogs-in-state-park advocates and ambassadors and oblige the signs by walking around the picnic area to return to your car at the pull-off along Highway NN.

WHILE YOU'RE IN THE AREA: We recommend visiting New Glarus Brewing Company. Their biergarten is dog friendly, atmospheric, and has amazing views. What else could you want? Well, in the summer, a little shade would be nice. Since there isn't much shade at the biergarten, we bring our own patio umbrella to slide into one of the many accommodating picnic tables. People sometimes look at us weirdly as we set up our umbrella, but then they are mostly jealous of our shade and sad they didn't think to bring their own umbrella.

Rocky Arbor State Park

As a kid, I watched the movie *FernGully: The Last Rainforest* a thousand times, and despite addressing some dark themes, the film enchanted me. As a result, I'm also enchanted by any place in Wisconsin that could be mistaken for a rainforest. The gorge in Rocky Arbor is one of the places where I feel completely transported to another world. The park's one-mile hiking trail goes out along the bottom of the gorge and then comes back along the top. The gorge is beautiful and ancient. The sandstone is about 500 million years old, and outcroppings jut out from the hillside with ferns and other vegetation dripping off of them, reminding me of the clocks in Salvador Dali's *The Persistence of Memory*.

With only one mile of hiking trail, it's unlikely that Rocky Arbor would be a destination in and of itself. But if you are planning to visit Wisconsin Dells, camping at Rocky Arbor is likely a cheaper and more scenic option than a resort or hotel, though certainly with fewer amenities. Even if you are just driving down I-90 through the Dells, you should stop at this park. Unlike other instances where there's a sign on the highway for a state park, so you exit, only to discover the park is still a great distance away, Rocky Arbor is just a couple of minutes off of I-90. This would certainly be a better pee break option for your pup than a gas station parking lot and is worth a road trip pitstop.

WORTH A MENTION: Mill Bluff State Park is also relatively close to I-90 and is about 34 miles north of Rocky Arbor, but of these two options, Lucky and I would recommend Rocky Arbor for a road trip pitstop.
WATER AVAILABILITY: Water is available near the park office.

BATHROOM AVAILABILITY: Vault toilets are available near the park office.

TRASHCAN AVAILABILITY: No trashcans on site; plan on carry-in/carry-out.

DESIGNATED DOG SWIMMING AREA: At the time of our last visit, there was no designated pet swim area, but I don't think you'd want to let your dog swim in the tiny stream that runs through the gorge anyway.

DESIGNATED DOG PICNIC AREA: At the time of our last visit, there was no designated pet picnic area. As always, check with park staff when you visit in case designations have changed.

RECOMMENDED HIKE: Nature Trail/Hiking Trail

HEADS-UP: In some instances, the trail at Rocky Arbor is referred to as "nature trail" and in other instances it's referred to as "hiking trail." Generally, dogs are not allowed on nature trails in Wisconsin state parks, but we've been assured that dogs are allowed on this hiking trail.

DISTANCE AND ELEVATION GAIN: 1.2 miles, 148 feet

DOG AND HUMAN FITNESS LEVEL: recreational rambler

TRAIL CONDITIONS/MATERIALS: The trail is mostly dirt, pine needles, and leaf litter, with some sections of intermittent exposed roots, which are mostly along the top of the gorge. There are two flights of wooden stairs, one on either end of the gorge and some wide-set wooden stairs leading to these staircases. The trail along the bottom of the gorge is narrow and best navigated single file; there are times when it may be difficult to step off the trail to let others pass. The trail along the top of the gorge is wider and can be navigated side by side. There is sufficient room for passing other groups along the trail atop the gorge.

TRAIL MARKINGS/EASE OF NAVIGATING: The trail is well established and easy to follow. There are posts with trail maps at the trailhead and where the trail to the campground intersects with the main trail.

THE EXPERIENCE: When you enter Rocky Arbor, go straight to park in the lot by the picnic shelter and playground. Walk to the trailhead at the southern end of the parking lot. A short distance into the woods, a sign indicates a wildlife observation blind is to the left. We went and checked it out because not only is it a very short distance from the main trail, but it is also a good place to hang out and wait for others to pass.

The trail continues a bit further into the woods and intersects with the first flight of wooden stairs that lead to the campgrounds. Skip the stairs for now and continue on the trail through the gorge. The steep hillside to the right is speckled with trees and occasional sandstone protrusions. Eventually, the stream becomes visible on the left, and a massive fallen tree tempts visitors far more daring than I to venture out on its trunk over the murky water and marshy vegetation. The trail continues parallel to the stream, and the surrounding vegetation gets thicker; the space between trees fills in with ferns and all sorts of other vibrant and lush green stuff. More sandstone edifices erupt from the side of the hill, and occasionally stretches of the trail get rocky. Eventually you'll encounter some squares of concrete that have been placed on the trail to prevent erosion or aid hikers, though now they are broken and askew.

The next major landmark is a giant sandstone boulder protruding, not from the hillside on the right, but from the stream on the left. It seems to float, like the bow of a ship, and it's adorned with a its own microcosm of the park around it; thick moss covers its surface and saplings grow from its top and sides. After passing the ghost ship boulder, the trail feels narrower and the forest thicker, until arriving at the next landmark, a large sandstone rock wall. The trees relinquish ground to the rock wall and a social trail heads up the hillside to its base. After the rock wall, the trail narrows again and slices through the thick undergrowth. The last point of interest before the trail turns to head up the side of the gorge is a view on the left of the marsh in the foreground and the forest distant in the background.

Climb the wooden stairs and the wooden staircase up to the top of the gorge. The trail now runs through the forest along the top of the gorge, paying homage to the arbor component of the park's name and only offering occasional views of the backsides of the sandstone rocks and the gorge below. On this portion of the hike, the trail is wide enough for side-by-side hiking but watch out for protruding roots. Eventually, you'll reach where the trail to the campground intersects with the main trail.

Take a right to stay on the trail toward the office. The descent back down into the gorge begins with a few wide-set wooden stairs with a wooden railing, and then a wooden railing ushers you along a short traverse before depositing you at the top of the wooden staircase. Use caution on the final few wooden stairs, which weren't in great shape at the time of our last visit. After reaching the bottom of the staircase, take a left to backtrack the short distance to the parking lot. If you and your dog are looking to log more miles, either do another loop or check out one of the other state parks in the area.

WHILE YOU'RE IN THE AREA: You should also visit Mirror Lake State Park and, if you must, Devil's Lake State Park.

Tower Hill State Park

The main attraction at Tower Hill State Park is the shot tower—a facility used between 1830 and 1860 to make lead pellets used in shotguns. Tower Hill is in the Driftless Region of Wisconsin, and like other state parks in the Driftless (such as Wyalusing, Wildcat Mountain, and Perrot), its topography includes bluffs carved out by adjacent rivers. These features made the location ideal for the shot tower because the molten lead droplets needed to fall a great distance into a pool of water. This location was also ideal for the shot tower because of its proximity to another natural resource: lead. The raw material needed to create the shot was abundant in this region, so it didn't have to travel far to get to the tower.

The process of making the lead pellets is interesting, but even more impressive is how one man pretty much single-handedly dug the 120-foot shaft in the sandstone cliff and the 90-foot tunnel between the shaft and the riverbank. Digging out the shaft and tunnel took Thomas Bolton Shaunce about two years, with some help from another miner named Malcom Smith. According to information at the park, Shaunce was never actually paid the $1,000 he was owed for his work, though he was eventually given some land as payment.

HEADS-UP: Tower Hill State Park is one of a couple of "seasonal" state parks in Wisconsin, which means the main entrance is open from May through mid-October. You can still visit during the off season; you just have to park at the entrance and then walk in. Thankfully Tower Hill is one of those parks where the scale of the map makes everything look like it's further away than it really is. Even if you did

Tower Hill State Park

Distance 1.3 mi
Elevation Gain 302 ft
RR/WW

N
W E
S

Mill Creek

Uphill

Going Up

Start & Finish

County Road Wisconsin

park at the entrance and walk in, it might be welcomed mileage. There are fewer than two miles of hiking trails in the park.

HEADS-UP: My pre-visit research usually includes reading some reviews of the park. In the case of Tower Hill, most visitors' reviews mentioned mosquitos. The segment of trail that runs along a slough in the course of Mill Creek must be responsible for the many biting reviews. The creek is less a flowing stream and more a stagnant puddle. At the time of our last visit, the mosquitos swarmed this segment of trail. We highly recommend taking precautions when visiting Tower Hill during mosquito season.

WATER AVAILABILITY: Water is available next to the historical marker by the picnic area shelter.

BATHROOM AVAILABILITY: A vault toilet is available near the picnic area shelter.

TRASHCAN AVAILABILITY: No trashcans on site; plan on carry-in/carry-out.

DESIGNATED DOG SWIMMING AREA: At the time of our last visit, there was no designated pet swim area, but I don't think you'd want to let your dog swim in the murky swamp waters of Mill Creek anyway.

DESIGNATED DOG PICNIC AREA: At the time of our last visit, there was no designated pet picnic area. In fact, there's a pretty blatant, "No Pets in Picnic Area" sign at the picnic area between the parking lot and campsites. As always, check with park staff when you visit in case designations have changed.

RECOMMENDED HIKE: Picnic Shelter to Shot Tower, Old Ox Trail to Tunnel Entrance, Tunnel to Campgrounds

DISTANCE AND ELEVATION GAIN: 1.3 miles, 302 feet

DOG AND HUMAN FITNESS LEVEL: recreational rambler/weekend warrior

TRAIL CONDITIONS/MATERIALS: This route has it all: pavement, pine needles, pinecones, dirt, grass, weeds, sand, stone stairs, and wooden stairs. There are some gradual climbs on this route as well as a couple of steeper sections. The trails are mostly wide and can accommodate walking side by side as well as passing other groups.

The exception is the segment of trail that goes from the tunnel to the shot tower, which climbs up and traverses along the edge of the bluff. This segment of trail is narrow and is bordered on one side by chain-link fence and on the other by rock wall covered in dense vegetation. Through this portion of the hike, there isn't anywhere to step off the trail and passing others would be incredibly challenging. Also, at the time of our last visit, this segment of trail was overgrown with vegetation, and the wooden stairs weren't in great condition. Use caution on these stairs as this is also the steepest section of trail.

TRAIL MARKINGS/EASE OF NAVIGATING: For the most part, the trails are well established and easy to follow. There are maps on posts at most trail intersections and there are occasional signs indicating the direction of the shot tower or the tunnel. The most challenging aspect of understanding the park map is recognizing when the trail is at the top or at the bottom of the bluff. At the time of our last visit, many of the maps included a message to "see enlargement of this area," regarding the trails around the shot tower and smelter house, but the enlargement didn't provide much additional detail. "Rock ledges" are indicated on the map, but that's a bit of a misnomer as far as the bluff is concerned. Where the tunnel entrance is marked on the map, there are two dotted lines of hiking trail, one on either side of a "rock ledge." On a two-dimensional map, these trails look like they run parallel to each other on either side of a rock wall. That is not the case. The trail closest to the water is at the bottom of the bluff, and the trail on the other side of the "rock ledge" is on the top of the bluff. And though there is a trail map at the intersection that takes you from the tunnel back to the top of the bluff, at the time of our last visit, the foliage around the trail was so overgrown, and the wooden stairs were in such a state of disrepair, that I seriously questioned whether this was in fact the trail.

THE EXPERIENCE: Park in the main lot by the picnic shelter and take the paved trail between the water spigot and the picnic shelter. Continue past the "Smelter House" sign and keep going on the paved trail as it leads into the woods. If you're referencing the park map, this is the left branch of the three trail options that begin at the picnic shelter. The trail is paved and benign to begin with but soon the grade gets relatively steep as it makes its way to the tower. There is a trail intersection just before the final climb to the shot house. Stay straight on the main trail which leads to a flight of stone stairs, and at the top of the stairs is the shot tower.

Here, at the highest point in the hike, the best views are from the vantage points on either side of the tower; though we found it difficult to get photos sans chain-link fence. I've ventured into the shot tower with Lucky to learn more about lead mining and the pellet-making process, but only when there were no other visitors in the area. Always be respectful of other visitors' space. If you do venture into the tower, make sure to peek down the shaft and take note, as this recommended hike also stops at the bottom of the shaft. Departing the shot tower, take Old Ox Trail, which is your only other option besides going back the way you came. Old Ox Trail is also wide, but rather than pavement this trail is mostly gravel with a bit of grass. As you amble on this trail, you'll navigate two intersections. At the first intersection keep going straight. At the second intersection, take the trail on the left.

The trail continues wide and flat as it cuts through the forest. This is the point at which we've noticed a higher concentration of mosquitos. The trail comes to a T-intersection, and a sign indicates the shot tunnel is to the left and a service road is to the right. Take the left to continue toward the tunnel. The trail here is wide enough for a vehicle, and it's clear from the parallel ruts that it has been driven on routinely. In between the ruts is a combination of sand, dirt, grass, and weeds. On the left the forest eventually defers to sandstone bluffs. On the right is a murky offshoot of Mill Creek. There is another trail map on a post, and a sign pointing straight ahead to the shot tunnel. For now, keep going straight to the tunnel. This portion of trail is hands down my favorite of this hike, so hopefully you can enjoy taking in the views of the sandstone bluff and the tunnel unmolested by mosquitos.

The trail dead-ends at the entrance to the tunnel. There is an interpretive sign informing visitors about white nose syndrome and how it is affecting the local bat populations. There's also a large wooden sign explaining how the tunnel was used to access the lead pellets at the bottom of the shaft. You can walk all the way into the tunnel to the bottom of the shaft which is behind what looks like chained prison cell doors. It's roughly 90 feet into the side of the sandstone cliff, and while it is not impossible to see unassisted, I use my phone flashlight to investigate while in the tunnel.

Once you're done checking out the tunnel, backtrack on the trail to the post with the trail map. According to the map, there is a fork in the trail in this general vicinity. But at the time of our last visit, the foliage around the trail was so overgrown, and the wooden stairs in such a state of disrepair, that I seriously questioned whether this was legitimately the trail or the remnants of shot tower operations of the past. Turns out, it's legit. The trail is just to the right of the post and begins to ascend the bluff via some stairs obscured by vegetation. You may have to do a little bushwhacking to get to the trail, and the stairs may not be super visible underneath the vegetation. Despite the dubious state of this segment of trail, Lucky and I recommend going for it because it adds a bit of novelty to an otherwise straightforward hike.

Start up the stairs and continue to climb the bluff via the series of wooden stairs and landings. This segment of trail is narrow and best navigated single file, as you are tightly squeezed between wooden railings or chain-link fence and the face of the bluff. I guess it's nice that they don't want you to fall, but the chain-link fence is another feature that made me question whether this was a designated trail or a restricted area. The chain-link is a consistent presence for this segment of trail that runs along the edge of the bluff. Stairs are also a consistent feature, until you reach a T-intersection. Continue straight, along the chain-link fence, which eventually deposits you at the top of a long and gradual flight of wooden stairs going back down to the campgrounds. At the bottom of the stairs, it's a short walk on a wide and paved road back to the picnic shelter.

If you'd like to get some more hiking in, we suggest doing another smaller loop made up of the middle and right branches of trail from the picnic shelter. That loop is about 0.4 miles and 108 feet of elevation gain. So, you know, not a ton more mileage, but a little something. And then you'll have pretty much hiked all the available trails.

Wyalusing State Park

Wyalusing State Park is one of our favorites, and we're pretty sure you'll like it too; it has something for everyone. If geology is your thing, there's millions of years of natural processes to study in the layers of sediment along the 500-foot descent from the top of the bluff to the shoreline. And Treasure Cave and Big Sand Cave are cool even if you're not interested in the processes that formed them.

If you love the mystery of Native American mounds, there are many here for your consideration. Wisconsin has the highest concentration of Native American effigy mounds in the world, and the Sentinel Ridge Mound Group is an excellent representation, with its series of conical (cone-shaped) and linear mounds, plus one bear mound. Many of the conical mounds are the final resting places of people from the Woodland Period who lived in this part of Wisconsin around 500 BC to AD 1250. And don't miss the information sign near the Passenger Pigeon Monument detailing the history of the Native American villages, camps, trails, and mounds. It's a good one.

If you're a conservationist, the Passenger Pigeon Monument is a must-see. It may seem strange to have a monument to an extinct bird that roamed all of eastern and midwestern North American here at Wyalusing State Park, but at one time, Wisconsin was home to the largest passenger pigeon colony ever recorded. Wisconsin was at one time also home to the revered conservationist Aldo Leopold, whose essay "On a Monument to the Pigeon" is a poetic and profound reflection on man's role in the extinction of the species. While the entire essay warrants a read, this quote is included on the interpretive sign at the monument, and I just had to include it here:

> We meet here to commemorate the death of a species. This monument symbolizes our sorrow. We grieve because no living man will see again the onrushing phalanx of victorious birds, sweeping a path for spring across the March skies, chasing the defeated winter from all the woods and prairies of Wisconsin. Men still live who, in their youth, remember pigeons; trees still live that, in their youth, were shaken by a living wind. But a few decades hence only the oldest oaks will remember, and at long last only the hills will know.

The essay goes on to explore the reasoning behind our sorrow. Leopold suggests, "The truth is that our grandfathers . . . were our agents in the sense that they shared the conviction, which we have only now begun to doubt, that it is more important to multiply people and comforts than to cherish the beauty of the land in which they live." Echoing that sentiment, the monument includes this inscription from ornithologist A. W. Schorger, "This species became extinct through the avarice and thoughtlessness of man."

The Passenger Pigeon Monument is honestly one of the most impactful I've encountered in our state park adventures. The weight I feel when I stand in front of this monument is the result of lessons not learned, behaviors unchanged, and avarice run amok. It's disheartening to realize we have made so little progress since this monument was erected in 1947; in fact, according to the 2019 IPBES Global Assessment Report on Biodiversity and Ecosystem Services, the rate of species extinction is accelerating.

Lucky and I try to be as environmentally friendly as possible, but I know there's always so much more we can do. We encourage all of you #wistateparkdogs to think about how you can help preserve our environment for future generations and take action to make it happen.

On a less somber note, here are some interesting tidbits I learned while reading up on the park. We're known as the Wisconsin Badgers thanks to early lead miners. The miners burrowed into the hillsides, and with no other place to live, they just stayed in the tunnels they had dug to access the lead, much like badgers who dig burrows for shelter. This is generic Wisconsin history though, as there were no successful mining ventures in Wyalusing State Park. But here's a little piece of interesting trivia that is specific to the park and the recommended hike: early European settlers of this area raised hogs, which they would let run wild in the winter to forage. Two opportunistic men came along, found the farmers' hogs running wild, butchered them, and then hid them in Sand Cave, which is essentially a big freezer during the winter. Then in spring, the men rafted the hogs to Prairie du Chien, which was ingenious albeit unlawful. If you visit Big Sand Cave, make note of its cooler temps.

HEADS-UP: While dogs are allowed to check out Treasure Cave, it might not be for all dogs and humans. Treasure Cave is accessed via two ladders. To be clear, these are ladders—not staircases. When we ventured, Lucky easily descended the first of the two ladders. He also methodically ascended the second ladder into the cave, which was steeper and longer. And then when it was time to go back down the ladder, he wasn't as sure. Here's how we made a safe descent: I went backwards down the ladder first with one hand on the railing and the other holding Lucky's collar. That way, I could control how quickly we both descended. This method worked well for getting us both down the ladder safely and soundly. In addition to the ladders, the entire approach to Treasure Cave and the cave itself are very tight spaces. On other visits, we've just waited at a distance for the rest of our group to explore the cave, especially if there are other groups already checking it out.

To hopefully save you some time fretting over which points of interest to check out, here are the Wyalusing points of interest by order of our most to least favorite:

1. Point Lookout—the best views in the park, easy. An effortless walk takes you to a panoramic view of the confluence of the Wisconsin and Mississippi Rivers and the adjoining portions of Wisconsin

Descending the ladder from Treasure Cave (Angela McNutt)

and Iowa stretching on to the horizon. It's so scenic couples get married here.

2. Passenger Pigeon Monument—an educational and somewhat somber point of interest. I enjoyed learning about the history of the passenger pigeon and contemplating my role in preserving the earth and its inhabitants.

3. Big Sand Cave—you won't be disappointed. The Big Sand Cave is such a cool natural feature and fun to get to. We think it's so cool that we selected Sand Cave Trail for the recommended hike.

4. Treasure Cave—an adventure to get to, especially with a dog. The easy part is the keyhole, which is an interesting geological feature and fun for photos. But then you have to navigate steep ladders to get to the cave. Once you're in the cave, there's not a lot of space, especially if there are other groups there already. But depending on your size and sense of adventure, you and your pooch could sneak into the smaller parts of the cave where the treasure is supposedly hidden.

5. Council Point—interchangeable with Signal Point. There are some views, but they aren't as good as those at Point Lookout.

6. Signal Point—interchangeable with Council Point. There are some views, but they aren't as good as those at Point Lookout.

7. Little Sand Cave—after seeing the Big Sand Cave, the Little Sand Cave is underwhelming. Plus, it's not that accessible/visible from the trail itself. There's a railing with a sign that lets you know it's there; otherwise, you might walk right past it.

8. The Knob—literally a stone picnic shelter. I'm not sure why this is a point of interest.

9. Paul Lawrence Interpretive Center—if interpretive centers are your thing, feel free to rate this higher on your personal list. I've been spoiled by an experience at the David R. Obey Ice Age Interpretive Center, and now most interpretive centers pale by comparison.

10. Pictured Rock Cave—only accessible via Sugar Maple Nature Trail, which is off limits to dogs. We ranked it last here because you won't be able to visit it with your dog. However, I did visit Wyalusing once without Lucky, so I took advantage of the

opportunity to check out Pictured Rock Cave. Afterwards, I had this to say: "[Pictured Rock Cave] is now my favorite sand cave at Wyalusing and quite possibly my favorite cave in Wisconsin!" I ultimately agree that this oasis is best protected from dogs—even the best behaved with the most respectful of owners. But if you get some you-time without your dog, I highly recommend hiking Sugar Maple Nature Trail to see Pictured Rock Cave.

WATER AVAILABILITY: Water is available at the Visitor Center at the entrance to the park, at the Homestead Picnic Area, and near the Point Lookout and Peterson picnic shelters.

BATHROOM AVAILABILITY: Flush toilets are available at the Visitor Center at the entrance to the park and near the Peterson Picnic Shelter. Vault toilets are available near most picnic areas.

TRASHCAN AVAILABILITY: Dumpsters at campgrounds are for registered campers only. Noncampers plan on carry-in/carry-out.

DESIGNATED DOG SWIMMING AREA: At the time of our last visit, there was no designated pet swim area, but I've taken Lucky down to the boat landing for a dip. The boat landing at Wyalusing is busy, so use caution if letting your dog swim here and be respectful of other visitors using the launch. To get to the boat landing, from the park entrance take State Park Lane into the park and then take a left on Long Valley Road. The boat launch is at the end of Long Valley Road. There is a main landing on the left where trailers back in and out of the water to launch larger vessels. Then there's a fishing pier, and then to the right of the fishing pier is a smaller paved ramp and a dirty beach area, possibly intended for launching canoes and kayaks. Lucky and I stick to the right side of the fishing pier, as it's the most out of the way. Also, before visiting, research water levels. If the Mississippi is high, the boat landing may be closed. During one of our visits in June, the boat landing was open, but part of the fishing pier was still under water. And as always, check with park staff when you visit in case designations have changed.

DESIGNATED DOG PICNIC AREA: At the time of our last visit, there was no designated pet picnic area, but the attendant suggested we use any picnic area other than the main picnic area. We usually eat lunch at the Green Cloud Picnic Area. There's a picnic shelter you can use as well as a picnic table outside of the shelter, but we like to set up our camp chairs closer to the edge of the bluff so we can enjoy the view while we eat. There is no water here, but there is a very new vault toilet. You may encounter hikers passing through on Sentinel/Ridge Trail. To get to the Green Cloud Picnic Area from the park entrance, take State Park Lane into the park and then take a left on Long Valley Road. Then take the first right onto the road that leads to the picnic area and the Passenger Pigeon Monument. The picnic area is the first parking lot on the right. If you keep going on the road up the hill, you'll end up at the Passenger Pigeon Monument.

Our other favorite spot is Henneger Point Picnic Area. We've never seen another visitor at this spot, so if you want maximum seclusion, this picnic area is for you. There are picnic tables and vault toilets at this picnic area though there is no water. Additionally, there's a Travel Wisconsin selfie station at this picnic area, but the vegetation is starting to obscure the view. To get to the Henneger Point Picnic Area, take the first left after you enter the park onto Homestead Camp Road. At the roundabout at the Homestead Campground, take the fourth exit, essentially making a left turn. Continue to follow the road through the Homestead Picnic Area, and then take a left onto Cathedral Tree Drive. Cathedral Tree Drive is a rough and bumpy road, but it's appropriately named as the trees make for a scenic drive. The road dead-ends at the Henneger Point Picnic Area. As always, check with park staff when you visit in case designations have changed.

RECOMMENDED HIKE: Sand Cave Trail + Little Sand Cave Loop
DISTANCE AND ELEVATION GAIN: 2.5 miles, 522 feet
DOG AND HUMAN FITNESS LEVEL: weekend warrior
TRAIL CONDITIONS/MATERIALS: These trails are mostly dirt, leaf litter, and occasional protruding roots and steppingstone rocks. In and around Big Sand Cave there's sand, naturally. As this route is mostly an out-and-back, the first portion of the hike is a steady descent down

the ridge, and the second half of the hike is a gradual ascent back up the ridge.

Big Sand Cave Trail starts out wide enough for walking side by side, but gradually narrows and is then best navigated single file. The Little Sand Cave Loop segment is especially narrow and best navigated single file. Passing others along the trail is easiest on Big Sand Cave Trail because the trail itself is a bit wider; there are places on Little Sand Cave Loop where passing could be managed where the terrain around the trail is flat and relatively devoid of vegetation. However, in other places, the terrain on either side of the trail is pitched as it traverses the side of the ridge. Use caution if attempting to pass along one of these narrow and pitched segments. Despite being narrow, you can often see far ahead of you on the Little Sand Cave Loop because of its route along the ridge, which comes in handy when having to plan a pass.

TRAIL MARKINGS/EASE OF NAVIGATING: The trail is well established and easy to follow. The trailhead is marked with a metal sign on a post that says "Sand Cave Trail." Along the trail there are semi-regular posts with Sand Cave Trail and hiker icons. There are also metal signs pointing out Big Sand Cave and Little Sand Cave, though we'd argue only the Little Sand Cave sign is necessary. Big Sand Cave is pretty obvious once you get there.

THE EXPERIENCE: The trailhead for Sand Cave Trail is by the Paul Lawrence Interpretive Center. Upon entering the park, take State Park Lane to the second parking area on the right. There's a metal sign on a post indicating the trailhead. Begin on the trail, which dips into the woods but runs somewhat parallel to the road until Walnut Springs and Sand Cave split at a Y-intersection. At the split, take the left branch to continue on Sand Cave Trail. Now, the trail heads deeper into the woods and remains fairly wide as it begins its descent down the ridge. At the first switchback, the trail makes a hairpin turn around a tree. The turn is reinforced with large flat stones. At this turn you may also notice some water trickling down the ridge, possibly headed for Big Sand Cave.

The trail continues to traverse the side of the ridge, and while it remains wide and mostly flat, there are occasional opportunistic roots protruding here and there. The next switchback occurs at the junction with the Little Sand Cave Loop. Take the hairpin left turn and continue to descend to Big Sand Cave. It's an easy hike to the end of the trail, where there's another Big Sand Cave sign as well as a "End of Designated Trail" sign. Getting up close and personal with the cave means going off the trail, so please be respectful of your surroundings if you do decide to leave the trail to explore.

The DNR describes Big Sand Cave as "a washed-out area of limestone with a small waterfall." At least the word "big" is in the name, but even that descriptor does little to convey the magnitude of this geological feature carved into the hillside. I can't get over how cool it is (literally and figuratively), and Lucky seems to like it too. After spending some time at the cave, head back up the trail, which is more strenuous now as you're retracing your steps back up the ridge. When you arrive back at the hairpin turn and intersection with Little Sand Cave Loop, take the left and begin the Little Sand Cave Loop.

A short distance later the trail forks. This is the beginning of the loop. We recommend taking the left branch, which means you'll be completing the loop clockwise and returning along the right branch. Now the trail is much narrower as it weaves through the woods along the ridge, and there are more noticeable changes in elevation. You reach the lowest point of elevation a little over a mile into the hike, and then there are noticeable but not necessarily strenuous ups and downs, until the ascent back up the ridge proper begins.

The trail continues through the woods, and then reaches a segment characterized by an even narrower path with dense understory on either side of the trail. This segment is short but could be a challenging section to pass on. Once you're through the dense understory, the trail dips and crosses a dried-up gulch. Then the trail gets extra narrow and extra crowded with vegetation again. Next, the trail arrives at a wooden barricade and takes a right. On the barricade, there's a sign that says "Little Sand Cave." Without this sign, I'm sure we would have hiked right past this point of interest. Depending on water levels, Little Sand Cave isn't very easy to see from behind the barricade, and what you can see may be underwhelming, especially after seeing Big Sand Cave first. Leaving Little Sand Cave, the trail continues along the ridge and then crosses the gulch again. Back on the other side of the gulch, the path widens a bit and remains so for the rest of the hike.

The trail comes back to meet with the very first segment of Little Sand Cave Loop, and just a bit further, it meets back up with Sand Cave Trail. At this intersection, take a left to backtrack on Sand Cave Trail to the parking lot. It's about 228 feet of climbing over the next 0.7 miles or so, which isn't horrible, but you'll likely notice the difference from when you hiked in on the trail. When you reach the intersection with Walnut Springs Trail, stay to the right, and finish the hike back at the parking lot for the Paul Lawrence Interpretive Center.

WORTH A MENTION: Lucky and I also really enjoy Sentinel Ridge Trail, though we like it best when we only have to hike it one way. Our favorite is starting at the top of the bluff, picking the trail up at Point Lookout, stopping about halfway at Green Cloud Picnic Area for lunch, and finishing the hike with a dip in the water at the boat landing. The last segment of this trail runs parallel to the train tracks. In this area, the trains still run very regularly, and the train and its horn are both very loud. Lucky doesn't seem to mind it too much, but I thought I would mention this for any pups who don't like trains or loud noises. One way, this hike is about 1.69 miles, and we like the route described above because it's mostly downhill from the top of the bluff down to the shoreline. In that direction, the hike gains 180 feet of elevation and loses 681 feet of elevation. So, if you don't have someone to pick you up from the boat landing, you'd be looking at 3.4 miles and 861 feet of elevation gain roundtrip. An out-and-back on Sentinel Ridge Trail would solidly fall in the avid adventurer category.

WHILE YOU'RE IN THE AREA: You should also visit Nelson Dewey State Park and the Wyalusing Public Beach, which is about 2.6 miles south of the park entrance. The beach is dog friendly but keep your pup on leash and be considerate of others. We've enjoyed much-needed swim sessions in the Mississippi to beat the summer heat as well as sunset snack sessions hanging out in our camp chairs on the beach. But if you are visiting in early spring/summer and the Mississippi is still high, the beach might be more muck than sand. It's still fun if you don't mind that kind of thing. Lucky doesn't mind it at all, and I do a lot of things I'm not thrilled about to make him happy.

Yellowstone Lake State Park

If you confuse Yellowstone Lake State Park with Yellowstone National Park, you're going to be disappointed. While Yellowstone National Park is known for natural geothermal features, Yellowstone Lake State Park is known for its manmade lake. The park exists for the lake, which exists for fishermen. At least when the lake was constructed between 1953 and 1954, it was paid for with money from the sales of hunting and fishing licenses. Every year, the lake is stocked with roughly 1,000 fish. So, if you want to fish or rent a boat, this is the spot for you. If you want scenic hiking trails, I guess it depends on your definition of *scenic*.

There are around 13 miles of hiking trails, but the trails feel like an afterthought to the lake—which they are, of course. The location was selected specifically because it was a good spot to build a lake. The trails are wide, grassy, and carve through uninspiring prairie and woodland compared to those of other Wisconsin state parks. And while there is a designated area for your dog to swim in the lake, it's hardly a dog beach. I guess what I'm trying to say is that, while there is always something to be appreciated when in nature, I wouldn't travel a great distance to visit Yellowstone Lake.

The most interesting thing about this park is its bat population. Four thousand little brown bats call Yellowstone Lake State Park home in the summer. These bats are pretty awesome. Not only have they been the subject of a documentary created by Bat Conservation International (BCI), but they also each eat up to 600 mosquitos an hour! This might be one of the only state parks where you don't need to wear bug spray for mosquitos (ticks are a different story).

WATER AVAILABILITY: Water is available at the park office, at the picnic area by the boat landing, and at the entrance to the campground near the amphitheater.

BATHROOM AVAILABILITY: Flush toilets are available in the park office. Vault toilets are available at the picnic shelter and the people swimming beach.

TRASHCAN AVAILABILITY: No trashcans on site; plan on carry-in/carry-out. But there was a trashcan outside of the concession stand near the boat rentals at the time of our last visit.

DESIGNATED DOG SWIMMING AREA: When visiting parks with Lucky, I like to stop in the office and ask the park attendant about the park's specific pet policies and areas. At Yellowstone Lake, when I asked the park attendant if dogs could swim in the lake, she told me there was a dog beach in the pet picnic area. As is often the case in Wisconsin State Parks, the term *beach* was being used very liberally. There is a point of access to the water from the pet picnic area on the south side of Lake Road. However, the postage-stamp-sized area of sand and rocks hardly constitutes a beach. This rocky spot is only big enough for one dog/owner duo to use at a time.

DESIGNATED DOG PICNIC AREA: The designated pet picnic area is accessible from Lake Road between the boat landing and the canoe landing. Signs mark the pet picnic area, which includes both picnic areas on the north and the south sides of Lake Road. The picnic areas each include their own parking lots, several picnic tables, and a couple of park grills. The picnic area south of Lake Road includes a point of access to the water for dogs to go swimming.

HEADS-UP: Most of the trails at Yellowstone Lake are multipurpose. In the summer this means four miles of trail, including Windy Ridge Trail, Savanna Loop Trail, and portions of Oak Grove Trail, are used for mountain biking as well as hiking. Thankfully, the trails are wide, but just be aware you could possibly encounter a mountain biker or two. The trail I've selected to recommend, Oak Ridge Trail, does not allow mountain biking.

RECOMMENDED HIKE: Oak Ridge Trail

DISTANCE AND ELEVATION GAIN: 1.6 miles, 181 feet

DOG AND HUMAN FITNESS LEVEL: recreational rambler

TRAIL CONDITIONS/MATERIALS: Most of the trails in Yellowstone Lake State Park are grass paths. Like plenty of other trails that double as hiking/cross-country ski trails, Oak Ridge Trail is a combination of grass and weeds, and depending on rainfall and the mowing schedule, the grass and weeds may be tall. Sections of the trail are marked by parallel vehicle ruts. The trails are wide enough to accommodate you and your dog walking side by side. There is plenty of room for letting groups pass. Oak Ridge Trail has some undulating terrain, but no significant elevation gains.

TRAIL MARKINGS/EASE OF NAVIGATING: The trails are well established and easy to follow. Oak Ridge Trail, and other trails at Yellowstone Lake, are well marked. Posts indicating which trail you are on and what activities are allowed on the trail appear frequently along trails. Intersections include trail maps and each trail at an intersection is marked with a post.

THE EXPERIENCE: Park in the lot for the picnic shelter and pick up the trail just to the left of and behind the picnic shelter. The trail is wide and cuts through some thick shrubs and understory before reaching the oak and hickory woodlands. A bench and trail map mark where Oak Ridge and Prairie Loop trails intersect. Stay to the right and continue on Oak Ridge trail. The next intersection is where the Oak Ridge loop begins. Hikers can take the loop in either direction. We recommend following the easy route for cross-country skiers and taking the loop counterclockwise. After passing through the two posts on either side of the trail, the forest gives away on the left to an expansive prairie and views of rolling hills in the distance. The forest stays on your right as you follow the edge of the prairie before passing back into the oak and hickory woodlands.

Upon returning to the beginning of the Oak Ridge loop, stay to the right and backtrack to the intersection with Prairie Loop. To complete the recommended hike, take a right at the intersection with Prairie Loop to backtrack to the parking lot. To extend your hike, you can take the left and hike the Prairie Loop (additional 0.8 miles) before backtracking to the parking lot.

WORTH A MENTION: The Wildlife Loop Trail is an easy one-mile walk that follows the edge of the lake for half of the route. The other half of the route goes through the wetlands, which are much more interesting in winter than in the summer. In the winter, when the water is frozen and the trees are barren, it's possible to see the composition of the marsh. In the summer, the dense vegetation prevents you from seeing past the edges of the trail.

HEADS-UP: In the winter, dogs are not allowed on trails that are groomed for cross-country skiing, which includes most of the trails in Yellowstone Lake. Our suggested winter hike route is the Wildlife Loop. The Wildlife Loop is especially enjoyable in the winter, as the barren trees and frozen water offer a unique view of the wetlands' composition. Also, in winter exercise caution on Blue Ridge Trail as this route doubles as a snowmobile trail.

THE WEST-CENTRAL REGION

Brunet Island State Park

I loved Brunet Island State Park. The water rivals that of Mirror Lake in reflectivity. The scenery is spectacular. If you're a canoer or kayaker, this park is a must-visit, and even if you aren't into water activities, there are some amazing spots to just set up a camp chair and read a good book overlooking the water. Consider this a glowing recommendation of the park's general ambiance and character. Now, on to the historical stuff.

The park's patron, Jean Brunet, was a French man—no surprise there. Brunet came over to the states with his family in 1818 and originally settled in St. Louis before heading north along the Mississippi and then the Chippewa River. He was the first to establish a dam and sawmill in Chippewa Falls before venturing further north along the Chippewa River and eventually building a house and trading post south of Cornell in the 1830s. According to historical accounts, Brunet was an all-around good guy and a true Renaissance Man. The city of Cornell was originally called Brunet Falls, but was renamed to honor Ezra Cornell, as in the founder of Western Union and cofounder of Cornell University. No joke.

Cornell was from New York and made a name for himself in the telegraph business first. Then he became an avid philanthropist. His first major contribution was giving a public library to the residents of Ithaca, New York. His next endeavor was to establish Cornell University in 1865. So why is it that Cornell, Wisconsin, is named after this New Yorker? That explanation starts with the Morrill Act of 1862.

The Morrill Act of 1862 created opportunities to form colleges in the US from the proceeds of federal land sales. These colleges are called land-grant colleges. So how the Morrill Act worked was each state was given a chunk of federal land, based on how many members of Congress the state had in 1860. The land was supposed to be used to create the college—either the college was to be built on the land or the money from selling the land was to be used to fund the college. Cornell saw this as an opportunity to start a college in Ithaca, but there wasn't enough federal land in New York to total the amount New York was supposed to get. In these cases, states were given federal land in other states where there was an abundance. Cornell convinced the state of New York to take timber lands in Wisconsin, and rather than sell the land immediately, New York kept the land and capitalized on its lumber. Cornell would come and visit the area, stay at Jean Brunet's inn, and the two would work together timber scouting and doing other lumber-type business things. New York eventually sold the land and made somewhere in the ballpark of $5 million, which went to Cornell University as an endowment.

So, I guess that's why they changed the name of the town to Cornell, though I don't really know what Wisconsin got out of this whole situation. Maybe economic development? At least when it came time to dedicate the state park in 1940, Wisconsin opted for Brunet as its eponym.

WORTH A MENTION: In 1977, a twister took out an 18-acre plot of hemlock trees in the middle of Brunet Island. The destruction was so bad the park was closed for roughly a year. Even now, you can tell where the tornado came through because birch trees have taken over where the hemlocks once stood.

WATER AVAILABILITY: Water is available at the park office, near the picnic shelter, beach, and playground.

BATHROOM AVAILABILITY: Flush toilets are available at the park office and at the beach.

TRASHCAN AVAILABILITY: No trashcans on site; plan on carry-in/carry-out. To assist you in this effort, there is a post with a trash bag dispenser at the southern end of the pet picnic area.

DESIGNATED DOG SWIMMING AREA: The designated pet area is near the boat mooring area, along the west side of the road between the north and south campgrounds. There is access to the Chippewa River shoreline at the boat mooring area, but it's not a beach or a boat launch. There are a couple of small depressions along the shoreline where a dog can more easily step into the water. Otherwise, it's a bit of a step down from the shore into the water, which could be intimidating for smaller dogs and for dogs like Lucky. Lucky prefers the most gradual of inclined entries into water despite his longish legs.

DESIGNATED DOG PICNIC AREA: The pet picnic area is near the boat mooring area, along the west side of the road between the north and south campgrounds. Signs on posts indicate the boundaries of the pet area and inform visitors that "pets are allowed in this area leashed and under control. Owners are responsible for clean-up of waste." There's a trash bag dispenser on the post at the southern end of the pet picnic area, and while not specifically a dog poop bag dispenser, it's the thought that counts. The area is relatively large and could accommodate a couple of groups at the same time; there are picnic tables, a park grill, a bench, and a campfire circle, which is surrounded by a stone bench.

RECOMMENDED HIKE: Pine Trail + Timber Trail + Spruce Trail

DISTANCE AND ELEVATION GAIN: 1.3 miles, 36 feet

DOG AND HUMAN FITNESS LEVEL: recreational rambler

TRAIL CONDITIONS/MATERIALS: The trails are mostly dirt and leaf/pine litter with some grass. The recommended route includes segments on the paved park road. The trails are mostly narrow and best navigated single file, but there is plenty of room to step off to the side of the trail to let others pass. This hike is completely flat.

TRAIL MARKINGS/EASE OF NAVIGATING: The trails are relatively well established and easy to follow. It's a small park, and at any given time along the recommended route you aren't too far from the park road. There are signs on posts identifying the trails at their beginnings and ends, and while there aren't markers along the official trail, there aren't any social trails to potentially lead you astray.

THE EXPERIENCE: There isn't a ton of hiking at Brunet Island. Clearly the main attraction here is the water. The trails that crisscross the island are perfect for land lovers looking for a leisurely walk, however. If you aren't camping at the park, we recommend parking at the boat

landing. After crossing the bridge onto the island, the road becomes
a one-way going clockwise around the island. The boat landing is the
first left after the road turns into a one-way.

This hike is a counterclockwise loop, which starts out on a tiny
segment of Spruce Trail. Access to Spruce Trail is at the northern
side of the parking lot; there is a Spruce Trail sign on a wooden post
at the entrance to the trail. This short segment cuts through the bit
of woods between the parking lot and the park road. Cross the park
road and reenter the woods at the Pine Trail sign. There are only two
trail intersections along this hike, and you'll arrive at the first just a
short distance into the woods. This is where Pine Trail splits: one
segment heads northwest and the other segment heads southwest.
Stay to the right to head northwest on Pine Trail. The trail continues
through the woods until it reaches the park road.

Take a left and hike on the park road until you reach the trailhead
for Timber Trail. Unlike some park roads, the road through Brunet
Island is nice and wide with a marked shoulder for pedestrians. Take
a left onto Timber Trail. The trail itself is narrow, but because the
trees were thinned out by that tornado in the 1970s, there's a lot of
space around the trail. Just after setting out on Timber Trail you'll
arrive at the second intersection, where that southwestern running
segment of Pine Trail connects to Timber Trail. Continue straight
(south) on Timber Trail. Along this segment there is more evidence
of the tornado's impact on the island. There are still plenty of fallen
trees in various stages of decomposition interspersed with the young
opportunistic birch. Further along Timber Trail, the trail widens a bit,
and as it gets closer to the south campground, you may start seeing
campers through the woods on your right. Timber Trail ends when it
reaches the park road.

Take a left on the park road and walk to the end of the parking lot.
Then cross the road, enter the parking lot, and pick up Spruce Trail at
the northeastern corner of the lot. The trail takes you through a short
section of woods before reaching the ballfield. If there isn't a game
going on, cut across the ballfield and pick Spruce Trail back up further
down the first base line. Now, the trail runs parallel to the Fisher

River, so you can catch glimpses of water through the trees. At the time of our last visit, there were a lot of dead trees along this section of trail, some precariously spanning the trail overhead, having fallen from one side of the trail and then gotten caught in the branches of a tree on the other side. We advise looking up occasionally. You've reached the end of the recommended hike when you end up back at the boat landing.

WORTH A MENTION: The park road would also be a nice walk. It's wide with a marked shoulder for pedestrians, and the scenery is pleasant the whole way around the loop.

WHILE YOU'RE IN THE AREA: In Cornell, Dylan's Dairy has a dog-friendly patio. You might also visit Lake Wissota State Park or stop in Jim Falls for their annual Sturgeon Fest, which includes a parade and demolition derby. If you go into Chippewa Ralls, Leinenkugel's Brewery has a dog-friendly patio. If you can find it, the Chippewa Moraine State Recreation Area is another great hiking option, and the David R. Obey Ice Age Interpretive Center is hands-down my favorite interpretive center. Finally, you might stop in Cadott, Wisconsin, to take your picture at the not-exactly-but-close-enough-for-a-photo halfway point between the Equator and the North Pole.

Buckhorn State Park

The history of the land that is Buckhorn State Park is not all that unique. Originally inhabited by the Ho-Chunk, the landscape in its natural state was "unbroken wilderness." And then it was broken. In the mid to late 1800s, loggers cut down the pine trees, and then farmers' cows grazed on the understory. In the 1920s, the farmers sold off their land to the Wisconsin River Power Company in anticipation of hydroelectric dams. For a while, the land was pretty much left to its own devices. Aspen, scrub oak, and jack pine started reestablishing themselves in the area. And then in 1940 the Castle Rock Dam was completed. The Wisconsin and Yellow rivers backed up to form the Castle Rock Flowage and a new peninsula, which is now Buckhorn State Park. Finally, in 1974 the Wisconsin DNR purchased the peninsula with intentions of returning it to a state of "unbroken wilderness."

As far as I can tell, those efforts are going well. Despite some of the park's oak trees succumbing to oak wilt, a deadly fungus that spreads through the oak's roots, killing the tree quickly, much of the park is being restored to its original habitat—one that does feel unique to this park. When we first visited Buckhorn State Park, I hadn't thought much about the ecosystems we'd be encountering, since so much of Wisconsin seems to be deciduous forest and prairie. I supposed I expected much of the same. But as we hiked, we found ourselves in an environment unlike anything we'd previously encountered. This unique area is the Buckhorn Barrens State Natural Area.

Before this land was broken, it was pine and oak savanna. Oak savannas exist in the transition between forest and prairie. Unlike prairies,

Buckhorn State Park

Distance 3.0 mi
Elevation Gain ?? Ft
RR

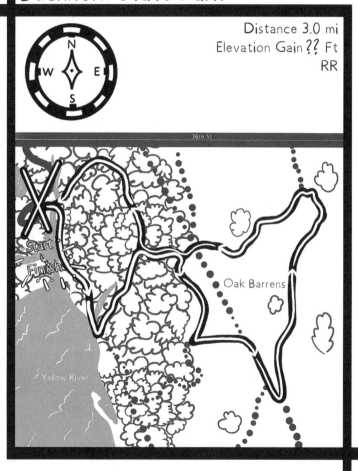

which are just grasslands, oak savannas are grasslands with occasional large oaks. And in fact, oak savannas are a rare find. According to the Wisconsin DNR website, "Intact examples of oak savanna vegetation are now so rare that less than 500 acres are thought to exist in a state similar to Euro-American settlement. This is less than 0.01 percent of the estimated 5.5 million acres of savanna historically found in Wisconsin." Barrens are also uncommon. They're like savannas, but they're established on sandy soils. Wisconsin is lucky to have both pine barrens and oak barrens. Thanks to the park's restoration efforts, Buckhorn Barrens State Natural Area offers park visitors a chance to experience and enjoy these rare ecosystems.

WATER AVAILABILITY: Water is available at the park office, near the beach picnic area, and the picnic area south of the amphitheater.

BATHROOM AVAILABILITY: Flush toilets are available at the park office. Vault toilets are available near the beach picnic area, near the boat launch by the accessible fishing pier, and near canoe launch B.

TRASHCAN AVAILABILITY: No trashcans on site; plan on carry-in/carry-out. There are dumpsters in the parking lot for the recommended hike with signs that say, "For Camper Use Only No Home Generated Trash Allowed," which I think opens a gray area. If your dog poops at the park, technically that trash wasn't generated at home. Just saying.

DESIGNATED DOG SWIMMING AREA: The designated dog area, for both swimming and picnicking, is located off Water Street, west of the Buckhorn Bridge. To get there, you'll leave the park, cross the bridge, and take an immediate right on the other side of the bridge—and I mean immediate. The first time we visited, we accidently passed it and had to go turn around in the boat launch parking lot. You'll know you've arrived when you see a small sand parking lot on the right, with yellow "State Park" signs, "Entering fee area" signs, "No campfires" and "No camping" signs, and one "Pet area" sign that was, at the time of our last visit, obscured by overgrown foliage. There are a couple of social paths that take you from the small parking lot down to the water.

I'm happy to report that this is a decent dog swimming area. Though small, I think the term *beach* is appropriate, and there are really two little beaches. The first one is more obvious as you approach the water, and the second is just at the end of a short social trail that goes around to the other side of a couple of trees. This second spot might be even a tad bit nicer than the first, but they are both perfectly pleasant. These two little beaches have all the criteria of a good dog swimming spot: a parcel of sand large enough to accommodate a couple of dogs and their humans, a gradual slope into the water, clear water devoid of excessive weeds and muck, and a location off the beaten path. And because this area is so removed from the rest of the park, we're less likely to interfere with anyone else's enjoyment of the park—and vice versa.

DESIGNATED DOG PICNIC AREA: The designated dog area, for both swimming and picnicking, is located off Water Street, west of the Buckhorn Bridge. For specifics on how to get there, see the

The dog swimming area at Buckhorn State Park (Danielle St. Louis)

"Designated Dog Swimming Area" info above. While there are no picnic tables, no park grills, no bathrooms, and no water fountains at the designated pet area, there are two little slices of Wisconsin paradise available for you to enjoy with your dog. It's just more of a BYO situation. It's not far from the road/parking lot to the beach, so bring your camp chairs and cooler and you'll be all set.

RECOMMENDED HIKE: Central Sands Nature Trail + Turkey Hollow Segment + Partridge Trail Loop

DISTANCE AND ELEVATION GAIN: 3 miles, none. Apparently, my GPS didn't register any elevation change. Or it malfunctioned. But the elevation chart looks like when someone flatlines on a medical drama.

DOG AND HUMAN FITNESS LEVEL: recreational rambler

TRAIL CONDITIONS/MATERIALS: The trails are primarily dirt, sand, and grass. There are several wooden bridges. The trails and bridges are all wide, characteristic of trails that are groomed for cross-country skiing in the winter (which these are). In many places the trails are wide enough for a vehicle as evidenced by the set of parallel tire tracks that mark much of the recommended route. There's room to hike side by side and plenty of space for passing others along the trails. The trails are all flat and can get waterlogged following heavy rains.

TRAIL MARKINGS/EASE OF NAVIGATING: The trails are well established and easy to follow. There are interpretive signs along Central Sands Nature Trail and brown metal or wood signs on wooden posts at trailheads and intersections indicating trails and directions. There are also trail maps at main intersections.

THE EXPERIENCE: Park in the lot by the south picnic shelter. To get to the lot, enter the park and take the park road until it reaches a T-intersection. At the T-intersection take a right, and then take the first left onto the drive for the parking lot. The connecting trail to get to Central Sands Nature Trail is at the east corner of the parking lot; it's marked with a brown metal sign pointing in the direction of campsites 4–7 and 13–15. There's also a sign that says, "No hiking or pets on trails when they are snow covered and skiable." Though most nature trails are usually off-limits to dogs, this sign suggests this is only the case for the Central Sands Nature Trail when it is snow covered. The trail heads toward the woods and arrives at the first of several wooden footbridges on this hike. Then the grass and dirt trail continues for a moment before crossing a second wooden footbridge, on the other side of which is the first trail intersection. Take a right, following the sign toward campsites 4–7 and 13–15. You're now heading counterclockwise around the Central Sands Nature Trail. The grass thins out and the trail turns to predominantly dirt and sand. The wide trail takes a straightforward path through the woods and then crosses another longer footbridge. After this third wooden footbridge, the trail's surroundings start to evolve. The forest becomes less dense around the trail and the understory becomes more prominent. After crossing another wooden footbridge there is an especially sandy segment of trail and a mound of sand and grass to the right of the trail. On the other side of the mound is the water. It's not a great spot for accessing the water—we'd save the swimming for the designated dog area—but it's not a bad vantage point to take in the view and take some photos. Then it's only a short distance further down the trail to the next intersection.

At the intersection, take a left to stay on Central Sands for a bit longer. Now, the trees are once again the predominant plants bordering the trail. Maybe because of the trees, the trail feels especially wide, though the parallel dirt tire ruts on either side of a mossy track suggest the width is consistent and equivalent to the previous stretches of Central Sands. At the next intersection, take a right to head in the direction of the Hunter parking lot. This is a short connector trail, which takes you to Turkey Hollow Trail.

Along this short connector trail, you'll cross into the Buckhorn Barrens State Natural Area. The change in environment isn't immediately obvious, but as you head down the trail, the forest begins to transition to barrens. Follow the Turkey Hollow Trail sign and then take a right to head south on it. You'll be traveling through the oak barrens—grasslands with occasional large oaks. At about a mile into this hike, you'll take a left onto the short connector trail that takes you from Turkey Hollow Trail to the Partridge Trail Loop. At the next T-intersection, take a right onto Partridge Trail, following the sign toward campsites 17–19. This segment of trail doubles as a service road, so the tire tracks may be more well defined (and potentially muddier).

At the next Y-intersection, take the left branch, and, in a moment, you'll see a Partridge Trail sign pointing to the left. This is where Partridge Trail and the service road part ways, so take the left to stay on Partridge Trail. The wide, mowed trail continues wandering north through the barrens, marked with occasional posts with hiker and hunter icons. The next intersection is another Y-intersection with a service road. Keep to the left, following the sign to stay on Partridge Trail.

Now Partridge trail heads southwest until it reaches the intersection with the main service road and the connector trail for Central Sands Trail. A metal "To Central Sands Nature Trail" sign stands at the entrance to the trail on the other side of the road. Cross the road and follow this sign and trail back to where the connector trail meets up with Turkey Hollow Trail. Rather than continuing straight on Turkey Hollow Trail, take a right onto the connector trail to get back to Central Sands Nature Trail. Backtrack along this segment of trail and exit the Buckhorn Barrens State Natural Area. The landscape begins to transition from barrens back to forest, and then you'll be back at the intersection for Central Sands Nature Trail. Take a right to continue counterclockwise on the Central Sands Nature Trail loop. Much like the first section of Central Sands, the trail is wide and grassy. You'll cross another wooden footbridge before arriving back at the very first trail intersection on this hike. Take a right to go back over the wooden bridge and back to the parking lot to finish the recommended hike.

If you're looking for a shorter hike, you can just do the Central Sands Nature Trail loop, which is about 1.4 miles, but you won't get to see the best parts of the barrens, which are along the Partridge Trail Loop.

Kinnickinnic State Park

The story of how Kinnickinnic State Park came into existence is an encouraging example of the difference regular people can make to save the environment. In the 1960s, residents recognized the importance of preserving the area where the Kinnickinnic (Kinni) and St. Croix rivers meet. Citizen groups like the Save the St. Croix Association and the Minnesota Wisconsin Boundary Area Commission fought to save the area from suburban sprawl. They lobbied the Wisconsin Natural Resources board to create a new state park in this area, and then, in 1972, three families donated portions of their land to the Department of Natural Resources for the creation of a state park. Because of the selfless efforts of these locals, Kinnickinnic State Park is available to us to enjoy today.

So what is so special about this area that the residents fought so hard to protect it? Well, the Kinni is a cold-water trout stream full of German brown trout and the St. Croix has a variety of fish to catch, including large walleyes—if fishing is your thing. Then there's the state natural areas of the Kinnickinnic River Gorge and Delta, which is one of the finest examples of river delta in Wisconsin (think plants galore). Between the variety of ecosystems within the park's boundaries, it's possible to see upwards of 85 species of birds in a day in the spring. During the migration season, more than 140 bird species make a pit stop in the river valley, so get out your binoculars, bird people! Oh, and because the delta at the mouth of the Kinni keeps the St. Croix from freezing, my favorites, bald eagles, hang out in the park during the winter. If that's not reason enough to visit Kinnickinnic State Park in winter, then here's another enticement: Kinnickinnic State Park officially allows skijoring! Your dog

Kinnickinnic State Park

Distance 3 mi
Elevation Gain 106 ft
RR

N
W E
S

St. Croix River

Dog Beach

Start
Finish

Dog Rd.

P

can pull you on your cross-country skis on Red, Blue, Brown, Pink, and Black when these trails are snow covered.

Something else that's been preserved in River Falls, Wisconsin, is the spirit of conservation. Some might say it's in their blood—or maybe it's something in the water—whatever it is, we could all aspire to be more like this community and work together to preserve our environment on a local level. Warren Knowles, the thirty-seventh governor of Wisconsin, a member of the Wisconsin Conservation Hall of Fame and a River Falls native, said many wise things, this among them: "While I recognize the need for global support for the environment, I have always thought that the slogan 'Think Globally, Act Locally' is an important plan of action for everyone." So, Lucky and I hope visiting Kinnickinnic State Park inspires you to act locally to support the environment because, as the people of River Falls have demonstrated, we can make a difference.

WATER AVAILABILITY: Water is available at the park office, at the St. Croix Overlook picnic area, at the picnic area by the swimming beach, and at the picnic area with access to the Yellow, Orange, and Blue trails.

BATHROOM AVAILABILITY: Flush toilets are available at the park office. Vault toilets are available at the St. Croix Overlook picnic area and at the picnic area by the swimming beach.

TRASHCAN AVAILABILITY: No trashcans on site; plan on carry-in/carry-out.

DESIGNATED DOG SWIMMING AREA: According to the Kinnickinnic State Park website, dogs can use "the water outside of the designated swimming area." The park attendant specified dogs could use the beach area to the south/southwest of the people swimming beach. Now normally, when there is a section of beach where dogs are allowed, it's usually the worst section of beach—you know, the section where people don't want to go. So, when we visited for the first time, I was anticipating a narrow, rocky strip of shoreline where Lucky could attempt to wade in the water a bit. I wasn't expecting someplace we'd want to spend any length of time. But when we got to the area the park attendant specified, what I saw amazed me. It

The dog swimming area at Kinnickinnic State Park (Danielle St. Louis)

was an actual beach! It was sandy and wide enough for plenty of picnic blankets, camp chairs, towels, sunbathers, and dogs.

To get there, park in the lot at the very end of the park road for the St. Croix Picnic Area and take the paved path down to the people swimming beach. Keeping to the left outside edge of the picnic area, walk toward the water. Once you hit the water, take a left. A little way down there is a stand of trees that creates a natural barrier between the people beach and the area the dogs can use. Always remember dogs should be on leash when not in the water, and of course, check when you visit in case designations have changed. Additionally, check seasonal water levels and water quality before your visit.

DESIGNATED DOG PICNIC AREA: The designated pet picnic area is by the parking lot for the sledding hill. After entering the park, it's the second parking lot on the left. There are a couple of picnic tables, a park grill, and a "Pets allowed in this area. Pets must be kept on a leash and cleaned up after" sign. The Blue and Brown trails intersect with this picnic area, so you may encounter hikers passing through. As far as pet picnic areas go, this one is fine. It's not on the water and it doesn't have any views, but it's perfectly pleasant. There is some shade, and it's large enough for a couple of groups to use it at the same time. If you're looking for something more scenic, you could try a picnic on the beach at the dog swimming area, but you'll have further to haul your lunch.

RECOMMENDED HIKE: Yellow + Green + Purple

DISTANCE AND ELEVATION GAIN: 3 miles, 106 feet

DOG AND HUMAN FITNESS LEVEL: recreational rambler

TRAIL CONDITIONS/MATERIALS: The trails are mostly grass, with some sections of dirt, sand, and sporadic weeds. The recommended hike also crosses the park road, which is paved. There are some sections along the Purple Trail with protruding tree roots. The Yellow, Green, and Purple trails are all groomed for cross-country skiing in winter, which means they are flat and very wide. They are wide enough to accommodate you and your dog walking side by side as well as able passing others along the trail.

TRAIL MARKINGS/EASE OF NAVIGATING: The trails are well established and easy to follow. There are frequent posts with colored bands that correspond to the color/name of the trail. Additionally, there are wooden signs with purple arrows at points along the Purple Trail, though the purple often looked blue to me. There are trail maps on posts or arrows at many intersections. There are also plenty of signs indicating where dogs are and are not allowed and signs reminding visitors, "Pets must be leashed at all times."

THE EXPERIENCE: Park at the third lot on the left after entering the park. It is one lot past the pet picnic area and has access to the Yellow, Orange and Blue trails. The recommended hike is a counterclockwise loop, so to get started, head toward the back of the picnic area and to the left. The Yellow trail runs along the back of the picnic area; you'll pick it up by the manual water pump. Take a left onto the Yellow trail, which is a wide, mowed grass path through the tall vegetation. Almost immediately, the Yellow trail crosses the Blue trail. Continue straight on Yellow, heading toward the park road. Cross the park road and keep going on the Yellow trail.

After crossing the park road, the trail is bordered on the right by the forest and on the left by former farmland that is being restored to prairie. There isn't much shade throughout this portion of the hike, in the event you set out on hot and sunny summer day. Next, the Yellow trail meets up with the Green trail. If you want a shorter hike, you could keep going on Yellow and cut straight across the prairie. But we recommend staying to the right picking up the Green trail. The Green trail keeps you hiking along the edge of the forest, essentially walking the perimeter of the prairie. Along the trail there is a bench for sitting and enjoying views of the prairie grasses and flowers, edged by forest in the background. Eventually, the Green trail departs the prairie and dips just inside the edge of the forest. A bit further into the woods, it dead ends at the Yellow trail. Stay to the right to head south on the Yellow trail for a short distance before reaching the intersection with the Purple trail. Once again, stay to the right, now jumping onto the Purple trail.

The Purple trail easily strolls through the old growth oak forest, with some variability in the trail materials below your feet. This segment of the trail is less consistently grass, with more weeds, sand and dirt mixing into the trail composition. Then, the Purple trail intersects the paved trail that leads down to the beach. If you want to take a detour to the beach, take a right and head down the paved trail. Otherwise, cross the paved trail and follow the purple arrow pointing to the continuation of the Purple trail.

The trail navigates the perimeter of the St. Croix picnic area. Stay to the right and along the edge of the picnic area, heading toward the monument stone. This segment of the trail is especially sandy with some exposed roots as it begins its approach toward the edge of the bluff. Head out to the overlook to take in the panoramic views of the Kinnickinnic Delta. Then hike back toward the picnic area. Stay to the right along the edge of the picnic area and follow the purple arrow on a post back into the forest. The trail strolls through the forest for a bit before reaching an intersection with the Orange trail. If you'd like a more difficult end to this hike, take a right onto the Orange trail, which features more challenging terrain but ultimately brings you back to the parking lot. Otherwise, stay to the left and on Purple.

A short distance after taking the left to stay on Purple, the trail dead ends at the Yellow trail. Take a right to head northeast on Yellow toward the parking lot. The trail emerges from the woods and is once again bordered on the left by prairie and on the right by woods. Next the Orange trail meets up and runs concurrently with the Yellow trail for a short distance. Keep to the left to follow Orange/Yellow toward the parking lot. At the next intersection, where Orange departs from Yellow, you can take either branch as both end up back at the parking lot. For simplicity's sake, stay to the left to take Yellow back to the picnic area and parking lot.

WHILE YOU'RE IN THE AREA: You should also visit Willow River State Park.

Lake Wissota State Park

The development of the land that is now Lake Wissota State Park followed a progression common to many areas in Wisconsin. The area used to be home to an abundant forest of white pines. After loggers cleared out the forests, farmers moved in. Then when hydroelectric power came onto the scene, a dam was constructed on the Chippewa River. The dam was completed in 1917, and the nearby farmland was flooded to make the reservoir. The resulting body of water was named Lake Wissota, a not-so-clever mash-up of Wisconsin and Minnesota. This progression from forest to farmland to lake resulted in damaging erosion of the land. So, from the 1950s to 1970s, the federal Soil Bank program paid farmers to plant trees to prevent erosion. The red pines that line Red Pine Trail are thanks to those early conservation efforts. Lake Wissota State Park opened in 1972, and now over a century after the lake's creation, the community is still trying to address the environmental impacts of the historical and contemporary land management practices. Among the environmental impacts has been the pollution of the lake's waters.

At the time of our last visit, the water at the beach was gross; even from a distance, we could see the water's green tint as children splashed each other. In 2002, the Environmental Protection Agency (EPA) assigned Lake Wissota an Impaired Water designation because of multiple issues including mercury and polychlorinated biphenyls (PCBs) in fish tissue and sediment, and phosphorus levels in the water. Local efforts by the Lake Wissota Improvement and Protection Association (LWIPA) have been attempting to address the issues, but there is a lot to overcome. The land's agricultural origins and longstanding agricultural practices result in runoff of sediment and nutrients into the lake. When phosphorous from fertilizers gets into the water, it fuels algae blooms, including dangerous blue-green algae blooms. The Lake Wissota Stewardship Project enlists landowners in the watershed to change their land management practices to conserve the land as well as to protect and improve the lake's water quality. By planting trees, restoring wetlands, and installing sediment retention basins, the water quality of Lake Wissota is slowly improving. The latest EPA assessment data from 2016 classified Lake Wissota's coastal waters as "good" for recreation, but the bays and harbors were still rated as "impaired" because of phosphorous and sediment.

It's impossible to deny the role human activity has played in creating the environmental issues that plague Lake Wissota, but thankfully we can also take action to restore the land and water. Through sustained local efforts, hopefully the lake will once again "sparkle like hundreds of diamonds on a sunny day" (Barbara Arnold, "A Dam Fine History: Lake Wissota and the Dam That Created It Turn 100 This Year").

WORTH A MENTION: Shout-out to Mary and Richard Anderson of New Richmond, who donated $5,000 to the Friends of Lake Wissota State Park. Mary and Richard visit the park regularly and camp with their three dogs. They requested that their donation be used in part to improve to the dog areas in the park (from the June 2, 2019, Friends of Lake Wissota State Park meeting notes). Mary and Richard, thank you for your generosity, which will benefit all dogs who visit Lake Wissota State Park.

WATER AVAILABILITY: Water is available at the park office, near the people beach, and at the picnic and play area across from the ball field.

BATHROOM AVAILABILITY: Flush toilets are available at the park office and at the picnic area across from the ball field.

TRASHCAN AVAILABILITY: There are dog poop-bag dispensers at both the northern and southern "leashed pet use areas," but there are no accompanying trashcans. Plan on carry-in/carry-out.

DESIGNATED DOG SWIMMING AREA: Near the northern pet picnic area, there is a little sign that says "Lake Access," with an arrow

Lake Wissota State Park

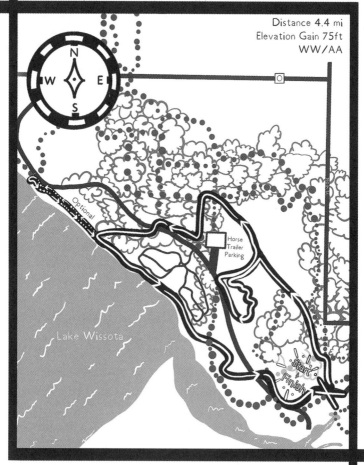

Distance **4.4** mi
Elevation Gain 75ft
WW/AA

N
W   E
S

Optional

Horse
Trailer
Parking

Lake Wissota

Start
Finish

pointing to a weathered wooden staircase. It's impossible to see past the first landing when standing at the top of the staircase, so here's what's down there: a tiny rocky area right on the lake's edge. The space isn't big enough for multiple groups to hang out at the same time, which makes the fact that you can't tell if anyone else is down there before you descend the stairs a bit of an inconvenience. The little lake access point felt crowded with just my friend Angela and me perched on rocks and Lucky wading around in the water. But it is very secluded, so if you're the only ones down there, it's not a bad spot to relax, have a snack, and enjoy looking at the water. And in our experience, we prefer it over the other lake access point for pooches.

At the time of our last visit, we couldn't get away from the second pet area fast enough. While the water further north had been clear and refreshing, the water at the southern pet area was some of the nastiest lake water we've ever seen. I held Lucky back for fear he might wade in the water, lap up a drink, and mutate into some sort of swamp monster. The water was slime green. Green water aside, this dog swimming area is more spacious than the northern lake access point, and by "more spacious" I mean maybe two dogs could frolic at a time. And unlike the rocky entry into the water at the northern access point, the entrance to the water at this southern spot is a gradual slope of sand, grass, and weeds. If the water quality were the same, we'd recommend this southern spot over the northern one based on ease of access and space. But water quality clearly trumps these other factors, so we hope the water is clear when you visit. Information about water quality can be found at the DNR website, or check with park staff when you arrive.

Park at the first lot on the right after entering the park to access the northern "leashed pet use area." It's also the lot for the overlook point. Then follow the "Lake Access" sign and take the stairs down to the lake's edge. To access the southern "leashed pet use area," park in the lot for the people beach, which is the third right after entering the park. After parking, head toward the picnic area and beach, staying to the right. There are numerous "Pets are not allowed in picnic areas"

The southern dog swimming area at Lake Wissota State Park (Danielle St. Louis)

signs—stay to the outside of the picnic area. After entering the "leashed pet use area" marked by a sign and the dog poop-bag dispenser, the dog swimming area is around the dense vegetation to the left. You can also hike to the southern swimming area via Lake Trail; however, the trail is super narrow and has been reinforced with wooden planks because the area can get waterlogged and mucky. Because of how narrow the trail is, we suggest you access the southern swimming area from the people beach and picnic area side where it is easier to manage potential encounters with other dogs coming and going from the swimming area.

DESIGNATED DOG PICNIC AREA: The northern "leashed pet use area" is a large clearing with several picnic tables and park grills next to a scenic overlook of the lake. There's even a dog poop-bag dispenser. While there's no water or restrooms or trashcans for those dog poop bags, the area is spacious and accommodating. It's nice, as far as pet picnic areas go. Multiple groups could use this area at the same time with plenty of space as a buffer between them.

Compared to the northern pet area, the southern pet area feels small and uninviting. At the time of our last visit, the dense plant life was encroaching on the southern pet area. There was one lone picnic table in a very small clearing next to the lake and a single park grill at the outer edge of the area. While there is a dog poop-bag dispenser and water and restrooms in the vicinity, this pet area is a sharp contrast to the people picnic area and beach just on the other side of the "Pets are not allowed in picnic areas" signs.

Park at the first lot on the right after entering the park to access the northern "leashed pet use area." It's also the lot for the overlook point. To access the southern "leashed pet use area," park in the lot for the people beach, which is the third right after entering the park. After parking, head toward the picnic area and beach, staying to the right. The "leashed pet use area" is marked by a sign and the dog poop-bag dispenser. You can also hike to the southern pet area via Lake Trail; check out the dog swim area section for our thoughts on that option.

RECOMMENDED HIKE: Staghorn + Jack Pine to Eagle Prairie + Prairie Wildflower + Red Pine Trail + Lake Trail + Jack Pine

DISTANCE AND ELEVATION GAIN: 4.4 miles, 75 feet

DOG AND HUMAN FITNESS LEVEL: weekend warrior/avid adventurer

TRAIL CONDITIONS/MATERIALS: The trails on this recommended hike are predominantly dirt and grass or mowed grass paths, and most of the trails are wide enough to accommodate walking side by side and passing other groups. Encroaching prairie grasses can make Prairie Wildflower Trail feel narrow, despite the wide mowed grass path. The exception on this route is Lake Trail, which has some very narrow sections and is generally best hiked single file. Passing other groups on the narrowest sections of Lake Trail would require stepping off the trail, which may be challenging in some places. The entire route is flat.

TRAIL MARKINGS/EASE OF NAVIGATING: The trails are well established and easy to follow. There are wooden signs at many

trailheads with trail names and trail maps. There are also wooden
signs and trail maps at some intersections. At other intersections,
one branch may be labeled while others aren't, which was the case
at the intersection of Eagle Prairie Trail and Red Pine Trail at the time
of our last visit. Additionally, there are posts with icons to indicate
prohibited activities (i.e., no horses) at some trailheads. While it's
always clear where the trails are, a park map is a helpful resource to
navigate the many connections between trails.

HEADS-UP: This recommended hike is borderline avid adventurer
because of the length. It's on the longer end of hikes I tend to
recommend, but I like this route because it's a giant loop and it takes
you through a decent chunk of the park with lots of opportunities to
add on or reduce mileage.

HEADS-UP: The only trails that are designated for "hiking only" are the
Prairie Wildflower Trail and the Self-Guided Beaver Meadow Nature
Trail. The rest of the trails in the park are multiuse hike-bike or hike-
bike-horse trails.

THE EXPERIENCE: Take the park road past the ball field, and then park
in the lot on the left. The trailhead for Staghorn Trail is marked with a
wooden sign and a trail map. Head straight north on Staghorn Trail,
which is more than vehicle-width wide and marked by parallel tire
tracks. The tire tracks disappear as the grass thickens and the trail
turns into a mowed grass path. Almost immediately, you'll reach the
intersection with Jack Pine Trail. Take the left and head down Jack Pine
for a moment to a Y-intersection. Take the right branch at the
intersection and head down Eagle Prairie Trail. These trails are
multiuse hike-bike, so it's possible you might encounter a bike or two.

Eagle Prairie Trail begins as a wide, mowed grass path through
prairie punctuated by pine trees. At the next intersection Fox Trail
connects with Eagle Prairie Trail. Fox Trail is a hard left, so veer
straight/right to stay on Eagle Prairie Trail as it continues to head
northwest. Now, Eagle Prairie skirts along the edge of the prairie, with
a notable contrast of prairie grass on the left and forest on the right.
At the next intersection, Eagle Prairie Trail ends at the intersection
with Red Pine Trail. We recommend taking a stroll through the prairie,

so take a left to hike southwest on Red Pine Trail to the Prairie Wildflower Trail loop. I normally find prairies boring, but this one is impressive. At the time of our last visit, the bright yellow and purple flowers were repping "sota" so hard, the prairie could have been mistaken for a Vikings crowd at a home game. After completing the prairie loop, double back on Red Pine Trail to the intersection with Eagle Prairie Trail.

Back at the Eagle Prairie Trail and Red Pine Trail intersection, take the left and continue northwest on Red Pine Trail. This section of Red Pine is extra-wide and more dirt and sand than grass, and now the forest of trees is on the left and the prairie grasses are on the right. The trail turns fully into the woods just before crossing the horse/bike trail. Stay straight through the intersection on Red Pine Trail, beginning the short section of trail where the horse-bike trail and the hike-bike trail overlap. Thankfully, only moments later, the trail arrives at another intersection; take a left here to take Red Pine south. There's a couple of different routes you can take in this area, but we recommend taking this first left so you are back on the hike-bike trail as quickly as possible, minimizing the amount of time you'd have to worry about intercepting horses.

This next segment of the hike is my favorite of the whole route because of the towering red pines that flank either side of the trail. The pines are tall and narrow, like giant skinny asparagus, but they are impressive, nonetheless. At the next intersection, take a right to continue on Red Pine Trail as it runs parallel to the park road, though you won't likely see the road through the dense understory. At the next T-intersection, take a left to cross the park road. After crossing the road, continue straight on the trail as it heads west toward the lake and then intersects with Lake Trail. You have two options at this intersection: take a right if you want to head up to the northern pet picnic and swimming area, which will add a little less than a mile to this recommended hike, or take a left to skip the northern pet picnic area.

After taking the left to head southeast along Lake Trail, you may notice signs warning of poison ivy. Be careful: watch out for the pesky plant, especially if you are stepping off the trail to let others pass. As you head southeast on Lake Trail, the views of the lake below you are mostly obstructed, but there are a couple of spots where you can get closer to the edge of the bluff and can see the lake. It is also through this section of the hike where the trail is best navigated single file and where passing others could be tricky because of the narrow trail and the potential poison ivy. As Lake Trail passes the family campgrounds, which are on the left, the right side of the trail is lined by wooden railings—to presumably prevent anyone from taking a tumble down the side of the bluff. After passing by the campgrounds and the wooden railings, you'll come to another intersection.

The intersection is where Lake Trail intersects with the other end of Red Pine Trail. The "To Beach" trail will take you to the southern pet area and includes an especially narrow segment of trail, which could be tricky for passing. Pass on the southern pet area for now and take a left to follow Lake Trail back up to the park road. After crossing the road, continue straight on the trail to the first intersection. Take a right at the first intersection to take Jack Pine Trail south parallel to the road and then east behind the ball field and back to the parking lot, completing this recommended hike.

WHILE YOU'RE IN THE AREA: You might also visit Brunet Island State Park or stop in Jim Falls for their annual Sturgeon Fest, which includes a parade and demolition derby. If you go into Chippewa Ralls, Leinenkugel's Brewery has a dog-friendly patio. If you can find it, the Chippewa Moraine State Recreation Area is another great hiking option, and the David R. Obey Ice Age Interpretive Center is hands-down my favorite interpretive center. Finally, you might stop in Cadott, Wisconsin, to take your picture at the not-exactly-but-close-enough-for-a-photo halfway point between the Equator and the North Pole.

Merrick State Park

Our first visit to Merrick State Park lasted about 15 minutes. It was the weekend right after my traumatic experience at Governor Thompson State Park, and I was having flashbacks. The grass on the trail was long, the bugs were bad, and a storm was rolling in. We bailed about a quarter of a mile into the hike and went home. I wish I could say our subsequent visits were leaps and bounds better, but I can't. On another occasion the bugs were so bad (gnats specifically) that we ended up running most of our hike to avoid the aggressive swarms. In Merrick's defense, I tend to visit this park when the Mississippi River is high, which I imagine is somewhat responsible for the thriving bug population. Also, in Merrick's defense, the Mississippi River is the most compelling feature of this park, so it's probably better suited to visitors interested in boating, canoeing, kayaking, and fishing than hiking.

Given the river's prominence in this park, it seems fitting to expand on the history of the river as a way of introducing the park. The Mississippi River wasn't originally navigable for commercial purposes, so in 1845 grain producers from five neighboring states joined together to develop a channel down the Mississippi from Minneapolis to St. Louis. The channel, with its locks and dams, turned the river into a series of 15- to 30-mile-long pools, essentially transforming it into a series of lakes, including the more well-known Lake Onalaska.

Sticking with the river theme, the park's eponym, George Byron Merrick, was a steamboat pilot and historian. He grew up on the Mississippi and wrote the book *Old Times on the Upper Mississippi: The Recollections of a Steamboat Pilot from 1854 to 1863*. He died in 1931 and when the park was established in 1932, John Latsch requested it be named after Merrick. Check out the introduction to Perrot State Park for more on Latsch.

HEADS-UP: I highly recommend waiting until after the Mississippi recedes from its spring swell to visit Merrick. When the river is high, the south and island campgrounds and the lower boat landing are often closed due to flooding. Additionally, the park road may be closed right after the upper boat landing, restricting vehicle access to the Round Shelter picnic area and the pet picnic area. While the flooding doesn't affect your hiking options much (only one short trail to two outlook points are closed when flooded), it affects the overall ambiance of the park. What I imagine to be a quaint park in normal conditions feels more like a buggy ghost town when flooded.

WORTH A MENTION: If you live in the area, Merrick State Park seems like a great option for canicross (cross-country running with your dog). The trails are wide, flat, and deserted, save for the occasional wildlife.

WATER AVAILABILITY: The only water we were able to locate was in the campgrounds.

BATHROOM AVAILABILITY: Vault toilets are available near the upper boat landing and past the Round Shelter picnic area. There is a port-a-potty in the parking lot for the Nature Center.

TRASHCAN AVAILABILITY: Technically, the trash and recycling are for registered campers only, but you have to pass the RV dump station, trash and recycling area on your way out of the park. I imagine you'd be able to dispose of your poo bags in the trash without incident, even if you aren't a registered camper.

DESIGNATED DOG SWIMMING AREA: There is no designated dog swimming area. At the time of our last visit, the park attendant informed us that there weren't many restrictions on where dogs could go, as long as the dog is always on leash and picked up after. I let Lucky wade into the water at the upper boat landing when there were no boaters using the launch. Use caution if letting your dog swim at the boat landing, be respectful of other visitors, and as always, check with staff when you visit the park in case designations have changed.

DESIGNATED DOG PICNIC AREA: At the time of our last visit, the park attendant said there was a pet picnic area, though it was not indicated on the park map. There is a sign past the Round Shelter picnic area that indicates "Pet Picnic Area," and points in the direction of the lower boat landing and south and island campgrounds. This pet picnic area is in a spot that is prone to flooding, so we have yet to be able to access it. Given the relaxed attitude toward pets in Merrick, I think you'd be fine using one of the other picnic areas, especially if the designated pet picnic area is not accessible due to flooding. We've picnicked near the Nature Center, and no one seemed to mind.

RECOMMENDED HIKE: Nature Center Loop + North Campground Loop

DISTANCE AND ELEVATION GAIN: 3 miles, 48 feet

DOG AND HUMAN FITNESS LEVEL: recreational rambler

TRAIL CONDITIONS/MATERIALS: The trail is mostly dirt and grass. The segment parallel to the water is blanketed with pine needles. There are some wooden stairs down to the water from the north campgrounds. This route is flat, and the trail is wide enough to accommodate you and your dog walking side by side. There is enough room for passing other hikers and dogs.

TRAIL MARKINGS/EASE OF NAVIGATING: The trail is well established and easy to follow. It is sparingly marked with brown posts with hiker and arrow icons. These posts are typically found at trail intersections or turns, of which there aren't many. The most confusing portion of the trail is right before reaching the north campgrounds. According to the park map at the time of our last visit, it looks like the trail stays south of the campgrounds, but we couldn't find it, so we ended up going through the campgrounds. Going through the campgrounds was beneficial because we needed to get water anyway, and we were able to find a trailhead and get back on track further into the campgrounds.

THE EXPERIENCE: This recommended hike covers 90 percent or more of the hiking trails in Merrick and is roughly two loops: one by the Nature Center and one by the North Campground. The Nature Center loop is the shorter of the two, at a little less than 1.5 miles, and the North Campground loop is the longer of the two, at a little over

1.5 miles. Do both to get in an easy 3 miles or do one or the other for a shorter hike.

Park in the lot for the Nature Center. Access to the trail is behind and to the left of the Nature Center. Take a left onto the trail and follow it southeast along the water, which is Fountain City Bay and not the Mississippi River proper. This segment of trail that runs parallel to the water is the most enjoyable of the hike. The trail is flanked on both sides by tall pines that offer shade and carpet the dirt trail with pine needles. The trail enters a clearing where there's a picnic table and park grill before arriving at the upper boat landing.

Head up to the park road and take a left, walking on the road until you see the entrance to the trail on the right. Not long after passing the vault toilets, the trail splits. Both options end up at the same place, and they are almost equidistant. We recommend staying to the right. The trail is super flat and extra wide but has plenty of shade. Next the trail crosses the road to the main park office before going back into the woods. It gets a bit grassier and undulates more throughout this section. The trail then skirts behind the RV dump station, trash and recycling. Stay on the trail until you reach another split. At this intersection, stay to the right to exit onto the road just north of the Nature Center, completing the Nature Center Loop.

To shorten the recommended hike, head to the parking lot and call it a day. Otherwise, cross the road and follow the trail through the prairie toward the Nature Center. Take a right onto the trail, which looks more like an overgrown road. Two parallel tracks of gravel with grass in between run along the edge of the woods for a moment before dipping into the woods completely and turning into an intermittent dirt-and-grass trail. As the trail gets closer to running alongside the road, a random park grill stands at attention on the right—the lone remnant of a bygone picnic area.

Then the trail arrives at a parking lot (possibly the lot for the bygone picnic area?) and traverses along the left of the concrete parking stops. At the edge of the parking lot, the trail continues for a moment before reaching the campgrounds and essentially disappearing.

According to the park map at the time of our last visit, it looks like the trail stays to the south of the campgrounds, but we couldn't find the trail once we reached the campground. If you can find it, stick with the trail. Otherwise, continue through the campgrounds, staying to the left. Eventually, there is another trailhead on the left with a sign that says "Water Access," a hiker icon, and an arrow pointing up a short set of stairs.

Follow the trail to the post with hiker icons and arrows. Straight ahead is the landing of a flight of wooden stairs that leads down to the water. Take a right at the post and continue on the trail, which cuts through the woods momentarily before reaching the prairie and a Y-intersection. This portion of the trail north of the campgrounds is a loop, so you'll end up back at this intersection either way. We suggest taking the left branch to start a clockwise loop. This portion of the trail is technically running parallel to the water, but it's too far away to be seen through the trees.

Eventually, the trail turns to the right, away from the water as it begins to loop back. The trail throughout the loop is consistently wide and flat, and the scenery is uneventful except for a random manmade tree balance beam. There's no explanation for this tree balance beam, so I can only imagine it's the training grounds for some secret ninja army or the remains of a former team-building ropes course. There's a trail diverting off the main trail that goes to the left, past and beyond the tree balance beam. Stay to the right to keep going on the loop, through the woods and eventually back out to the prairie and the Y-intersection. Take a left to backtrack past the stairs down to the water and back to the campgrounds. From here, retrace your path south through the campgrounds and along the edge of the parking lot.

Finally, keep to the right to stay alongside the water, rather than returning to the Nature Center via the segment with the lonely park grill. The most pleasant sections of this hike are the trail segments that run parallel to the water, like this segment from the random parking lot to the upper boat launch. That's why this recommended hike starts out on the southern portion of that segment and ends on the northern portion; it's our hiking version of a compliment sandwich: the beginning is nice, the middle isn't very impressive, but the ending is nice again. When you reach the next intersection, take a left to go back to the Nature Center. From there, head back to the parking lot to finish the North Campground Loop.

WHILE YOU'RE IN THE AREA: You should also visit Perrot State Park.

Mill Bluff State Park

This park is a geologists' dream. Mill Bluff contains examples of large bluffs called *mesas*, smaller more abrupt bluffs called *buttes*, and even thinner bluffs called *pinnacles*, which range in height from 80 to 200 feet. Rocks of foreign composition have been found on the sides of the mesas and buttes, which used to be islands in Glacial Lake Wisconsin. The rocks were brought from great distances encased in icebergs. In 1971, Mill Bluff was established as a unit of the Ice Age National Scientific Reserve. It's pretty cool if you're into rocks.

If you're not into rocks, you may be less impressed with this park. With over two whole miles of hiking, it's not so much a destination park as it is a good place to stop and stretch your legs along I-90. Dogs are allowed on two of the three trails, so you have your pick: up a strenuous flight of 223 stone stairs from the 1930s to a view of I-90 and Camels Bluff in the distance or along a flat and grassy loop trail through an unremarkable and potentially buggy prairie and forest. Even if you do both trails, this visit will take you a couple of hours, tops, and leave you with plenty of time and energy to check out one of the other state parks nearby.

HEADS-UP: As you approach the park on Funnel Road, the most visible components are the pond, beach, and picnic shelter on the west side of Funnel Road. The main entrance to the park is less visible and on the east side of Funnel Road.

WATER AVAILABILITY: Water is available by each picnic shelter. One shelter is by the beach and the other is just past the park's main entrance, on the other side of Funnel Road from the beach.

BATHROOM AVAILABILITY: Vault toilets are available near the picnic shelters on either side of Funnel Road. One is by the beach and the other is just past the park's main entrance.

TRASHCAN AVAILABILITY: No trashcans on site; plan on carry-in/carry-out.

DESIGNATED DOG SWIMMING AREA: At the time of our last visit, there was no designated pet swim area. Check with park staff when you visit in case designations have changed.

DESIGNATED DOG PICNIC AREA: At the time of our last visit, there was no designated pet picnic area. Check with park staff when you visit in case designations have changed.

RECOMMENDED HIKE: Mill Bluff Summit

DISTANCE AND ELEVATION GAIN: 0.8 miles, 252 feet

DOG AND HUMAN FITNESS LEVEL: recreational rambler/weekend warrior

TRAIL CONDITIONS/MATERIALS: The trail from the parking lot to the base of the stairs is a wide and mostly dirt trail. You can easily walk side by side and pass others without having to step off the trail. The flight of 223 stone stairs was originally constructed in the 1930s, so it's in as good a shape as you can expect. The stairs are evenly spaced, and a pipe handrail runs along the left side, offering hikers additional stability and support. The trail up the stairs is narrow and best navigated single file. Passing here could be difficult, as the area alongside the stairs is steep. As a reminder, downhill traffic is supposed to yield to uphill traffic, but we recommend visitors with dogs always yield to visitors without dogs, no matter which direction you're going. Thankfully, there are occasional landings where you could pull off with your dog to let others go by. The trail on the top of the bluff is a combination of stone and dirt. It is wide except for when the trail splits into two narrow paths on either side of a stand of pines.

TRAIL MARKINGS/EASE OF NAVIGATING: The trail to Mill Bluff Summit is well established and easy to follow.

THE EXPERIENCE: When you turn off US-12 onto Funnel Road, the first visible sign of the park is the pond on the left. But take a quick right into the main entrance of the park and find a parking spot across from the picnic shelter. The trailhead is behind and slightly to the west of the picnic shelter.

The approach to the stairs up Mill Bluff is flat and wide. There's a bench at the base of the stairs, and from there, the path is unmistakable—up. At the top, take a left to check out the views from the observation deck. Turning around and walking past the stairs along the top of the bluff brings to you to its southern end. A sign says you should be able to see Volk Field from here, but the view mostly consists of trees and chain-link fence. After spending some time on top of the bluff, head back down the stairs. At the bottom of the stairs, take a left to backtrack on the trail to the main entrance and picnic shelter.

WHILE YOU'RE IN THE AREA: Since there's not a lot of hiking at Mill Bluff State Park, we recommend trying to visit another state park while you are in this area. Some of our favorites in the vicinity are Rocky Arbor, Natural Bridge, and Mirror Lake state parks. And if you must, Devil's Lake State Park is also nearby.

Perrot State Park

The real story behind Perrot State Park has very little to do with its eponym, Nicholas Perrot, a famous French trapper and fur trader, and everything to do with the less-famous John Latsch. Latsch owned a grocery store in Winona, Minnesota, in the early 1900s and would often jump in his canoe and head down the Mississippi to escape the stress of daily life. One day he was out in his canoe when a storm rolled in. Latsch pulled up his canoe at a landing and hunkered down to wait out the weather, but the landowner descended on him with his dog and gun and forced Latsch back out onto the river in the storm.

After getting back to Winona and drying off, Latsch vowed to make the banks of the Mississippi safe harbor for stranded canoeists. He started out his legacy of conservation by buying the parcel of land he had been kicked off of that fateful day. But he didn't stop there. Latsch purchased more than 18,000 acres, which, when he died in 1934, were valued at two million dollars. He was generous enough to donate some of that land to his neighbor state of Wisconsin for Perrot and Merrick state parks, and it was Latsch who modestly insisted on naming the park after Perrot. It's unfortunate Latsch was treated so inhospitably, but he made lemonade out of those lemons—lemonade we get to enjoy decades later and for decades to come.

HEADS-UP: Dogs are not allowed on the Black Walnut Nature Trail. Since black walnuts and the wood and shells of black walnut trees can be poisonous to dogs, we're ok sitting that trail out.

Perrot State Park

HEADS-UP: In spring and early summer when the Mississippi River tends to be high, sections of Riverview Trail may be closed and/or especially soggy.

WATER AVAILABILITY: Water is available at the main entrance to the park, where there is a spigot for filling bottles and even a dog water fountain. Additional water fountains/spigots are available throughout the park at the picnic areas.

BATHROOM AVAILABILITY: Flush toilets are available in the park office. Vault toilets are available at the picnic areas.

TRASHCAN AVAILABILITY: No trashcans on site; plan on carry-in/carry-out.

DESIGNATED DOG SWIMMING AREA: At the time of our last visit, there was no designated pet swimming area, but I've let Lucky take a dip at the boat launch as long as no one else was there. Use caution if letting your dog swim at the boat launch and be respectful of other visitors. As always, check with park staff when you visit in case designations have changed.

DESIGNATED DOG PICNIC AREA: At the time of our last visit, there was no designated pet picnic area. We've seen people picnicking with their pups at both East Brady's and West Brady's picnic areas. Check with park staff when you visit in case designations have changed.

RECOMMENDED HIKE: Brady's Bluff Loop (going up Brady's Bluff West and coming down Brady's Bluff East, taking Riverview back to Brady's Bluff West)

HEADS-UP: Going up Brady's Bluff West is a steep and challenging climb, but in my opinion, I'd prefer to go up the steeper side (west) and down the more gradual descent (east). Also, the view of the Mississippi River from Brady's Bluff East is amazing and easier to look at while going down this trail than up it. If you'd rather do a more gradual climb up and a steeper descent, do the recommended hike in reverse.

DISTANCE AND ELEVATION GAIN: 2.7 miles, 833 feet

DOG AND HUMAN FITNESS LEVEL: avid adventurer

TRAIL CONDITIONS/MATERIALS: Brady's Bluff West is a combination of grass, dirt, gravel, and stairs made of stone and wood. The sections of stone stairs are original to the 1930s and the wooden stairs are from 1995, so you'll notice a difference in the stairs' conditions. The stone stairs, while still solid, are more irregular and require more attention to foot placement. Brady's Bluff West is super narrow in places, especially toward the top of the trail where you and your dog have to squeeze between a wooden handrail and the side of the bluff on some irregular and winding 1930s stone stairs. This section could be difficult for an unsure dog and/or owner. There are some sections where passing is possible and other places where passing is impossible. If the trail is busy, be prepared to take a break on one of the many landings while you wait for others to pass. These are great opportunities to catch your breath and drink some water.

Brady's Bluff East is mostly a narrow dirt trail that switchbacks down the side of the bluff. There are some stone stairs. Riverview Trail is also a dirt and grass trail of variable widths with some wooden stairs and a wooden footbridge. Passing on these trails is possible but should be done carefully. We recommend walking single file on all trails.

TRAIL MARKINGS/EASE OF NAVIGATING: These trails are well established and easy to follow. The successive flights of stairs up Brady's Bluff West offer a defined route for you to follow. Intersections are marked with posts and brown signs indicating which trails go in which directions. There are also trail maps at some intersections, in addition to the trail marker signs.

THE EXPERIENCE: The trailhead for Brady's Bluff West is just across the street from the parking lot above the boat landing. This trail is the shortest way to get to the top of Brady's Bluff, reaching the peak in a smidge over 0.5 miles of hiking, so it's pretty much all climbing. A few stairs start you off, giving you a small preview of what's to come. The trail alternates between a narrow flat dirt track and irregular stone stairs, and then the sections between sets of stairs get shorter and shorter and the stone stairs start getting more and more irregular. In one longer and more intense stretch of these stairs, the trail on either side of the narrow staircase has been widened by wear, and short wooden retaining walls have been added to prevent further erosion.

Then modern engineering offers a section of wood and gravel stairs that are wide, gradual, and a welcome change of pace at this point in the hike. This section transitions to a more traditional wooden staircase, and then a gravel path takes you along a scenic outlook. Here you can take a break on a bench and look out past a wooden guard railing at Trempealeau Bay.

Next, the trail alternates between stone stairs and flights of wooden stairs. Closer to the top of the bluff, the stairs are built into the side of the cliff face. Now, the stairs have hand railings for both physical assistance and safety. The final stretches of stone stairs are winding and squeeze between the side of the bluff and a wooden handrail. When you break above the tree line, you'll find yourself in a goat prairie (a dry type of prairie found mainly on south-southwest-facing slopes that get a lot of winter sun in the Upper Mississippi Valley in the Driftless Area) where a bench offers a spot to rest and read about the geology of Perrot State Park. There isn't much shade here, however, and with the peak of the bluff in sight, power through on the dirt trail to the shelter, where you'll be rewarded with shade and the best views in the park.

The first time Lucky and I summited Brady's Bluff, it was 90 degrees and humid to boot. When we made it to the shelter, we both flopped down and Lucky actually looked tired. After catching our breath and drinking some water, I peeked out of the shelter and was taken aback by the sprawling view of Trempealeau Mountain, the Trempealeau Bay, and the Mississippi River. As I took in the view, I shifted my focus from the landscape in the distance to the sky nearby and saw numerous hawks taking to the air. I pondered whether Lucky could appreciate what we were seeing. Does he feel any wonder at the view? Any sense of accomplishment for summiting this bluff? On that day (like many others), he looked at me with his typical "what's next?" face.

At the top of the bluff, pick up Brady's Bluff East just to the right of the shelter if you're looking at it. The trail is narrow, and the initial length along the side of the ridge gets rockier and steeper until it turns into an actual rock staircase. Wooden railings help you stay on course as the trail turns to switch back along the ridge. From this point forward, the rest of the descent is more gradual, with one more switchback before the trail leads into the woods. The trail is a bit wider throughout this section, though we still recommend walking single file. A small rock outcropping along the edge of the trail makes a nice spot to take a rest and a few photos before continuing down the trail. The trail once again enters the woods and remains under the tree canopy until reaching the park road.

A wooden footbridge and then some stone stairs lead to a trail intersection of Brady's Bluff East and Perrot Ridge Trail. Stay to the right to continue on Brady's Bluff East, which eventually ends at the park road. To get back to West Brady's parking lot cross the park road and go through East Brady's picnic area to the trailhead for Riverview Trail/Perrot Ridge Trail. This segment of trail strangely vacillates between being a single-file footpath and a double-rutted overgrown road. At the first intersection, take a right on Riverview Trail to head back toward Brady's West.

Riverview Trail is mostly dirt and grass, and relatively wide throughout this first section. It narrows a bit before reaching a flight of wooden stairs and narrows further after the stairs. Now, the water and railroad tracks are more visible through the trees as the trail weaves through the woods and up a slight incline. Then the trail narrows even more; actually, the dirt path may be the same width, but an overgrowth of understory closes in on both sides. Thankfully, this section is short; eventually, the overgrown understory retreats, and the trail returns to a narrow dirt path for another stretch above and along the water and railroad tracks.

Next, the trail heads further inland, and as it does so, it widens and gets grassier. After the trail transitions back to mostly dirt, a couple wooden stairs take you part of the way down toward the water and railroad tracks. A bit further, a few more wooden stairs take you the rest of the way down to the water, which at this point is no longer the actual Mississippi River but a small stagnant pond of Mississippi River water. You'll cross a short wooden footbridge, and then the trail continues along the stagnant pond water's edge. Parts of this segment may be especially muddy and soggy, depending on the time of year and river and weather conditions.

After the Mississippi River pond segment, the trail widens again and continues through the woods until it reaches the intersection of the Mississippi and Trempealeau rivers. You can see the Trempealeau through the trees, and a short social path on the left takes you out to the water's edge where you can sit on a concrete column and watch the train and boats go by. Back on the trail, you'll now be walking alongside the Trempealeau River, heading north. There may be a soggy section or two, again depending on the river and weather conditions. A flight of wooden stairs leads up to the park road, and the trail continues on the left side of the guardrail. Once you're past the guardrail, the trail becomes less defined as it cuts through a grassy clearing and then the parking lot for the boat launch. Stay to the left through the clearing and parking lot and stop for a dip in the water if no one's using the boat launch before heading up the hill through the picnic area to West Brady's parking lot to complete the hike.

WORTH A MENTION: Riverview Trail is a nice recreational rambler option if you're looking for something with little to no elevation gain. It hugs the edge of Trempealeau Bay and continues along the edge of the Mississippi River, offering occasional views of both. As you go along this trail, alternate between taking in views of the water and keeping an eye out for aquatic creatures like frogs, toads, turtles, and yes, snakes! With only short offshoots that connect to the parking lots along the main road, this trail is easy to navigate. Riverview Trail is mostly grass and dirt with a couple short sections of gravel and sand. This trail is mostly flat, with a few wooden stairs, and it's mostly narrow, making walking single file the best option.

WORTH A MENTION: If you're looking for something even more challenging than Brady's Bluff West, check out Perrot Ridge Trail. I think this route is more challenging because it has less engineering to help you out on the climb up to the ridge. At the trailhead, a sign says "Natural Terrain Trail. Difficult at times. Steep and irregular grades," and the trail is exactly that, especially when starting at East Brady's parking lot and doing the trail clockwise. There are even times when you have to scramble (use your hands to assist you on your climb). And for all the work, the views from Perrot Ridge aren't as impressive as those from Brady's Bluff.

WHILE YOU'RE IN THE AREA: You should also visit Merrick State Park. "Should" is probably too strong a suggestion; Merrick is close by, but the hiking at Perrot is preferable. If you didn't go to Merrick, you wouldn't really be missing out on anything. Just saying.

Rib Mountain State Park

Many of Wisconsin's "mountains" started out as hills and were then renamed to, I suppose, better capture their magnitude relative to their surroundings. Rib Mountain is among Wisconsin's more impressive hills; it's the fourth highest point in Wisconsin—behind first-place Timm's Hill by only 28 feet. For some context, Timm's Hill rises 1,951 feet above sea level. Mt. Elbert, the highest peak in Colorado, tops out at 14,440 feet and Mount Whitney, the tallest mountain in California and in all the contiguous United States, reaches 14,505 feet. So, it seems appropriate that Timm's Hill would retain its hill designation and it seems aspirational to call Rib Mountain a mountain. Though, characteristic of a mountain, the north side of Rib Mountain is lined with ski lifts and runs that are part of the Granite Peak Ski Area. The first skiing competition was held on Rib Mountain in 1938. Also, many members of the 10th Mountain Alpine Division, which served in the Italian Alps during World War II, were from the Wausau area and learned to ski at Rib Mountain. So that's cool.

The other distinct feature of Rib Mountain is that it's made of quartzite, a very hard metamorphic rock that, in many places, erupts from the ground at all angles. And as you might expect, where there's quartzite, there's a quarry. The quarry is worth a look, especially to read the messages spelled out at the bottom in rocks and tree limbs. It's as if survivors of a shipwreck constructed giant SOS messages, but instead spelled out "Boys Suck" and "Send Dudes." These were some very conflicted castaways.

Rib Mountain State Park

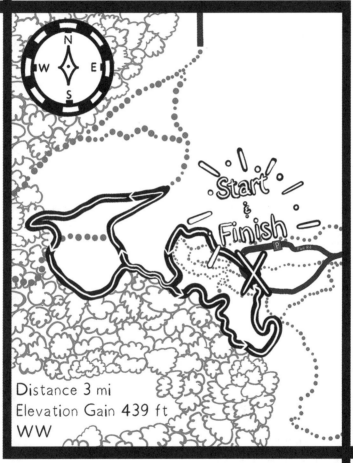

Start & Finish

Park Rd

Distance 3 mi
Elevation Gain 439 ft
WW

HEADS-UP: The south side of the mountain is more adventurous and steeper; it's where you can find the most physically demanding trails in the park. On the north side of the mountain, the trails are relatively flat; it's where you can get in some mileage without a lot of labored breathing. If you want a bigger challenge than the recommended hike, check out the Yellow Trail, which offers several route options and more climbing.

WORTH A MENTION: Quarry Trail is a bit of a misnomer. This trail doesn't go around the quarry or offer any views of the quarry. You should hike Turkey Vulture Trail or the Homestead Loop trail if you'd like to see the quarry.

WATER AVAILABILITY: Water is available at the park office. Additionally, there's a concession stand open late spring, summer, and early fall.

BATHROOM AVAILABILITY: A flush toilet is available at the park office. Vault toilets are available at the lower picnic area by the amphitheater and by the trailhead for the Blue Trail.

TRASHCAN AVAILABILITY: There's a dumpster by the concession stand.

DESIGNATED DOG SWIMMING AREA: None, as there are no bodies of water at this park.

DESIGNATED DOG PICNIC AREA: At the time of our last visit, there was no designated pet picnic area. The attendant on duty seemed surprised when I inquired about one. He told us we could use any of the picnic areas if Lucky was on leash. He also recommended we take our lunch with us on our hike and do a little picnic overlooking the quarry. This was an excellent recommendation we're happy to pass along. As always, check with park staff when you visit in case designations have changed.

RECOMMENDED HIKE: Red Trail + Quarry Trail + Homestead Loop Trail + Quarry Trail + Red Trail

DISTANCE AND ELEVATION GAIN: 3 miles, 439 feet

DOG AND HUMAN FITNESS LEVEL: weekend warrior

TRAIL CONDITIONS/MATERIALS: The Red Trail is a narrow dirt trail with quartzite protruding from the ground regularly and haphazardly. When my sister and I visited Rib Mountain together, I was happy she had just purchased and was wearing a thicker-soled hiking shoe that offered more protection from the rocky terrain. The southern section on the Red Trail is more challenging and better suited for the sure of foot. The Red Trail is also very narrow and best navigated single file. Passing other hikers and dogs may be difficult in some sections. The Quarry and Homestead Loop trails are both wide dirt trails with fewer quartzite protrusions to navigate. Passing others on these trails is much easier. Though this route does include some elevation gain, the climbs are mostly gradual, and the frequent benches are a nice opportunity to stop and take a rest if needed.

TRAIL MARKINGS/EASE OF NAVIGATING: Less than a quarter of a mile into our hike on the Red Trail my sister started laughing. Curious, I asked what was up, and she explained, "I always hear about these people who go out for a hike and get lost in the woods, and I always wondered how that's possible. How hard can it be to follow a trail? But I keep looking up and wondering 'Is this the trail? or is that the trail?' and now I understand how people get lost!" Thankfully, despite a few moments of uncertainty, the trails at Rib Mountain are marked well enough that we made it from the Red Trail to the Quarry Trail without becoming a cautionary tale.

The Red Trail markers are metal posts with a red tag at the top, and the trail markers are frequent enough that you can usually see one up ahead of you if you look hard enough. The Quarry Trail and Homestead Loop trails are well established and easy to follow. Both trails are well marked with frequent metal posts with a tag with the trail name on it. At the time of my last visit, the DNR map thoroughly and accurately depicted the location of every bench along the trails, so the benches are useful landmarks for tracking progress along a trail.

THE EXPERIENCE: Park at the concession stand lot and pick up the north section of the Red Trail from there. The trail proper begins after crossing the park road, where it skirts along the edge of the ridge and offers views of the ski runs and the city of Wausau. The Red Trail's narrow and rocky conditions are best navigated single file, but the area on either side of the trail is open enough to allow for stepping aside so others can pass. At the first bench, stay to the right to continue on the Red Trail. The trail meanders through the forest passing by occasional rock outcroppings, and then, about a half-mile into this hike, it reaches the intersection with Quarry Trail. If you'd like to do a shorter hike, continue straight and complete the rest of the Red Trail. Otherwise, take the right onto Quarry Trail.

After taking the right onto Quarry Trail, you may notice the trail is a bit wider than the Red Trail and there are fewer rocks protruding out of the trail at odd angles. After a short distance, the trail reaches another intersection where this short connection segment reaches the loop portion of Quarry Trail. Take the right branch to head northwest/counterclockwise on the Quarry Trail loop. You won't see the quarry along this stretch of the trail (or anywhere on Quarry Trail for that matter), but don't worry, you'll get an up-close and personal view a bit further into the hike. For now, the trail meanders through the woods with just enough variability in trail conditions and scenery to keep things interesting. Then, Quarry Trail comes to a bench at the intersection with the Homestead Loop Trail. At this intersection, take a right to start a counterclockwise route on the loop portion of Homestead. Though this takes you northeast and away from the quarry for a bit, it's an enjoyable way to tack on a little more mileage and time in the woods. At the next intersection and bench the loop portion of Homestead meets the stick portion of Homestead. Take a left to continue heading counterclockwise on Homestead loop. This segment begins a gradual climb up to the rim of the quarry.

The trail brings you to what could be deemed an overlook. From here, you're able to get up close and personal with the quarry to the extent you're interested. The quarry makes an excellent rest stop: it's about halfway through this recommended hike and is a cool spot to hang out, eat a snack, drink water, and read the messages spelled out in rocks below while hawks cruise by overhead. After taking in the views and fueling up, stay on the Homestead Loop Trail for a quick second as it turns away from the quarry. The trail heads back into the woods where it meets up with Quarry Trail and a segment of Turkey Vulture Trail. Take a right at this intersection to head counterclockwise on the loop portion of Quarry Trail, which coincides with the Vulture

Trail for a quick second. No sooner do these trails overlap than they part ways. Follow the trail marker and take the left, which keeps you on the loop portion of Quarry Trail. Next, you'll reach the intersection where the loop portion of Quarry Trail started. Take a right to backtrack along the connector segment of Quarry Trail to the T-intersection with the Red Trail. Next, take a right to head south to complete the Red Trail loop.

The southern section of the Red Trail is more technical and challenging than the northern portion, but it's solidly in the weekend warrior category. The trail is again narrow with frequent rock protrusions, so walking single file is recommended. Additionally, there are a few narrow and rocky areas that are a bit awkward for Lucky to navigate with his backpack. Passing on this section of trail can be challenging, especially along the segment that traverses the edge of the cliff. During one of our visits, we had to scramble up the rock outcroppings to let a family with children pass on the trail, which had us both channeling our inner mountain goats. Despite mild huffing and puffing, this section of the Red Trail goes by quickly and offers some nice views of the southern side of Rib Mountain. If you start out on this more challenging section of the Red Trail and then decide it's not for you, the Blue Trail offers an "out," cutting off the final 0.4 miles of the Red Trail and taking you past the South Observation Deck and Sliding Rock. Continuing on the Red Trail, you'll descend to a low point of 1,670 feet before turning to climb back up the side of the mountain. As it climbs, Red Trail meets up with the Lower West Yellow Trail, and the two run concurrently for a moment. Continue straight up, and then, at the next Y-intersection where the two trails part ways, take the left branch to stay on the Red Trail. The Red Trail dips back south for a moment before turning north for the final push up to the CCC Gazebo. After passing the gazebo, the trail arrives at the park road. At the road, take a left and head back to the concession stand parking lot to complete this recommended hike.

Roche-A-Cri State Park

Even though one of the main attractions at Roche-A-Cri State Park, the Roche-A-Cri Mound, is off limits to dogs, this park was still worth a daytrip. About 15,000 years ago, the mound was an island in Glacial Lake Wisconsin. Today it reaches more than 300 feet above the now dry lakebed around it. Made of Cambrian sandstone, the mound is long and narrow, with a flat top and craggy cliff sides. The mound and the woods that surround it are both state natural areas (SNAs). Areas are given this designation for several reasons, including having an outstanding natural community, being a critical habitat for rare species, being an ecological benchmark area, having a significant geological or archaeological feature, or being an exceptional site for research and education. Roche-A-Cri checks off a few of these categories.

Most obvious, Roche-A-Cri Mound is a significant geological feature, but less obvious is the significant archaeological feature at the base of the mound. Petroglyphs and pictographs that date back to around 900 AD and 1500 AD respectively depict ancient messages. Archaeologists can only guess as to their meaning, but interpretive signs offer their speculations, and assistance for locating the marks on the stone. Unfortunately, between centuries of natural weathering and contemporary vandalism, the petroglyphs and pictographs are difficult to detect, and in time they may disappear altogether.

The forest surrounding the mound earned the SNA designation for its outstanding natural community. The old-growth pine and oak forest with its vibrant shrub layer and ground layer consisting of more than 220 species of plants dominates the SNA, but other minor natural communities are part of the designated area as well, including dry sand prairie and oak barrens. Much like Buckhorn State Natural Area in Buckhorn State Park, the land in this region used to be dominated by prairie and oak savannas. Restoration efforts have been underway to restore these native communities, which can be observed best via Turkey Vulture Trail.

WORTH A MENTION: Roche-A-Cri is a great option for winter hiking/snowshoeing with your pup as the trails aren't groomed for cross-country skiing.

HEADS-UP: While the park is open year-round, the main entrance is closed in the winter. If you visit during the winter, park in the lot on the north side of Czech Avenue, west of State Highway 13.

WATER AVAILABILITY: Water is available at the park office and at the picnic area by the Roche-A-Cri Mound.

BATHROOM AVAILABILITY: Vault toilets are available at the park office and at the picnic area by the Roche-A-Cri Mound.

TRASHCAN AVAILABILITY: No trashcans on site; plan on carry-in/carry-out.

DESIGNATED DOG SWIMMING AREA: None, as there are no bodies of water at this park.

DESIGNATED DOG PICNIC AREA: At the time of our last visit, there was no designated pet picnic area. As always, check with park staff when you visit in case designations have changed.

RECOMMENDED HIKE: Mound Trail + Acorn Trail

DISTANCE AND ELEVATION GAIN: 3.8 miles, 72 feet

DOG AND HUMAN FITNESS LEVEL: recreational rambler/weekend warrior

TRAIL CONDITIONS/MATERIALS: The trails are predominantly dirt and grass. The platform for viewing the petroglyphs is wooden, and there is a gradual flight of wooden stairs down from the platform to the park road. This route crosses the paved park road twice. The width of Acorn Trail varies. For the most part it is wide enough for walking side by side, but there are narrower sections, especially as you approach the petroglyphs. Passing others along the trail is possible but may require stepping off the trail, especially in the narrower segments. The trail is very flat with a few undulations that barely register as changes in the terrain.

TRAIL MARKINGS/EASE OF NAVIGATING: The trails are well established and easy to follow. There are frequent posts with hiker icons along the trail to keep you assuredly on the correct course. Wooden signs indicate trails/directions, and there are posts with trail maps at intersections; however, at the time of our last visit, the maps weren't all legible and some of the "You Are Here" dots were missing. Even without the dots, it is possible to determine where you were on the map given the size of the park and landmarks. Additionally, areas where dogs are not allowed are thoroughly marked with signs.

THE EXPERIENCE: Park in the lot by the main picnic area and access to the Roche-A-Cri mound observation deck. While dogs aren't allowed up the mound, if you're with a group you might start by taking turns climbing Top of the Rock Trail to check out the view. Otherwise, skip the mound and just get started hiking. The trailhead for the recommended hike is on the west side of the park road. Follow the paved path past the water fountain to the trail. This wee portion of Mound Trail dead-ends at Acorn Trail. When you reach the intersection, Mound Trail ends, and Acorn Trail is to the left and right. Take a right onto Acorn Trail, beginning a clockwise loop. For the next mile and a half, the trail is well established and easy to follow as it meanders through the woods. It's wide enough for hiking side by side, and there's room enough for passing others without having to depart the trail.

At the next intersection, Acorn Trail connects to Chickadee Rock Nature Trail. While both branches ultimately lead back to the eastern end of Mound Trail, we recommend taking the left branch and continuing on Acorn Trail. After a bit, the trail emerges from the woods and crosses over the park road. After this, Acorn Trail continues to head south toward the petroglyphs. On the way to the petroglyphs there are two three-way intersections: first where Mound Trail connects to Acorn and second where a short trail connects Acorn to the campgrounds. In both cases, continue straight to stay on Acorn Trail. The next intersection you encounter is with the service road. There's a sign that points to the right and says, "To Petroglyph." There's also a sign reminding visitors to stay on the designated trail in this portion of the park, which is a state natural area. While it's always best to stay on designated trails, it's even more important in state natural areas like this one.

Acorn Trail brings you to the eastern side of the parking lot near the petroglyphs. Take the wooden ramp up to the platform to view the petroglyphs and pictographs. Once you're ready to continue with the recommended hike, take the wooden stairs that lead back down from the platform. Cross the park road and pick Acorn Trail back up on the other side. Just ahead is Carter Creek. There's a nice spot to stop along the creek and enjoy the view and then there's a three-way intersection where Acorn Trail connects to Spring Peeper Trail. Stay to the right to continue the clockwise loop on Acorn Trail. Just after this intersection is another with Turkey Vulture Trail. If you'd like to extend your hike and get in a bit more mileage, take the left onto Turkey Vulture Trail. While the name gives you no indication, this trail has some real ambiance as it crosses and then meanders near Carter Creek before entering the prairie. To complete the hike without adding on Turkey Vulture Trail, continue straight on Acorn Trail through woods to complete the loop. You'll end up back at the intersection with the western end of Mound Trail. Take a right onto Mound Trail, and you'll quickly be back at the parking lot.

Wildcat Mountain State Park

The story of how Wildcat Mountain got its name is much like the tall tale of a fisherman's epic catch. In the 1800s, a bobcat was menacing local farmers' sheep. Not wanting to lose any more of their livestock, the farmers formed a hunting party. They tracked down the bobcat and shot and killed it near what is now the park's main overlook. The farmers commemorated the spot as Wildcat Hill, but over the course of time and recounts of the story, the bobcat remained a bobcat and the hill grew into a mountain. Now, Wildcat is one of a handful of "mountains" in Wisconsin, despite being the 122nd highest point in the state.

Wildcat Mountain overlooks the Kickapoo River, one of the most popular destinations for canoers and kayakers in Wisconsin. Kickapoo means "that which goes here, then there" in Algonquin and describes the meandering course of the river, which was used by early Native Americans to travel between their permanent homes and temporary hunting camps. Because it was so heavily trafficked, the Native Americans also referred to the Kickapoo as the "river of canoes." Eventually, the Native Americans and their canoes were replaced by fleets of lumber rafts as Europeans arrived and logged the white pines and hardwoods until they were almost completely gone.

The logging industry had many effects on the landscape of Wisconsin beyond the most obvious. Due to the severe deforestation of the area, water levels in the Kickapoo decreased. It's estimated the Kickapoo used to have 15 times as much water in 1845 as it does now. The loss of trees was the beginning of a chain reaction: once the trees were cleared, erosion accelerated, especially as farmers moved in and started plowing the cleared land. Without the trees, the drainage patterns of the springs feeding the river changed, causing the springs to dry up. Now we're left to imagine what the Kickapoo might have been like in its unadulterated state, as the Native Americans once knew it.

On that solemn note, I'd like to share one lighter piece of Wisconsin history I dug up while reading up on Wildcat Mountain. Wildcat Mountain State Park was once the location of a ginseng operation. Ginseng was plentiful in the woods, and Wisconsin developed quite the reputation as a ginseng producer. Vernon County was, at one point, the largest producer of ginseng in America. The ginseng was exported to China, where they believed the more the root looked like the human form, the more effective it would be at curing disease and prolonging life. Wisconsin still plays a major role in the ginseng industry, but now 95 percent of US ginseng comes from Marathon County, about two hours north/northwest of Wildcat Mountain State Park.

WORTH A MENTION: If you're in the area in the winter, hike the Ice Cave Trail to see its eponym. The trail to the Ice Cave is not in the main section of the park. Driving from the park office, take a left onto Highway 33 and then a right onto County Highway F. The parking lot for Ice Cave Trail is on the right, just before the bridge over Billings Creek. Take the short, easy walk along Billings Creek to the end of the trail where a small spring flows over a depression in the sandstone rock. In the winter, this spring turns into a giant icefall. The icefall at its largest can reach 20 feet high and 10 feet thick and may even appear to be blue because the thick ice acts as a filter, absorbing red light.

HEADS-UP: Wildcat Mountain has more than 20 miles of trails, but most of those miles are horse trails. Hiking is permitted on horse trails, but because Lucky is reactive, I typically avoid potential horse encounters. Additionally, the Hemlock Nature Trail is off limits to dogs, which means if you want to climb Mount Pisgah, you'll have to leave your dog at home. This leaves visitors with dogs one legit hiking option and two meanders. Old Settler's Trail is a little more than two miles long, while Observation Point Trail and Ice Cave Trail are barely-long-enough-to-be-called-a-trail trails. Observation Point and Ice Cave trails are recreational rambler trails and are appropriate for dogs of all sizes.

WATER AVAILABILITY: Water is available at the park office, near the upper and lower picnic shelters, and by the front door of the maintenance shop when the office is closed.

BATHROOM AVAILABILITY: Flush toilets are available at the park office. Vault toilets are available near the upper and lower picnic shelters and near the trailhead for Ice Cave Trail.

TRASHCAN AVAILABILITY: No trashcans on site; plan on carry-in/carry-out.

DESIGNATED DOG SWIMMING AREA: At the time of our last visit, there was no designated pet swim area. Check with park staff when you visit in case designations have changed.

DESIGNATED DOG PICNIC AREA: At the time of our last visit, there was no designated pet picnic area. Check with park staff when you visit in case designations have changed.

RECOMMENDED HIKE: Old Settler's Trail

HEADS-UP: Old Settler's Trail is not for the faint of heart, but it's fun and the only horse-free option for getting in some mileage with your dog at this state park. You'll likely work up a sweat on this moderately challenging hike. In general, I would not recommend this trail in inclement weather or for dogs or humans that aren't sure of foot. And when passing other groups along the narrow and technical segments of the trail, use caution, as stepping off the side of the trail could be dangerous.

DISTANCE AND ELEVATION GAIN: 2.5 miles, 554 feet

DOG AND HUMAN FITNESS LEVEL: weekend warrior/avid adventurer

TRAIL CONDITIONS/MATERIALS: Old Settler's Trail is mostly dirt, some exposed rock, and lots of tree litter. There are flights of wooden stairs, some of which are steep. There's crushed limestone between the stairs coming down from the picnic area. Additionally, there are a couple of wooden footbridges along this route. The trail is narrow and best navigated single file. In some areas, passing others would be especially difficult because stepping off the trail could be dangerous. This is especially true of the segment of Old Settler's Trail immediately north of Taylor Hollow Overlook. While flat and easygoing at times, there are stretches of moderate climbing along this trail.

TRAIL MARKINGS/EASE OF NAVIGATING: Old Settler's Trail is well established and easy to follow. The trail doesn't intersect with any other named hiking trails, but it does intersect with a short connector trail that leads to the amphitheater. This intersection is marked with a wooden sign indicating the trail name and direction, and there's also a trail map attached to the post. There are infrequent hiker icons on posts marking the trail, but the lack of additional signs or icons along the trail isn't problematic as the trail is well worn and there aren't many social trails to potentially confuse you.

THE EXPERIENCE: Park at the Upper Picnic Area parking lot and walk north toward the picnic shelter. The trailhead is just past and to the right of the picnic shelter. You'll hike this segment of the trail twice, on your way out and on the way back, but it's much more enjoyable on the way out. The trail descends a moderately graded staircase. To call it a staircase might be generous—it's irregularly spaced wooden stairs and no handrails. Once you reach the bottom of the stairs and set out on the trail proper, it becomes clear that you are traversing the side of a very steep hill on a narrow trail. For most of the first half-mile or so, stepping off the trail to let others pass could be potentially dangerous, as the ground on either side of the trail is at a steep angle.

Where the stick portion of Old Settler's Trail meets the loop portion, take a right to complete the loop counterclockwise. Next the trail crosses a wooden bridge spanning a gulch, and then it meanders through forest and past rock outcroppings. During this stretch of Old Settler's Trail, it would be easier to pass others; while the trail is still narrow, you're at least on more level ground. Then, at the edge of a sizable pine plantation, the trail meets the short connector trail that leads to the amphitheater. Take a left to stay on Old Settler's Trail and experience one of our favorite segments of this hike.

The pines here were obviously planted. Their uniform parallel rows defy nature but create a stunning effect and make for some pretty cool photos too. After crossing through the pine plantation, the trail reaches Taylor Hollow Overlook. The overlook is a bit overgrown.

Trees obscure much of the view, but there's a bench for taking a break and having a snack. Unlike other trails in other parks, there aren't many places along this trail where I would stop for a snack. So, if you want to snack, Lucky and I recommend you do it here or wait until after your hike.

From the Taylor Hollow Outlook, the narrow trail begins its descent initially by turning away from the outlook for a few feet and then sharply switching back to a harrowing flight of stairs that runs along the side of the rock outcropping. This section of the trail is very narrow and features an especially steep slope on the right-hand side of the trail. The last time we hiked this trail we didn't encounter another soul until this stretch, which is of course the worst place to pass on this route. If necessary, you can scramble up the hillside to the rock outcropping on the left to let others pass but do so with extreme caution. The soil on the hillside is soft and sandy, and when we executed this move to let the mother-child duo pass us, it was difficult to get traction and establish reliable footing. Some treats paid the price and fell out of my training pouch when I lost my footing. Lucky, extremely committed to "leave no trace," wanted to go to their rescue, but we had to abandon them for safety reasons.

After reaching the bottom of the harrowing stairs, the remainder of the trail is much less technical and continues through both hardwood and pine forests. The trail remains narrow, but at least it's possible to step off the trail onto level ground in this section in order to let others pass. There's another surreal section through parallel pines and another smaller wooden footbridge over a stream before the trail reaches the end of the loop. Back at the intersection where the loop of Old Settler's Trail connects to the stick, take the right to head back up the flight of wooden stairs to the picnic shelter and parking lot.

Willow River State Park

If you live in the west-central or northern regions of Wisconsin, you may have heard of and even visited Willow River State Park. But, coming from the southeastern side of the state and now living in the south-central region, Willow River was never on my radar—but it should have been. In 2018, Willow River was the third most visited state park, with 944,300 visitors. First, as always, was Devil's Lake with 2,674,386 visitors, and second was, no surprise here, Peninsula State Park with 1,191,551 visitors. (If you include the Kettle Moraine State Forest—South Unit, with 1,484,771 visitors, then Willow River was in fourth.) Willow River's location is certainly a factor in its popularity; it's a quick 10-minute drive from Hudson, Wisconsin, and a 30–40-minute drive from the Twin Cities. But location alone doesn't account for the closing-in-on-one-million visitors a year attendance. To reach that level of popularity, there must be something extra-special worth seeing. And at Willow River, there is.

The must-see at Willow River is Willow Falls. After our first visit, my initial review of the falls said, "The coolest freaking waterfalls in all of Wisconsin. Seriously." I stand by that assessment but offer this elaboration. Willow Falls is idyllic. The tiered falls are wide and welcoming to waders of all ages. Though the park provides an obvious trail and viewing areas marked by railings, they don't restrict visitors to these official places. In fact, the cover of the park brochure features a group of youngsters playing in the middle of the falls. Going into the falls is what you do here. Daily, the scene at the falls resembles a Norman Rockwell/Bob Ross mash-up of American life on a happy landscape: swimsuit-clad teenagers jostling for social status by stunting in front of friends, and parents trying to wrangle their children out of the falls to feed them lunch, all on a backdrop of cliffs, forest, and falls.

We haven't been able to enjoy the second main attraction at Willow River State Park as it was out of commission for the last few years. Little Falls Lake was drawn down in 2015 to rebuild Little Falls Dam and was just refilled in 2020. The Little Falls Dam was originally constructed in 1920 by the Willow River Power Company for hydroelectric power. At almost one hundred years old, the dam's structural integrity was becoming compromised. It wasn't designed or constructed to handle contemporary flood flows. I suspect that now that the lake is reinstated, Willow River will easily reach over one million visitors a year.

HEADS-UP: I did not recommend trails over by the falls as the Recommended Hike for a couple of reasons but mostly because they are the most popular hiking destinations in the park. While I'm not recommending the hiking by the falls, I am recommending you go explore the falls. But before you do, here's what you need to know. The trail down to the falls from the Willow Falls parking lot is a road. It's paved and extra wide, but the grade is not for the faint of heart. It's steep—like feet sliding into the toes of your shoes kind of steep. So wear good shoes (not flip-flops). Then, the stairway to get to the overlooks is metal with wide grating. The climb is strenuous and feels like you're climbing up a never-ending urban fire escape. Lucky was a little unsure of the treads, and it took some coaxing to get him all the way to the top. Dogs with smaller paws may find the stairs especially challenging.

To get into the falls, you must venture on social trails that can be tricky to navigate. We found it easiest to access the falls from the southern bank of the river. But the cliff on the north side of the falls is a cool spot to hang out, even though it can be more challenging to get to from the official trail. In the summer, the falls attract huge crowds. Visitors use the falls like a local swimming hole and splash pad. People bring their young children, camp chairs and coolers, set

A beautiful and busy day at the falls, Willow River State Park (Angela McNutt)

up camp in the shallow water, and run in and out of the falls playing games and cooling off. It could be overstimulating for a dog; I know it was a lot for Lucky to handle. If you want to spend a day wading in the falls, I recommend you bring your water shoes and leave your dog at home. Or, if you want to bring your pooch, visit earlier or later in the season or on a day when the weather isn't great, so the falls are less crowded.

WATER AVAILABILITY: Water is available at the park office and at the picnic area by the beach.

BATHROOM AVAILABILITY: Flush toilets are available at the park office, near the boat launch, at the picnic area by the beach, and the picnic area by the dam. Vault toilets are available by the Nature Center.

TRASHCAN AVAILABILITY: No trashcans on site; plan on carry-in/carry-out.

DESIGNATED DOG SWIMMING AREA: At the time of our last visit, there was no designated pet swimming area. Dogs are allowed in Willow Falls but must always remain on leash. Little Falls Lake was drawn down in 2015 to rebuild Little Falls Dam and wasn't refilled until 2020. It's possible the designated dog swimming area might be by the boat launch near the pet picnic area, in which case it would be a pretty nice spot.

DESIGNATED DOG PICNIC AREA: The designated pet picnic area is by the boat launch. To get there, take the park road past the 300 campground and then turn into the first parking lot on the right. Then, take the dirt trail at the northeastern corner of the parking lot down to the picnic area. There is a sign on your right as you head into the clearing that confirms, "Pets Allowed in this Area Pets Must Be Kept On Leash and Cleaned Up After." The pet picnic area is a large, shaded area with picnic tables and park grills; multiple groups could use it at the same time and have plenty of space. As a heads-up, Little Falls Trail (green) runs through the pet picnic area. It's a paved trail and allows bikes and rollerblading, so a heads-up if your dog isn't a fan of speedy people on wheels. Overall, this is a pleasant place to have a picnic, and I'm sure is even more pleasant when there's water in the lakebed.

Little Falls Lake was drawn down in 2015 to rebuild Little Falls Dam and wasn't refilled until 2020, so Lucky and I haven't had a chance to experience the lake yet. I bet that with the lake refilled, this picnic area will likely be one of our favorites!

RECOMMENDED HIKE: Trout Brook Trail (Purple)

DISTANCE AND ELEVATION GAIN: 1.4 miles, 31 feet

DOG AND HUMAN FITNESS LEVEL: recreational rambler

TRAIL CONDITIONS/MATERIALS: Trout Brook Trail alternates between gravel, dirt, grass, and weeds with dirt tire tracks. It is super wide and flat. There is plenty of room for walking side by side and for passing others along the trail.

TRAIL MARKINGS/EASE OF NAVIGATING: The trail is well established and easy to follow. It is marked with occasional wooden posts with purple bands around the tops. There are two of these posts on either side of the trailhead. Then there's a wooden "loop" sign where the stick meets the loop portion of the route. There is only one intersection, where the Nelson Farm Trail comes across the river on a wooden bridge and connects with Trout Brook Trail. While there aren't any signs on the southern side of the bridge, there is a trail map on the northern side of the bridge. This route is about as straightforward as they come.

THE EXPERIENCE: Park in the giant parking lot by the picnic area near the beach. It is almost all the way to the end of the park road, just before the dead-end parking lot and picnic area for Little Falls Dam. After parking, walk west toward the park road. The trailhead for Trout Brook Trail is just across the road from the entrance to the parking lot and the wooden sign for the beach.

Trout Brook Trail is what we like to call a "lollipop" trail—a loop on a stick. The hike starts out on the stick portion, and the trail is wide and gravely as it enters the woods. The stick portion runs parallel to Willow River, though the river snakes through the woods while the trail runs relatively straight. So, the river is visible from the trail for a moment, but then its curved path takes it away from the trail. After catching your first glimpse of the river, the trail transitions to predominantly grass with parallel dirt tire tracks. Another short segment through forest and thick understory leads to another touchpoint with the river. Then the trail arrives at the bridge that spans the river and connects with the Nelson Farm Trail. Though this recommended route doesn't take you over the bridge, we recommend walking out onto it to take in the view of the river and to take some photos. The next segment of the trail is especially pleasant as the river remains mostly visible. After the bridge, there's a small clearing with a bench near the water.

Just after passing by the bench, the stick portion of Trout Brook Trail reaches the loop portion where the trail splits into two branches. We hike the loop counterclockwise. Taking the right branch, the trail turns inland, away from the river through pine stands and prairie.

When you arrive back at the beginning of the loop, you can meander back along the stick portion of the trail, revisiting the river at the bench and bridge and passing back through the forest before popping back out on the park road, completing this recommended hike.

WHILE YOU'RE IN THE AREA: You should also visit Kinnickinnic State Park to the south or Interstate State Park to the north.

Local and 24-Hour Veterinarians

I hope you never have to read this section, but in the event your dog needs medical attention during your state park adventuring, I've included information for the closest local veterinarian and 24-hour emergency veterinarian offices here, based on travel time from the park.

THE NORTHERN REGION
Amnicon Falls State Park

Local
Superior Animal Hospital
36 E. Second Street
Superior, WI 54880
715-392-6211
15 miles from Amnicon Falls State Park

24 Hour
Affiliated Emergency Veterinary Services
2314 W. Michigan Street
Duluth, MN 55806
218-302-8000
18 miles from Amnicon Falls State Park

Big Bay State Park

Local
Country Care Pet Hospital
939 W Bayfield Street
Washburn, WI 54891
715-373-2222
22 miles from Big Bay State Park

24 Hour
Affiliated Emergency Veterinary Services
2314 W. Michigan Street
Duluth, MN 55806
218-302-8000
85 miles from Big Bay State Park

Copper Falls State Park

Local
Care Animal Clinic
10186 State Road 27
Hayward, WI 54843
715-634-5050
55.6 miles from Copper Falls State Park

24 Hour
Affiliated Emergency Veterinary Services
2314 W. Michigan Street
Duluth, MN 55806
218-302-8000
91 miles from Copper Falls State Park

Council Grounds State Park

Local
Merrill Veterinary Clinic
1301 E. Main Street
Merrill, WI 54452
715-536-9177
3.6 miles from Council Grounds State
  Park

24 Hour
PAW Health Network Animal Emergency
  Center
1420 Kronenwetter Drive
Mosinee, WI 54455
715-693-6934
30.7 miles from Council Grounds State
  Park

Interstate State Park

Local
Valley View Veterinary Hospital
821 US Highway 8
Saint Croix Falls, WI 54024
715-483-1551
3 miles from Interstate State Park

24 Hour
Affiliated Emergency Veterinary Service
11850 Aberdeen Street NE
Blaine, MN 55449
763-754-5000
43.1 miles from Interstate State Park

Pattison State Park

Local
Happy Tails Animal Hospital
1327 Banks Avenue
Superior, WI 54880
715-718-2130
12.9 miles from Pattison State Park

24 Hour
Affiliated Emergency Veterinary Services
2314 W. Michigan Street
Duluth, MN 55806
218-302-8000
18 miles from Pattison State Park

Straight Lake State Park

Local
Interstate Veterinary Hospital
421 5th Street
Centuria, WI 54824
715-646-2312
15.8 miles from Straight Lake State Park

24 Hour
Animal Emergency & Referral Center of
  Minnesota
1163 Helmo Avenue North
Oakdale, MN 55128
651-501-3766
67.8 miles from Straight Lake State Park

THE NORTHEASTERN REGION

Governor Thompson State Park

Local
Crivitz Veterinary Clinic
811 FJ Street
Crivitz, WI 54114
715-854-2751
16 miles from Governor Thompson State
  Park

24 Hour
Green Bay Animal Emergency Center
2141 Lime Kiln Road
Green Bay, WI 54311
920-494-9400
76.7 miles from Governor Thompson
  State Park

Hartman Creek State Park

Local
Waupaca Small Animal Hospital
780 Bowling Lane
Waupaca, WI 54981
715-258-3343
7.7 miles from Hartman Creek State Park

24 Hour
Animal Referral Center
4706 New Horizons Boulevard
Appleton, WI 54914
920-993-9193
44.7 miles from Hartman Creek State
  Park

High Cliff State Park

Local
Sherwood Animal Hospital
N521 Knight Drive
Sherwood, WI 54169
920-989-3200
2 miles from High Cliff State Park

24 Hour
Fox Valley Animal Referral Center
4706 New Horizons Boulevard
Appleton, WI 54914
920-993-9193
16.4 miles from High Cliff State Park

Lost Dauphin State Park

Local
Animal Hospital of De Pere
703 N 9th Street
De Pere, WI 54115
920-336-5774
9.1 miles from Lost Dauphin State Park

24 Hour
Green Bay Animal Emergency Center
2141 Lime Kiln Road
Green Bay, WI 54311
920-494-9400
16.1 miles from Lost Dauphin State Park

Newport State Park

Local	24 Hour
Northern Door Pet Clinic	Animal Referral Center of Green Bay
10393 Northwoods Drive	2141 Lime Kiln Road
Sister Bay, WI 54234	Green Bay, WI 54311
920-854-4979	920-494-9400
11.9 miles from Newport State Park	89.4 miles from Newport State Park

Peninsula State Park

Local	24 Hour
Northern Door Pet Clinic	Animal Referral Center of Green Bay
10393 Northwoods Drive	2141 Lime Kiln Road
Sister Bay, WI 54234	Green Bay, WI 54311
920-854-4979	920-494-9400
6.7 miles from Peninsula State Park	71.5 miles from Peninsula State Park

Potawatomi State Park

Local	24 Hour
Animal Clinic of Sturgeon Bay	Animal Referral Center of Green Bay
130 S Madison Avenue	2141 Lime Kiln Road
Sturgeon Bay, WI 54235	Green Bay, WI 54311
920-743-2628	920-494-9400
5.2 miles from Potawatomi State Park	45.6 miles from Potawatomi State Park

Rock Island State Park

Local	24 Hour
Northern Door Pet Clinic	Animal Referral Center of Green Bay
10393 Northwoods Drive	2141 Lime Kiln Road
Sister Bay, WI 54234	Green Bay, WI 54311
920-854-4979	920-494-9400
13.2 miles from Northport, Wisconsin	90.9 miles from Northport, Wisconsin

Whitefish Dunes State Park

Local	24 Hour
Door County Veterinary Hospital	Animal Referral Center of Green Bay
3915 Old Highway Road	2141 Lime Kiln Road
Sturgeon Bay, WI 54235	Green Bay, WI 54311
920-743-7777	920-494-9400
10.9 miles from Whitefish Dunes State Park	61.3 miles from Whitefish Dunes State Park

THE SOUTHEASTERN REGION

Big Foot Beach State Park

Local
Lake Geneva Animal Hospital
801 E Townline Road
Lake Geneva, WI 53147
262-248-4790
2.6 miles from Big Foot Beach State Park

24 Hour
VCA Milwaukee Emergency Center for
   Animals
3670 S 108th Street
Greenfield, WI 53228
414-543-7387
45.2 miles from Big Foot Beach State
   Park

Harrington Beach State Park

Local
Cedar Grove Veterinary Services
23 Highway RR
Cedar Grove, WI 53013
920-668-6212
5 miles from Harrington Beach State
   Park

24 Hour
Lakeshore Veterinary Specialists
207 W. Seven Hills Road
Port Washington, WI 53074
262-268-7800
10 miles from Harrington Beach State
   Park

Kohler-Andrae State Park

Local
Sheboygan Veterinary Clinic
1103 Indiana Avenue
Sheboygan, WI 53081
920-452-2899
5.6 miles from Kohler-Andrae State Park

24 Hour
Lakeshore Veterinary Specialists
207 W. Seven Hills Road
Port Washington, WI 53074
262-268-7800
24.5 miles from Kohler-Andrae State Park

Lakeshore State Park

Local
Milwaukee Vet Clinic
107 E Seeboth Street
Milwaukee, WI 53204
414-310-8997
1.2 miles from Lakeshore State Park

24 Hour
Mayfair Animal Hospital
11619 W. North Avenue
Wauwatosa, WI 53226
414-897-8840
10.3 miles to Lakeshore State Park

THE SOUTH-CENTRAL REGION

Aztalan State Park

Local
Tyranena Veterinary Clinic
805 N Main Street
Lake Mills, WI 53551
920-648-8400
3.1 miles from Aztalan State Park

24 Hour
VCA Veterinary Emergency Service &
    Veterinary Specialty Center
4902 East Broadway
Madison, WI 53716
608-222-2455
28.7 miles from Aztalan State Park

Belmont Mound State Park

Local
Family Pet Hospital LLC
1620 Means Drive
Platteville, WI 53818
608-348-9581
7.3 miles from Belmont Mound State
    Park

24 Hour
VCA Veterinary Emergency Service &
    Veterinary Specialty Center
1612 N High Point Road
Middleton, WI 53562
608-831-1101
57.8 miles from Belmont Mound State
    Park

Blue Mound State Park

Local
Starlight Veterinary Clinic
10902 Eckel Road
Blue Mounds, WI 53517
608-437-8387
1.7 miles from Blue Mound State Park

24 Hour
VCA Veterinary Emergency Service &
    Veterinary Specialty Center
1612 N High Point Road
Middleton, WI 53562
608-831-1101
22.3 miles from Blue Mound State Park

Cross Plains State Park

Local
Petcare Clinics, S.C.
1845 Bourbon Road
Cross Plains, WI 53528
608-798-4545
6.2 miles from Cross Plains State Park

24 Hour
VCA Veterinary Emergency Service &
    Veterinary Specialty Center
1612 N High Point Road
Middleton, WI 53562
608-831-1101
6.2 miles from Cross Plains State Park

Devil's Lake State Park

Local
Baraboo Valley Veterinary Clinic
403 South Parkway
Baraboo, WI 53913
608-355-2882
3.1 miles from Devil's Lake State Park

24 Hour
VCA Veterinary Emergency Service &
   Veterinary Specialty Center
1612 N High Point Road
Middleton, WI 53562
608-831-1101
35.1 miles from Devil's Lake State Park

Governor Dodge State Park

Local
Dodgeville Veterinary Service
105 County Highway YZ
Dodgeville, WI 53533
608-935-2306
3 miles from Governor Dodge State Park

24 Hour
VCA Veterinary Emergency Service &
   Veterinary Specialty Center
1612 N High Point Road
Middleton, WI 53562
608-831-1101
41.2 miles from Governor Dodge State
   Park

Governor Nelson State Park

Local
Pineview Veterinary Clinic
6000 County Highway K
Waunakee, WI 53597
608-850-7387
2.1 miles from Governor Nelson State
   Park

24 Hour
VCA Veterinary Emergency Service &
   Veterinary Specialty Center
1612 N High Point Road
Middleton, WI 53562
608-831-1101
6.6 miles from Governor Nelson State
   Park

Lake Kegonsa State Park

Local
Stoughton Veterinary Service Animal
   Hospital
1900 US Highway 51/138
Stoughton, WI 53589
608-807-1007
6 miles from Lake Kegonsa State Park

24 Hour
VES/VSC Madison
4902 East Broadway
Madison, WI 53716
608-222-2455
8.6 miles from Lake Kegonsa State Park

Mirror Lake State Park

Local
Noble Hound Animal Hospital & Pet
　Resort
490 Bunker Road
Baraboo, WI 53913
608-253-2275
3.8 miles from Mirror Lake State Park

24 Hour
VCA Veterinary Emergency Service &
　Veterinary Specialty Center
1612 N High Point Road
Middleton, WI 53562
608-831-1101
42.2 miles from Mirror Lake State Park

Natural Bridge State Park

Local
Sauk Prairie Small Animal Hospital and
　Shamrock Pet Resort
E11340 County Road PF
Prairie Du Sac, WI 53578
608-643-2451
11.9 miles from Natural Bridge State
　Park

24 Hour
VCA Veterinary Emergency Service &
　Veterinary Specialty Center
1612 N High Point Road
Middleton, WI 53562
608-831-1101
33.4 miles from Natural Bridge State
　Park

Nelson Dewey State Park

Local
South West Veterinary Services
451 Canal Street
Bloomington, WI 53804
608-994-2724
15.3 miles from Nelson Dewey State Park

24 Hour
VCA Veterinary Emergency Service &
　Veterinary Specialty Center
1612 N High Point Road
Middleton, WI 53562
608-831-1101
99.1 miles from Nelson Dewey State
　Park

New Glarus Woods State Park

Local
Country View Veterinary Service of New
　Glarus
1106 State Road 69
New Glarus, WI 53574
608-527-2212
2 miles from New Glarus Woods State
　Park

24 Hour
Madison Veterinary Specialists &
　Emergency Care
2704 Royal Avenue
Madison, WI 53713
608-274-7772
28.7 miles from New Glarus Woods State
　Park

Rocky Arbor State Park

Local
Dells Animal Hospital
4135 State Highway 13
Wisconsin Dells, WI 53965
608-253-7361
6.6 miles from Rocky Arbor State Park

24 Hour
VCA Veterinary Emergency Service &
    Veterinary Specialty Center
1612 N High Point Road
Middleton, WI 53562
608-831-1101
49.1 miles from Rocky Arbor State Park

Tower Hill State Park

Local
Spring Green Animal Hospital
506 Rainbow Road
Spring Green, WI 53588
608-588-3535
3.5 miles from Tower Hill State Park

24 Hour
VCA Veterinary Emergency Service &
    Veterinary Specialty Center
1612 N High Point Road
Middleton, WI 53562
608-831-1101
29.9 miles from Tower Hill State Park

Wyalusing State Park

Local
Southwest Veterinary Services, S.C.
37460 US-18
Prairie du Chien, WI 53821
608-326-6464
9 miles from Wyalusing State Park

24 Hour
VCA Veterinary Emergency Service &
    Veterinary Specialty Center
1612 N High Point Road
Middleton, WI 53562
608-831-1101
90.3 miles from Wyalusing State Park

Yellowstone Lake State Park

Local
Argyle Veterinary Svc
201 S State Street
Argyle, WI 53504
608-543-3082
8.6 miles from Yellowstone Lake State
    Park

24 Hour
Madison Veterinary Specialists &
    Emergency Care
2704 Royal Avenue
Madison, WI 53713
608-274-7772
46.8 miles from Yellowstone Lake State
    Park

THE WEST-CENTRAL REGION
Brunet Island State Park

Local
Cornell Veterinary Clinic
409 S 8th Street
Cornell, WI 54732
715-239-6482
2.5 miles from Brunet Island State Park

24 Hour
Animal Emergency & Referral Center of
  Minnesota
1163 Helmo Avenue N.
Oakdale, MN 55128
651-501-3766
112 miles from Brunet Island State Park

Buckhorn State Park

Mauston Pet Hospital and Veterinary
  Clinic
512 Gateway Avenue
Mauston, WI 53948
608-847-6024
13 miles from Buckhorn State Park

24 Hour
VES/VSC Madison
4902 East Broadway
Madison, WI 53716
608-222-2455
87.8 miles from Buckhorn State Park

Kinnickinnic State Park

Local
Kinnic Veterinary Service
1333 N Main Street
River Falls, WI 54022
715-425-5182
9.8 miles from Kinnickinnic State Park

24 Hour
Animal Emergency & Referral Center of
  Minnesota
1163 Helmo Avenue North
Oakdale, MN 55128
651-501-3766
24 miles from Kinnickinnic State Park

Lake Wissota State Park

Local
Chippewa Veterinary Clinic SC
14961 81st Avenue
Chippewa Falls, WI 54729
715-723-3655
4.7 miles from Lake Wissota State Park

24 Hour
Animal Emergency & Referral Center of
  Minnesota
1163 Helmo Avenue North
Oakdale, MN 55128
651-501-3766
90.5 miles from Lake Wissota State Park

Merrick State Park

Local
Winona Veterinary Hospital
4136 W 6th Street
Winona, MN 55987
507-452-4811
13.6 miles from Merrick State Park

24 Hour
BluePearl Pet Hospital
121 23rd Avenue SW
Rochester, MN 55902
507-424-3976
64 miles from Merrick State Park

Mill Bluff State Park

Local
Tomah Veterinary Clinic, S.C.
1600 Superior Ave
Tomah, WI 54660
608-372-4879
10.4 miles to Mill Bluff State Park

24 Hour
VCA Veterinary Emergency Service &
    Veterinary Specialty Center
1612 N High Point Road
Middleton, WI 53562
608-831-1101
82.2 miles from Mill Bluff State Park

Perrot State Park

Local
Van Loon Animal Hospital
W7683 Old Highway 93
Holmen, WI 54636
608-588-8120
10 miles from Perrot State Park

24 Hour
BluePearl Pet Hospital
121 23rd Avenue SW
Rochester, MN 55902
507-424-3976
65.6 miles from Perrot State Park

Rib Mountain State Park

Local
Marathon Animal Hospital
1025 S 17th Avenue
Wausau, WI 54401
715-845-1919
6 miles from Rib Mountain State Park

24 Hour
PAW Health Network—24 Hour Animal
    Care Center
1420 I-39 Frontage Road
Kronenwetter, WI 54455
715-693-6934
10.8 miles from Rib Mountain State Park

Roche-A-Cri State Park

Local
Adams Marquette Veterinary Service Inc
W8881 WI-82
Oxford, WI 53952
608-586-5768
29.5 miles from Roche-A-Cri State Park

24 Hour
PAW Health Network—24 Hour Animal
    Care Center
1420 I-39 Frontage Road
Kronenwetter, WI 54455
715-693-6934
71.9 miles from Roche-A-Cri State Park

Wildcat Mountain State Park

Local
Animal Acres
Vet Road
Hillsboro, WI 54634
608-489-3420
6.7 miles from Wildcat Mountain State
    Park

24 Hour
VCA Veterinary Emergency Service &
    Veterinary Specialty Center
1612 N High Point Road
Middleton, WI 53562
608-831-1101
85.2 miles from Wildcat Mountain State
    Park

Willow River State Park

Local
Animal Care Center of Hudson
591 Lenertz Road
Hudson, WI 54016
715-386-8878
3.6 miles from Willow River State Park

24 Hour
Animal Emergency & Referral Center of
    Minnesota
1163 Helmo Avenue North
Oakdale, MN 55128
651-501-3766
18.2 miles from Willow River State Park